HOSTILE AND
MALIGNANT PREJUDICE

PSYCHOANALYTIC IDEAS AND APPLICATIONS SERIES

Recent titles in the Series
(for a full listing, please visit www.karnacbooks.com)

HOSTILE AND MALIGNANT PREJUDICE

Psychoanalytic Approaches

Edited by

Cyril Levitt

KARNAC

First published in 2015 by
Karnac Books Ltd
118 Finchley Road, London NW3 5HT

British Library Cataloguing in Publication Data

A C.I.P. for this book is available from the British Library

  ISBN 978 1 78220 111 3

Edited, designed and produced by The Studio Publishing Services Ltd
www.publishingservicesuk.co.uk
e-mail: studio@publishingservicesuk.co.uk

www.karnacbooks.com

CONTENTS

Hermann Beland is currently a psychoanalyst (DPV, IPA, DGPT) in private practice in Berlin. He is a supervisor and training analyst, German Psychoanalytic Association (DPV), and has occupied leading positions in the DPV from 1984–1992. He has published numerous papers about the theory and technique of psychoanalysis and has written extensively on anti-Semitism, the role of projection in destructive outbreaks and wars, and in collective mourning.

Tomas Böhm, MD, was a psychoanalyst in private practice in Stockholm, Sweden, a training analyst and supervisor in the Swedish Psychoanalytic Association, and a couples' therapist. He was the author of several books, on love relations, xenophobia, orthodoxy, and revenge. He lectured about moral courage, bystanders and tolerance in connection with the international exhibition on Raoul Wallenberg, and wrote regular columns about love relations in a Swedish magazine. He was also a hobby jazz musician. Tomas passed away following a massive brain haemorrhage in May 2013.

Adeline Fohn, PhD, is a clinical psychologist who worked at the Université Catholique de Louvain (Belgium) as a researcher in psychology. She collected life narratives of Jewish children who survived the Second World War in hiding and highlighted the long-lasting effects of their traumatic experiences related to the Holocaust. Her PhD thesis is entitled "Trauma, memories and *après-coup*: the experience of hidden Jewish children in Belgium".

Ignacio Gerber is a psychoanalyst and a member and professor at the Brazilian Psychoanalytic Society of São Paulo (SBPSP). Dr Gerber has published many articles in Brazil and abroad. Originally majoring in civil engineering, he specialised in soil mechanics, and he worked as a consultant on more than 5000 projects concerning major structures until 1980. He is also a practising violin-cellist and choir conductor.

Susann Heenen-Wolff is a psychoanalyst and training and supervising analyst in the Belgium Society of Psychoanalysis (IPA). She is also a professor of clinical psychoanalysis at the University of Louvain-la-Neuve (UCL) and at the Free University of Brussels (ULB). She publishes in French, German, and English (mostly in the *International Journal of Psychoanalysis*).

Jorge Kantor is a training and supervising analyst at the Peruvian Psychoanalytic Society (SPP). He is currently the President of the SPP and he was Director of the Institute, Scientific Secretary, and Treasurer of the SPP. He was Director of the Internship Programme at the Centre of Psychoanalytic Psychotherapy. He was one of the first male members of COWAP and has written several articles on gender issues and on logic and psychoanalysis, with a special interest in the notion of time.

Cyril Levitt was the chair of the Committee on Prejudice (Including Antisemitism) of the IPA, 2009–2013. He trained at the Toronto Institute of Psychoanalysis and chairs its Library and Archives Committee. For thirty-eight years, he has been a professor in the Department of Sociology at McMaster University and has served as past chair of that department. He is the Director of the Lawrence Krader Research Project at McMaster University. Professor Levitt is also a psychoanalyst in private practice in Toronto.

Henri Parens, MD, Professor of Psychiatry, Thomas Jefferson University, and a training and supervising analyst (adult and child) at the Psychoanalytic Center of Philadelphia. He is the author of over 250 publications, including twenty-two books, eleven authored and nine co-edited, five scientific films, one DVD documentary, one CD, and one television series for CBS of thirty-nine half-hour programmes. His principal research and prevention efforts include the theory and development of aggression and the prevention of violence and malignant prejudice, especially by means of formal parenting education.

Marcelo Nelson Viñar Munichor, MD, is a psychoanalyst, and a Teaching Member of the Uruguayan Psychoanalytical Association. Since 1990, he has co-ordinated a Field Investigation Group concerning marginalised adolescence and juvenile offenders. He is President of the Uruguayan Psychoanalytical Association (APU) and he served as President of the Latin American Psychoanalytical Federation (FEPAL). He is a member of the Board of Representatives of the IPA and the author of many articles and books.

Vamık D. Volkan, MD, is an emeritus professor of psychiatry at the University of Virginia School of Medicine, an emeritus training and supervising analyst at the Washington Psychoanalytic Institute and the Senior Erik Erikson Scholar at the Austen Riggs Center in Stockbridge, Massachusetts. He was the director of the University of Virginia's Center for the Study of Mind and Human Interaction, and is a past president of the International Society of Political Psychology and the Virginia Psychoanalytic Society.

The Publications Committee of the International Psychoanalytical Association continues, with this volume, the series "Psychoanalytic Ideas and Applications".

The aim of this series is to focus on the scientific production of significant authors whose works are outstanding contributions to the development of the psychoanalytic field and to set out relevant ideas and themes, generated during the history of psychoanalysis, that deserve to be known and discussed by present psychoanalysts.

The relationship between psychoanalytic ideas and their applications has to be put forward from the perspective of theory, clinical practice, technique, and research, so as to maintain their validity for contemporary psychoanalysis.

The Publications Committee's objective is to share these ideas with the psychoanalytic community and with professionals in other related disciplines, in order to expand their knowledge and generate a productive interchange between the text and the reader.

Hostile and Malignant Prejudice: Psychoanalytic Approaches, edited by Cyril Levitt, is the result of the work of the Committee on Prejudice (Including Anti-Semitism) of the International Psychoanalytical Association, and is part of its Outreach Mandate.

Divided into four parts, this book approaches the problem of prejudice from a variety of different frames, both theoretically and clinically, including such features as the difference between ordinary and malignant prejudice, its development in childhood and its prevention, the international implications of hostile and malignant prejudice, as well as a series of very interesting chapters on the subjects of secrecy and the denial of trauma, collective mourning, xenophobia, and anti-Semitism. It seems to me that this book represents a very good example of the functioning of a working group which is able to produce good psychoanalytical ideas and applications, which is the exact aim of this book series. Special thanks are, therefore, due to the editor and to all the contributors to this valuable volume.

Gennaro Saragnano
Series Editor
Chair, IPA Publications Committee

Introduction

This book is divided into four parts. Part I, "The origin of prejudice in childhood: theory and practice", comprises a seminal paper by Henri Parens whose theoretical and empirical work on prejudice, in terms of its origins in early childhood, represents the cutting edge of psychoanalytic work in the field, and provides the foundation upon which the rest of the book stands. Part II, "Theory", comprises three chapters by senior analysts in different countries: Ignacio Gerber (Brazil), Marcelo Viñar (Uruguay), and Vamık Volkan (USA), representing different aspects of psychoanalytic theory in relation to hostile and malignant prejudice. Part III, "Applications", is composed of the works of five psychoanalysts that focus on the application of psychoanalytic theory and techniques specific to manifestations and consequences of hostile and malignant prejudice: Hermann Beland (Germany), Tomas Böhm (Sweden), Jorge Kantor (Peru), Susann Heenen-Wolff, and Adeline Fohn (Belgium). Part IV, "Conclusion: realistic expectations", comprises a concluding essay emphasising the difficulties facing psychoanalysis, indeed, any and every approach to dealing with hostile and malignant prejudice related to the seeming intractability of the problems associated with overcoming this endemic blight upon the human condition.

Collectively, these essays represent the cutting edge of psycho-analytically orientated approaches to the understanding, treatment, and informed social policy engagements with hostile and malignant prejudice.

Beginning in 1970, Parens and his team worked with a group of mothers and their newborn children twice weekly in two-hour observation and intervention sessions. His initial study ran over the course of seven years, then continued with three follow-up studies that in turn ran for well over three decades. One of the purposes of these studies was to document the changes effected by Parens and his co-workers' interventions in helping to shift the mothers' parenting modality from "growth disturbing to growth promoting". The focus of this research related to comparing the aggression profile of the children participating in the study to the population from which the sample was drawn. The initial study and follow-up work confirmed what other studies have also found: "a stable positive correlation between *the quality of the child's attachment to his/her mother (primary caregiver[s])* and *the child's aggression profile*". Parens succinctly summarised the main conclusion of the work as follows: *Excessive Unpleasure (EU) (psychic pain) generates High-Level Hostile Destructiveness (HL-HD): "EU → HL-HD"* whereby excessive unpleasure is ameliorated by growth-promoting parenting. High-level hostile destructiveness (HL-HD), as a measure of aggression, is a function of excessive unpleasure.

Parens, himself a Holocaust child survivor, became interested in examining how his findings on aggression and violence might be applied to reducing prejudice. Parens came to the conclusion that we all have benign prejudices, as a result of identifications with our parents and relatives and our stranger anxiety, which is a normal developmental stage. In other words, we all have prejudices that lead us to prefer our own, without necessarily developing hostility towards others. There are a number of factors active in generating hostility, anger, hatred, and rage towards other groups. The first and most important of these is the ambivalence in the relationship to primary care-givers. Even (or especially) the best of parents must frustrate the child's wishes and actions in the interest of healthy ego development. The child reacts by developing hostile trends against those that they love and need most. To defend against these hostile trends, the child employs the defences of inhibition, displacement, splitting, projection, rationalisation, and denial. Later, they develop "reality distorting defences", such as reductionism, caricaturing, deprecation, and vilification of others that are factors in organising malignant prejudice. The "hostilification" of prejudice is a spectral phenomenon that runs from mild antipathy without further consequence to genocidal wishes and actions.

This developmental pattern, which might help organise hostile and malignant prejudice on the basis of existing benign prejudices, may be further exacerbated by the presence of trauma of various sorts, and by certain aspects of education, both in the family and in social institutions where vilification of other groups is practised and inculcated. Traumatic experiences might induce extreme anger responses, which could, in turn, be channelled against target groups and populations in the form of revenge for some actual or historical grievance. The need to have enemies is an outlet for the rage engendered by the reaction to trauma. Parens goes on to suggest ameliorative actions that can be undertaken to prevent or lessen the development and organisation of hostile and malignant prejudice. The title of this present work is heavily influenced by Parens' research and writings.

In the first chapter of Part II: "Theory", Marcelo Viñar takes us into the borderland between psychoanalysis and philosophy, by means of his reception of some of the main ideas found in the book: *La Science Face au Racisme* (Frankel et al., 1981). He subjects the concepts of race and racism to a historical critique by exposing the error of ethnocentric self-reference among the assumptions of those engaged in the "natural science" of race from the mid-nineteenth century. The purported objective findings of a dispassionate science, underlying the concepts of racial superiority and inferiority, are shown to be nothing but a popular prejudice dressed in scientific garb, whereby the underlying political prejudices of race and racism are completely occluded. Does this not call into question all scientific thinking as objective, neutral, and impartial? Yes and no. The "territory" mined by psychoanalysis is the unconscious, and whereas its method is burdened by the power of the drives, fantasy, and illusion, which casts doubt on our ability to always act with neutrality and objectivity, we do not relinquish the attempt, so that we may approach this ideal asymptotically. In the matter of racism and racial superiority, Viñar is unequivocal: psychoanalysis and all thinking people of good will are united in their vocal and unswerving opposition.

In order to fully explicate the genesis of racism and malignant prejudice, psychoanalysis must open itself up to the study of cultural and political trends. He cites the example of Melanie Klein working with a child during the London blitz, without taking note of the trauma inflicted by the falling bombs and the destruction that they unleashed upon London. Without abandoning our bedrock understanding of the importance of infantile and childhood sexuality and aggression, we must, out of necessity, be open to a multi-causal approach to understanding the genesis of hostile and malignant prejudice. Taking this argument further, Viñar suggests that the technological changes which have led to instantaneous communication and the further socialisation of the subject, necessitates that psychoanalysis become more "relational" in its orientation, and that it must go beyond the endopsychic realm of the individual subject to consider the individual as a kind of "cell" within the larger social organism. The individual in psychoanalysis is a henad and not a monad, that is, one in relation to others, many, and the social whole, and not an isolated and closed unity. In this way, Viñar implicitly links psychoanalysis with the Durkheimian tradition of sociology in which the individual is considered to be a "homo duplex", a constellation of two opposing elements, the psychobiological (egoism) and the social (altruism) that is superimposed upon it. We must focus on the interaction effects of the endopsychic and cultural if we are to truly come to grips with the genesis of hostile and malignant prejudice.

Viñar gets to the heart of the matter when he identifies the problem as the "Other", the stranger, "difference". Why is it that we too frequently approach "difference" with anger, hatred, and hostility? Why is the toleration of difference so fraught with the potential for violence? The stranger, the one who is different, about whom there is mystery, is always ready at hand to become the object of our negative projections, to unsettle us in our own identities, to become objects of scorn or worse. In several passages, Viñar asks the question of how the tolerance and inclusion of those who are different can be turned around into violent exclusion and exterminatory eradication. The question is not answered, and neither do we expect an answer. The question requires in part an answer that is empirical and political. Why Germany responded to the economic crisis with Nazism and America with social democracy requires an analysis of German and American history, culture, and politics, as well as comparative child-rearing practices, values, and norms. At one point, the author suggests that only an (aristocratic?) few can maintain the spirit of tolerance and openness to difference, in the face of the temptation to vilify, exclude, and practise violence upon "the stranger", "the Other". However, this answer gets us only as far as the Righteous Gentiles of the Holocaust, or Sir Percy Blakeney as the Scarlet Pimpernel. The seriousness of Viñar's challenge to us, in his chapter, is that of working together with other disciplines to answer the tough questions.

Ignacio Gerber, in the second chapter of Part II: "Theory", continues to work in the borderland between psychoanalysis and philosophy, in which he embeds his thoughts about prejudice. He argues that psychoanalysis joins quantum physics and paraconsistent mathematics in challenging the assumptions of classical logic's law of the excluded third. He bases his work in part upon the ideas of the psychoanalyst Matte-Blanco, according to whom human beings live a dualism–monism, that is, they have two ways of being in the same psyche, conscious, and unconscious. The unconscious, as Freud pointed out, does not respect the laws of contradiction, a hallmark of the secondary process and conscious thought. There is a balance that must be achieved in order to avoid psychopathology. A similar balance must be maintained between the constructive force of Eros, and the destructive and aggressive trends. Hostile and malignant prejudice result when people can no longer maintain this balance, when the life force and aggression work on their own against one another, in attempting to achieve mastery over one another. The split between the two drives leads to one of two opposite trends: the denial of difference, in which case the likelihood is perversion, or the more destructive trend, which exacerbates difference to the point at which the humanity and dignity of the Other is called into serious question.

Gerber points out that the union of positive science with evolutionary theory in the nineteenth century created a pseudo-scientific theory of racism, which was used to justify colonialism, slavery, mistreatment of indigenous peoples, forced conversions, forced expulsions, theft of land, and other forms of inhuman practices. Racial differences were linked to biology, or attributed to a positivistic stage theory of cultural development that ranked cultures according to a specious theory of progress. Gerber then tackles Freud's later drive theory, by asking the question concerning the origin of violence and its relation to fear. In the realm of the unconscious, we are faced with contradictory trends and emotions, which exist in conflict vying for expression and dominance. Gerber uses the Eastern device of the *koan* as a way of posing problems that cannot be addressed by formal logic, the logic of the excluded middle. The *koan* as a way of posing issues arising from deep conflict is not merely a metaphor. He argues that the relations between the mind's conscious and unconscious processes are similar to the relations between classical (Newtonian) and quantum physics. He suggests that the quantum realm exists, in what Lawrence Krader (2010) suggested is a different order of nature (i.e., a different order of space–time) than the material order. By extension, one could argue that the same could be said of the mind's conscious and unconscious processes. Concordance has yet to be established between these different orders, if such concordance is even possible.

In answer to the question regarding the priority of fear or violence, one of the crucial questions we must address in thinking about hostile and malignant prejudice, Gerber comes down clearly on the side of fear. The fundamental fear is that of exclusion, being cut off from a humanity that has become our expected environment over the course of evolution. It is this fear that, in a variety of ways, leads to violence, and the violence to renewed fear. The first suggestion Gerber makes, which he calls a pragmatic utopia, is to work on reducing the grounds of fear, which will, in turn, lead to a reduction in violence, including violence that arises out of hostile and malignant prejudice. His second suggestion for a pragmatic utopia concerns the construction of a society where the feminine spirit prevails. His understanding of the feminine spirit is sure to raise the ire of many, since some will argue that it is a construction of patriarchy and not something linked to biology in a fixed way. In the end, he argues in favour of a union between both the masculine and feminine principles, whereby the former informs the ego, while the latter informs the id in a helpful complementarity. Such pragmatic utopias, Gerber argues, will diminish the potential for violence associated with hostile and malignant prejudice.

In the final chapter of Part II: "Theory", which provides a bridge to Part III: "Applications", Vamık Volkan introduces us to large-scale group prejudice, thus taking up both Viñar's relational and political dimension and Gerber's emphasis on the treatment of the "stranger", the "Other". Volkan, perhaps more than any other psychoanalyst today, has contributed to the understanding of large-group psychology, theoretically, clinically, and practically. He takes up this challenge in different ways from the other authors within this compendium concerning the psychology of nations and peoples. His contribution to this volume is both personal, based upon his experiences growing up within a Turkish family on Cyprus during the Second World War, and at the time of the ethnic clashes between Greek and Turkish Cypriots after the war. He links the personal, political, and psychological in a moving way. The goal of his chapter is the development of large-group psychology, elements of which focus on shared mental processes within a group having significant political, social, and historical consequences. Focusing on the large-group identity, he examines the impact of large-group regression, externalisations or projections, and large-group mourning. As he explains it,

> A large group regresses when there is a shared threat or harm done to its large-group identity, and it utilises massive externalisations or projections in order to strengthen the large-group identity, and it mourns when various types of losses are associated with harm to the large-group identity.

From among the twenty signs and features of societal regression, which he earlier identified, Volkan focuses here on "chosen glories" and "chosen traumas", the former referring to historically significant achievements or victories which the groups' ancestors experienced decades, centuries, or even millennia ago, the latter signifying losses and defeats at the hands of others, which, as a kind of collective *après-coup*, may be reactivated and given heightened significance in the present. Chosen glories and traumas are shared mental representations that link the current generation to a mythologised view of the past, the chosen glories being positive, the basis for extolling the victories, and the heroism that knits the present generation's ethnic group, nation, religious affiliation, etc., to the history of the group's positive victories and achievements. Chosen traumas, on the other hand, recall the negative shared mental representation of significant defeats, tragedies, losses of territory and honour, etc., at the hands of other groups. These serve to enhance the commitment to the group through the generation of collective feelings of revenge, retribution, and self-sacrifice. The mechanism for the transgenerational transmission of the chosen trauma is a collective parallel to projective identification within individual psychology. The adults put their own "traumatised self and object images" into their children, who lack the experiential context in which these images developed in the adult victims. With chosen traumas, this inculcating of traumatised images occurs within hundreds, thousands, or even millions of younger group members, and tends to heighten the social solidarity of the group concomitantly with the denigration of the group or groups responsible for inflicting the trauma.

The second mechanism that Volkan discusses is the process whereby unwanted aspects of the self are externalised or projected on to opposed groups. In his chapter, Hermann Beland has demonstrated how this mechanism was operative throughout the history of Christianity in relation to the Jews. An example closer to home for Volkan concerns the Greeks purging their language of the Turkish words after achieving their independence from the Ottoman Empire. In purging Greek of the Turkish words that had been part of their language for centuries, Volkan suggests that the Greeks were ridding themselves of their inner Turk, an unwanted part of themselves.

Large-group mourning is the third mechanism involved in the promotion of a chosen large-group trauma. The loss suffered by the group at the hands of another large group with a different group identity is experienced as a serious narcissistic blow, which might lead defensively to an exaggeration of the group's narcissism and, in turn, may develop into a "masochistic large-group narcissism", which engenders a feeling of superiority and entitlement within the collective psyche of the group which mourns the loss suffered in the chosen trauma. In relation to these three mechanisms that might play in response to the distortions occasioned by the acceptance and exaggeration of the chosen large-group trauma, Volkan develops a schema of consequential steps that lead to a potential outbreak of violence between large groups.

In his final considerations, Volkan writes a little about his own work with his patients, and in league with other analytic colleagues, with bringing together groups of people from opposing "hostile" large groups to counteract the forces in play which bring about the further "hostilification" of the psychology of group conflict. Although the numbers involved in such encounters are small in comparison with the polities from which they come, and the participants might not constitute a representative sample of their nations or large groups, Volkan and his colleagues have had considerable success in creating a greater openness, diminishing narcissistic exaggeration and feelings of group superiority and entitlement, separating out the real grounds for conflict from the psychological illusions and distortions, following the adoption and exacerbation of chosen traumas, and focusing on their potential resolution on the basis of compromise.

In the first chapter (Chapter Five) of Part III: "Applications", Susann Heenen-Wolff and Adeline Fohn bring us back from the philosophical heights of Viñar's paper to an empirical question concerning the role of secrecy in the denial of trauma among Jewish children who were hidden from the Nazis and their collaborators in Belgium during the Holocaust. Based upon group psychoanalytic work and interviews with sixty child survivors in Belgium in 2007, the focus comes from the concept of *après-coup* or *Nachträglichkeit*, as Freud put it. This key concept for Heenen-Wolff's and Fohn's work refers to the phenomenon of a kind of delayed reaction to a trauma sustained much earlier (which might not have been experienced as such at the time), but becomes activated by a much later experience which gives the original traumatic event a new meaning on account of the associative linkage between the present and past event.

The children interviewed by Heenen-Wolff and Fohn were either hidden in some physical hiding place, or concealed in plain sight by posing as non-Jewish children. In both cases, these children had to keep their Jewishness a secret. Separated from their parents, siblings, relatives, and community at a young age, they developed feelings of both shame for their origins as a kind of identification with the aggressor and a deep sense of guilt in relation to their survival, as well as a sense that they had somehow been responsible for their "hiddenness" and for the loss of their families. Their chapter focuses on two of the sixty formerly hidden children. Careful to alert the reader to the fact that the children did not all react to their trauma in the same way, they point out that the situation of the younger children was different to that of the older ones, that some renounced their Jewishness by formal conversion and others did not. The authors seek to show how the life trajectories of the two cases presented can be seen as a response to the secretiveness, the splitting, shame, and guilt that developed in reaction to their situation and their treatment. Silent for years after the war ended, these children experienced an *après-coup* when confronting certain situations that reactivated the trauma, giving it a different meaning and significance. Such circumstances were varied, and included, among others, the rise of anti-Semitic parties and the social phenomenon of survivors coming together to tell their stories to a more receptive public in the 1980s and 1990s.

Heenen-Wolff and Fohn argue that elements such as secrecy, shame, or guilt, are also found among children in Rwanda, Bosnia, and elsewhere where mass ethnic and racial violence has occurred.

In Chapter Six, the second in Part III: "Applications", Hermann Beland presents us with a courageous, thoughtful, and insightful analysis of the German psyche[1] in relation to the Holocaust during the post-war years. Building upon the work of Rüsen (2001), Mitscherlisch and Mitscherlisch (1968), and Bohleber (2007), he argues that the initial response of the Germans to the Holocaust was to project their guilt feelings on to a relatively small group of Nazi leaders, and cast themselves as victims of the war, bombings, death of loved ones, and the loss of part of their country. The second period, which coincides with the youth and student rebellion of the 1960s, was characterised by the identification of German youth with the victims, and the discrediting their parents' and grandparents' generations. The third stage, and the most critical for Beland, relates to his chapter's main theme, the coming to grips with the loss of one's own national goodness. To be German today requires an acceptance of the deeds of the Nazi generation as German deeds, as their own deeds. In reading this section of Beland's paper, I was struck by the similarity of this acceptance of the crimes of the earlier generation of Germans, to whom the current Germans stand as progeny both genetically and culturally, and the portrayal of the "wicked son" in the Passover Haggadah, whose wickedness lies in his distancing himself from the exodus, thus cutting himself off from his people. However, whereas the "wicked son" cuts himself off from the national experience of redemption, the Germans, during the first two periods outlined above, cut themselves off from the national experience of the perpetration of genocide.

It is often argued that, although Christian anti-Semitism prepared the way for the exterminatory anti-Semitism of the Nazis, it was different in that Jews could always avail themselves of conversion to Christianity as a way of self-preservation. Beland challenges this interpretation by suggesting that the same deep mechanisms at work in Christian anti-Semitism were continued with formal variation in racist anti-Semitism. Christian thinkers from Augustine to Luther and Pascal, and on into the twentieth century, were engaged in massive projections of their own anti-Christian proclivities on to the Jews, as

Freud (1912–1913) had argued more generally regarding Christian anti-Semitism. All the charges and prejudices against the Jews ought to be conceived as split off and projected elements of the German-Christian unconscious.

In the final section of this chapter, Beland writes autobiographically about his experiences in meetings and seminars with Israeli and Jewish colleagues that made him feel enormously uncomfortable. He puzzled over why the Israeli and Jewish colleagues were so intent on coming together with Germans such as himself, and he concluded that they wanted to know his horror. They wanted to learn what it was like to belong to a national group that instigated, planned, and carried out, in an industrial and scientific fashion, mass murder and genocide. At first, Beland could not answer, but he came to recognise the necessity of facing the question for himself and for others.

In his chapter, Tomas Böhm presents us with an approach to prejudice and anti-Semitism that is partly influenced by the work of Melanie Klein and her followers. Böhm begins his chapter with the assertion that love is more precarious and fragile than evil or hatred. In the Kleinian schema, at the beginning of psychic life the paranoid–schizoid position characterises the inner world of the neonate and young child and the vagaries of unconscious fantasy life always threatens to pull the developing individual from the depressive position back into the paranoid–schizoid. The frustrating care-giver is perceived as a persecuting figure, a bad mother, or breast, split off from the good. This leads to a black and white universe, whereby that which is inside is all good and that which is outside is all bad. The more mature depressive position is a platform for integration and compromise, where there is nuance as opposed to black and white thinking.

Hostile and malignant prejudices are a mechanism of the paranoid–schizoid position, through the projection of what is bad inside to some other individuals or groups outside. The sexual desires of repressed white southern men in the USA, for example, before the civil rights movement, were projected on to African-American men who were often castrated before they were lynched, the pretext for this "punishment" being that they looked leeringly at a white woman. Similarly, greed and vulgarity, which lie deep within the psyche of anti-Semites as their own intolerable qualities, are projected on to the Jews. The hatred of these unconscious trends which lie within can be given free reign through the hatred of the Jew, by means of this projective identification. This process is thus directly linked with the splitting of the ego, whereby unacceptable aspects are split off and projected, as the above examples illustrate. Although hostile and malignant prejudices are not congruent with all forms of splitting and projection, they lend themselves well to it, which keeps all the good within the group while the outside groups are utilised as containers for that which is bad.

Strict ideologies of a religious, political, or social nature foster the kind of black and white thinking that is associated with the schizoid–paranoid position. Charismatic leaders may also use their "talents" (backed up by their terror apparatus) to foster a we/them attitude within their subjects. What prevents "friendly" competition between groups, say for example, in sports, from taking a hostile or malignant colouration is the degree of playfulness involved, which ensures that whatever regression does take place occurs in the service of the ego. When the stranger or outsider provokes anxiety within us, it causes a xenophobic reaction. This reaction, which might simply be a fear of the unknown, may also relate to a fear of our unknown parts, if, as Kristeva maintains, the self is not a homogenous construct, but, rather, a more or less loosely put together whole with different or even conflicting parts. The splitting, which is a key feature of the paranoid–schizoid position, can be activated and reactivated time and again over the course of a life, through retraumatisation and external influences due to societal vicissitudes, such as propaganda, charismatic leadership, or totalitarian and fundamentalist movements.

Böhm then reviews for us various theories of anti-Semitism, beginning with Freud, then including Chasseguet-Smirgel and Arieti. Following a lead from Chasseguet-Smirgel, he discusses the perverse elements in anti-Semitism. If one of the hallmarks of a perverse thought system is the denial of difference, such as boundaries between the generations and the sexes, then the Jew represents a mixture of different elements *par excellence*. He is both the normal citizen and something strange and mysterious, with occult powers of intellect, innovation, and mobility. The Jew is weak and strong, public and private, inferior and superior. As Böhm puts it, the Jew "will attract racists like a magnet".

Böhm concludes his chapter by offering a kind of social democratic alternative to the regressive forces that pull us back into the schizoid–paranoid position. Democracy cultivates the acceptance of difference. Levelling the inequality in society, by means of a social democratic programme, counteracts the corrosive force of envy.

Jorge Kantor, in the final chapter (Chapter Seven) in Part III: "Applications", provides us a view into the operation of widespread prejudice regarding race, class, and culture in Peru, a prejudice which might manifest itself in a similar way in other Latin American countries. (When I worked with a group of anthropologists in Mexico City, I learnt of a similar widespread prejudice of race, class, and culture in that country and was then told that it was rife in Latin America more generally.) Accordingly, one's position in the status hierarchy is determined by the degree to which "white blood" predominates in a family. European characteristics are privileged over the "Indian" elements. Since the majority of the population is, to one degree or another, *mestizaje*, or mixed race, there is a stigma and prejudice against the majority of the population. Since almost everyone has *mestizaje* characteristics, there is an element of self-loathing in most individuals, and when an individual uses an epithet referring to another as an "Indian", he is denying an aspect of himself. When a baby is born, the "white" qualities are highlighted and praised and each family takes credit for those qualities, while the "Indian" features are scorned, downplayed, and imputed to the other family (the narcissism of minor differences).

These elements of prejudice and discrimination are transmitted intergenerationally within families through identification processes with family members. In order to illustrate these points, Kantor presents four vignettes from sessions with an analytic patient, John, whose father was from a wealthy "European" family from Lima, and whose mother was from a *mestizaje* background from a small town in the countryside. By means of these four vignettes, Kantor is able show the subtleties of racial prejudice, interwoven with themes of sexuality and development, idealisations, identification, patterns of aggression, and the self in conflict. These analytic excerpts show how deeply the racial divide reaches into the individual psyche and explains John's intrapsychic conflict. The prejudices of which John gives evidence are not unlike Volkan's transgenerational transmissions of chosen glories and traumas, in that they are unlike identifications that come from the developing child, but, rather, resemble projections that are put into the child by family and the surrounding community. The hostility between his father's urban, wealthy, educated world and his *mestizaje* mother's poor, rural world constitutes the background against which his sadomasochistic sexual trends are nourished. Robust, integrative, adult sexuality with strongly erotic and tender trends is not achieved. Rather, the sexual realm is suffused with the alternatives: fuck or be fucked. As Kantor points out,

> The vignettes illustrate the operation of features of a racial radar, in which Peruvian people are placed into different worlds; a kind of gradient of colour and ethnicity, in which the paternal family is positioned at one end and the maternal family at the other.

This culture pattern through identification and transgenerational transmission produces the conflicted self with a tendency to perverse, sadomasochistic sexuality, and a polity that is stunted in its capacity for democratic growth and maturity. John's associations are suffused with primary process thinking and the cultural split in Peru itself has infected the psyche of the analyst as well as the analysand. It is a struggle with which the analyst must also engage in his clinical work.

In the final chapter of the book, by way of a conclusion, I take a position against the grain of most of the other chapters. I felt it was important to call attention to some of the most difficult problems in dealing with possible responses to hostile and malignant prejudice. I write about the difficulty of finding objective points of reference that all parties of the conflict could use to temper their own national, ethnic, religious, political, historical interests and viewpoints. I have tried to show that not all chosen traumas are equal, and that some chosen traumas actually choose the people involved. I have attempted to show how some of the institutions that ought to be fair arbiters of justice have become politicised and, thus, have become a part of the problem rather than a part of the solution. Given more time, I would have pointed out that sometimes nations and peoples must use force to put down the stated threat, such as genocide, ethnic cleansing, exploitation, or oppression. We seem to have forgotten some of the lessons from the 1930s, and the terrible consequences of appeasement. Of course, this does not mean that we should scorn every attempt to resolve conflicts peacefully and diplomatically, but force should be a regrettable last resort. Our wisdom would lie in the ability to discern those circumstances which are amenable to diplomacy and peaceful resolution from those in which such means, while promoting peace in the short run, will lead assuredly to a more costly and difficult confrontation in the long run. Nevertheless, I conclude by suggesting that there is much that we can do by way of enlightenment when it comes to working with children and their parents. We can, for example, provide psychoanalytic tools to professionals who treat problems of hostile and malignant prejudice in their own work. I would not call this a proposal for establishing a pragmatic utopia as Ignacio Gerber uses the term, but I can see the efficacy in this approach for reducing the potential for hostility based on race, ethnicity, religious affiliation, etc.

The chapters that follow represent some of the cutting-edge work on the problems of hostile and malignant prejudice by leading psychoanalysts working within this area. It illustrates the theories based upon clinical work and metapsychology, by means of specific applications in different places and cultures. It is truly an international effort objectified in the form of a book that ought to interest psychoanalysts as well as the educated lay public concerned about issues of prejudice. On the occasion of concluding this work, we wish to recall the memory of our colleague, the late Elizabeth Young-Bruehl, who contributed to this field of research, as she did to other aspects of psychoanalytic theory and its applications, and whose sudden untimely death cut short her further work within the field.

We dedicate this book to the memory of one of our contributors, an active member of our Committee on Prejudice, and our friend, Tomas Böhm, who passed away quite suddenly in May 2013.

Note

1. Terms such as "the German psyche" are a vague, if commonly used, designation to express a dominant trend or trends in a relatively homogeneous population. It does not include all individuals but it does imply that all individuals must deal with these trends, even if they are not included in them. Beland recognises this explicitly at the end of his chapter, where he refers to the problematic nature of linking individual pathology with collective phenomena. Freud recognised the same problem in *Totem and Taboo*, *Group Psychology and the Analysis of the Ego*, and in *Civilization and Its Discontents*.

References

Bohleber, W. (2007). Remembrance, trauma and collective memory. *International Journal of Psychoanalysis, 88:* 329–352.

Frankel, C., Fresco, N., Guillaumin, C., Hiernaux, J., Jacob, F., Jacquard, A., Langaney, A., Olender, M., & Poliakov, L. (1981). *La Science Face au Racisme.* Paris: Seuil, Le Genre Humain.

Freud, S. (1912–1913). *Totem and Taboo. S.E., 13:* 1–161. London: Hogarth.

Freud, S. (1921c). *Group Psychology and the Analysis of the Ego. S.E., 18:* 69–143. London: Hogarth.

Freud, S. (1930a). *Civilization and Its Discontents. S.E., 21:* 57–145. London: Hogarth.

Krader, L. (2010). *Noetics: The Science of Thinking and Knowing.* New York: Peter Lang.

Rüsen, J. (2001). Holocaust-Erfahrung und deutsche Identität. Ideen zu einer Typologie der Generationen. In: W. Bohleber & S. Drews, (Eds.), *Die Gegenwart der Psychoanalyse - die Psychoanalyse der Gegenwart* (pp. 95–106). Stuttgart: Klett-Cotta.

PART I

THE ORIGIN OF PREJUDICE IN CHILDHOOD: THEORY AND PRACTICE

CHAPTER ONE

Malignant prejudice:
its development and prevention*

Henri Parens

A model of prejudice

This model of prejudice evolved in sequence through a series of research projects that started with my study on the development of aggression in early childhood (Parens, 1973, 1979[2008]). This prejudice model addresses:

- the obligatory development of prejudice in humans;
- a stratification of qualitative levels of prejudice;
- its key contributors and psychodynamics;
- guidelines for the prevention of malignant prejudice;
- key obstacles to its prevention.

I should note that the thrust to my considering the notion or feasibility of preventing, or at least reducing, occurrences of malignant prejudice came from the findings that emerged from our observational

---

* This chapter is a condensation of two previously published and more detailed articles (1) "Malignant prejudice—guidelines toward its prevention" (Parens, 2007b) and (2) "Attachment, aggression and the prevention of malignant prejudice" (Parens, 2012).

research on the development of aggression in early childhood: in fact, from infancy on. As I have described (Parens, 1973), the entire enterprise of this series of projects—from the development of aggression to the prevention of malignant prejudice—was launched by an adventitious finding that struck me of much consequence: that infants do not behave as prescribed by the then extant psychoanalytic theory of aggression, that is, Freud's amended death-instinct-based theory of aggression (Hartmann, Kris, & Loewenstein, 1949). These findings led me to propose a revision to the psychoanalytic theory of aggression (Parens, 1979[2008]). The relevance of this revision lies in the fact that the experiences we have during the course of growing up highly determine how hostile we become as adults, and how readily we may become an advocate of malevolence towards others.

Through the course of clinical work and research, I have found that among those experiences that forge the degree to which we become hostile, none is larger than the quality of experiences we have at the hands of our primary care-givers. There is significant consensus among researchers in mental health and social sciences that there is a strong correlation between qualitative strategies of child rearing and the quality of their children's relationships, their adaptation to life and society, and, specifically, their hostile–destructive aggression profiles (see Parens, 2011, Chapters Two and Three for reviews of pertinent literature). Indeed, in our own research on aggression, we found meaningful support for this correlation (Parens, 1993). Furthermore, we found that how parents handle their young children can be optimised by means of psychodynamically informed parenting education strategies (Parens, 2008a; Parens & Rose-Itkoff, 1997; Parens, Scattergood, Duff, & Singletary, 1997a,b). Briefly, here is evidence from our project's documentation.

Positive correlation between quality of attachment and aggression profiles

During the course of seven years of twice a week two-hour observation–intervention sessions with mothers and their newborns, then continuing for nearly four decades in three follow-up studies, we found, as have others (see Aichhorn, 1944; Beebe, 2005; Bowlby, 1946; Brazelton, 1981; Eissler, 1949; Egeland, Yates, Appleyard, & van Dulman, 2001;

Gilligan, 1997; Kernberg, 1966; Sroufe, Egeland, Carlson, & Collins, 2005), a stable positive correlation between the quality of the child's attachment to his/her mother (primary care-giver(s)) and the child's aggression profile.

Within eighteen months from the start of our study in 1970 (Parens, 1979), on the basis of our parenting optimising intervention, we saw the mothers' interactions with their children shift significantly in their parenting behaviour from "growth-disturbing to growth-promoting". This was ascertained in our nineteen-year follow-up study, and confirmed in our thirty-two and thirty-seven-year follow-up studies. On a ten point scale, a shift *in the mothers' self-evaluations* of over five points, while *the staff* recorded a shift of just less than four points along three of the four parameters, resulted in a significant change in the character of their parenting from "growth-disturbing" to "growth-promoting" (see Table 1; Parens, 1993).

A key factor links the quality of attachment and the child's aggression profile as explained by the "multi-trends theory of aggression" (Parens, 1979[2008]). This multi-trends theory of aggression holds that the trend, which is neither inborn nor biologically generated and is constituted of the range of affective expressions of hostile destructiveness (HD), that is, from anger to hostility, rage, hate, etc., is

Table 1. Changes in parents' functioning.[1]

Change in parenting parameters (Means) on 10-point scale	Parent self-ratings (n = 8*)			Stat. sig. (Wilcoxon)	ECDP** staff ratings (n = 10)			Stat. sig. (Wilcoxon)
	Before	After	*Diff.*		Before	After	*Diff.*	
Understanding child & rearing	3.2	8.6	*5.4*	p < 0.02	3.4	7.3	*3.9*	p < 0.01
Shift in ambivalence	3.2	8.4	*5.2*	p < 0.02	5.5	8.2	*2.7*	p < 0.01
Effectiveness of parenting	3.4	8.7	*5.3*	p < 0.02	4.3	8.1	*3.8*	p < 0.01
Self-worth and competence	3.4	9.0	*5.6*	p < 0.02	4.1	7.9	*3.8*	p < 0.01

*One mother did not return self-rating; one other mother lost to the project was included in staff evaluation (in the project only one year, her changes were minimal).
**ECDP = The Early Child Development Program, H. Parens, Director.

structured through experiences of excessive psychic pain in the context of object relatedness (Parens, 1979 [2008]). That experiences of "Excessive Unpleasure, i.e., psychic pain (EU) generate Hostile Destructiveness (HD)" in humans is the critical factor that links the quality of attachment and the child's aggression profile. This means that: ". . . given a child's average-expectable biological endowment, the way parents rear their child will directly affect the character of that child's aggression profile" (Parens, 2012, p. 173).

Let's keep in mind that, when we think of prevention, "HD can be *moderated* or it can be *heightened* by experience".

I emphasise that the cardinal hypothesis pertinent for prevention is: "Excessive Unpleasure (psychic pain) generates High-Level HD: 'EU → HL-HD'".

The evidence observed and documented on paper and in film during the seven-year project, and in the three follow-up studies, strongly suggests that optimising the mothers' child-rearing strategies led to both favourable attachments and favourable aggression profiles in their children (Table 2).

Note: While our study sample is small (sixteen children), the two parameters critical to the children's outer-directed anger and hostility are significantly more favourable than the population from which they come.

Finding convincing observational evidence—even if from a small subject population—of the bettering of the mothers' child rearing and of the mother–child relationships, we developed parenting education

Table 2.   Anger and hostility in ECDP children.

*FAI parameters	ECDP av. (n = 12)	FAI av.	Cut off "mild" to "moderate"	Stat. significance (2-tailed T-test)
Anger	37.8	50.10	45.0	p < 0.05
Trust/mistrust	6.1	6.07	6.0	NS
Passive aggression	8.8	10.11	9.0	NS
Violence potential	5.1	7.96	7.0	p < 0.05

* FAI = Fitzgibbons Anger Inventory.

Two permissions to interview not granted by one father, FAI not available; two lost to project; one not applicable.

materials, all in the service of the prevention or reduction of experience-dependent emotional disorders in children, including a
reduction in their hostility, hate, and violence. This effort at the
reduction of hostility, hate, and violence opened up a further avenue
of possible intervention.

From correlations of attachment and
aggression to the study of prejudice

Driven by unconscious motivations, given my life experiences, which I
detailed in my Holocaust memoirs (Parens, 2004), it makes sense that
I would make the leap from generating strategies for the reduction of
excessive hostility in humans to searching for ways to reduce prejudice.

In starting that study, I objected to the statement that "we all have
prejudices", but I found myself compelled to see, in my labouring
over the details of psychoanalytic developmental theories and my
own research and clinical findings, that, as Figure 1 shows, yes we do
all have prejudices.

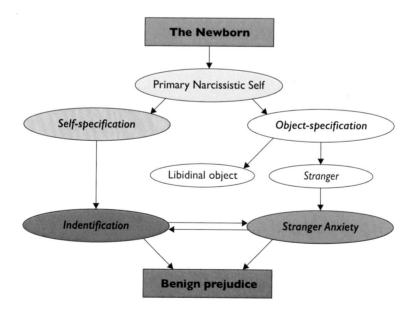

Figure 1.   The development of benign prejudice.

Normative developmental factors that make us all prejudiced

I came to realise that two factors do so, factors essential to the child's emerging and developing identity and sense of self, an achievement that evolves in reciprocity with the formation of primary relationships. In 2007, I detailed that (1) *identification* and (2) *stranger anxiety* predispose us all to having prejudices (Parens, 2007a). Let me briefly address each in turn.

The role of identification in self-specification

As I try to illustrate in Figure 1, we know that the development of self is intimately linked to the development of one's relationships. Mahler proposed that the development of self, from its nucleus in primary narcissism, is forged during the separation–individuation process. Also, as Freud hypothesised in 1939 regarding the child's self-development, resulting from seemingly obligatory identifications with his primary care-givers, the child will bear the stamp "Made in Germany", which I specify as "Made in the X, Y, or Z Family". Two major factors bring about this specific, distinctive identity stamping:

1. Our *genes*, which make their enormous biological *genotypic* contributions to our being like our parents.
2. It is especially those identifications with our primary love objects that give us our specific *phenotypic* stamp "Made in My Family". This, in turn, leads to our becoming members of our specific community, since, as Freud (1940a) proposed, our parents are to us the representatives of the community to which we belong.

With regard to the development of prejudice, this critical self-specification factor, identification, plays a powerful role in that part and parcel of identification is the taking on of familial and, therewith, societal–cultural mores. These will include familial–cultural prejudices, whether they are in favour of accepting as equally valuable or as not equally valuable people different than ourselves. The multimodal communications of parents and later neighbours that convey such biases are compelling and make these accepting or hostile biases toward "others" an unavoidable part of one's identifications.

Lorenz, Spitz, and Bowlby[2] are the foremost *attachment* pioneers. In the summation of his studies on the structuring of the libidinal object, Spitz (1965) detailed two complementary object specification factors: "separation anxiety" and "stranger anxiety". Note that while identification is a self-specification factor, separation anxiety and stranger anxiety are object specification factors. Stranger anxiety carries with it the potential for the rejection of objects different than those to whom the child attaches, or with whom the infant centrally identifies. Let's look more closely at this key contributor to the development of prejudice.

Stranger anxiety and the roots of xenophobia

Mammal neonates are biologically "pre-wired" to attach to others. In altricial organisms[3] such as Homo sapiens, attachment is profoundly experience-dependent. Of large consequence to the question of prejudice, stranger anxiety, the earliest manifestation of rejecting "others", plays a crucial role in the formation of love-relationships. In observing infants grasping the significance of the structuring of the libidinal object, Spitz (1965) proposed four cardinal indicators of this process.

1. With *the social smiling response*, which emerges between five and ten weeks of age, the infant engages in and "invites" an emotional dialogue with the objects involved in their care. Within months, the infant's attachments progressively become specific. While object-specificity becomes observable from about approximately five to six months on, this object specification, in fact, evolves and stabilises only gradually over the first twenty four to thirty six months.[4] During this period, the infant's attachment, not yet securely set, is vulnerable to derailment. This is evidenced in the following infant behaviours.
2. *Separation anxiety* emerges from about five months on, when on separations—even if only brief—the infant experiences the threat of loss of the object due to the infant's inability to evoke the internal representation of the attachment object when it is out of the infant's visual field. By eighteen months, the infant can evoke the object representation and separation anxiety may decrease. Similarly,
3. *Reunion reactions* affirm the recovery and the evolving attachment to specific objects. Critical to our present concern is
4. *Stranger anxiety* affirms the infant's recognition that *not all objects are his or her objects for attachment.*

I have proposed that stranger anxiety serves attachment to specific objects by containing and directing the infant's inborn object-attachment tendency away from any non care-giving object, toward the care-giving objects. I have suggested, as did Spitz (see below) that this normal developmental factor, stranger anxiety, plays a key role in the predisposition to prejudice.

The thoughts I have pulled together, represented in Figure 1, shed light on those normal developmental factors that facilitate the organisation of prejudice within us. They explain well why "We all have prejudices". But what kind of prejudice is this? Does this normal preference for "one's own kind" lead to our wanting to depreciate, harm, and destroy strangers, those "others"? I have proposed that the factors so far addressed readily explain the tendency in us to develop prejudice, but it is *benign*, it does not carry the wish to harm others.

We cannot account for prejudice that leads to harming or destroying others on the basis of these developmental factors alone: I would say even where identification with familial and cultural mores brings intense negative prejudice against "others".

It is hostile destructiveness in the form of hate that forges our benign prejudice into prejudice of a very different kind.

What hate? What wishes to destroy are we talking about? I have rejected the theory that infants come into the world driven by an instinct to destroy (Parens, 1979), and, like Spitz (1965, pp. 157–160), I have also rejected Szekely's (1954) view that children come into the world with an inborn xenophobia. My work has led me to propose that ambivalence in primary relationships is the most central and powerful contributor of the generation in humans of the wish to harm or destroy "others". Let me clarify.

The large dilemma created in the child by ambivalence

Longitudinal child observation documents decidedly indicate that hating those we love, ambivalence, creates in the child a large dilemma. In our research, we saw a striking cluster of defences young children erect when very angry with their mothers. By twelve months of age, we had seen much evidence of *displacement*, *inhibition*, and even *splitting of object representations*. By eighteen months of age, we saw clear evidence of *projection*, *rationalisation*, and *denial*: "I didn't do that;

it was an accident". Then, especially organising of prejudice, starting from five to six years on, we saw behaviours from which we could infer "reality-distorting defences", suggesting *reductionism, caricaturing, depreciation,* and *vilification,* defences that play a key role in the organisation of what I have called "malignant prejudice" (Parens, 1999, 2007a).

I have tried to summarise my findings to date, as I have searched to understand the psychogenesis and dynamics of the hostilification of benign prejudice into hostile and malignant prejudice and represented them in Figure 2, taking note of critical interacting individual and group forces that, I believe, lead to its development.

First, let us take a further step in the evolution of my model of prejudice, in order to elaborate on the hostilification of benign into malignant prejudice. Akhtar (2007) is right in proposing that there are gradations of prejudice beyond what I have so far mentioned. A patient's associations drew my attention to the need for a state of hostilification of benign prejudice that falls well short of being malignant prejudice. What my patient's associations drew to my attention is so well known as to approach the banal. In essence, it is no more than that the person says, "Well, you know, Jews are greedy!", or "Oh, Blacks are just so lazy!", or "You just don't know; is this Muslim a terrorist?!" It is ugly. However, it has not taken the turn to wanting to destroy them; it does not fuel ethnic cleansing; it is not malignant prejudice. But it certainly is distorting, pejorative, and, all in all, hostile. This is *hostile prejudice*. In contrast, *malignant prejudice* can and has led to murder and genocide.

The role of trauma in the hostilification of benign prejudice

Trauma is a major contributor to what generates HD in humans. Much hurtfulness happens to people, but people are vigorous: not all intense pain is traumatising. It is when one's adaptive capacities are overwhelmed by highly painful events of shocking meaning to the self that we experience it as traumatising; it triggers and generates high level HD in us. Various parameters determine the degree of psychic pain we experience: the *nature* of the traumatic event; the *age* and *state* of self at the time of occurrence; who is the perpetrator; whether it is episodic or chronic; what meaning we give to the event; and, highly

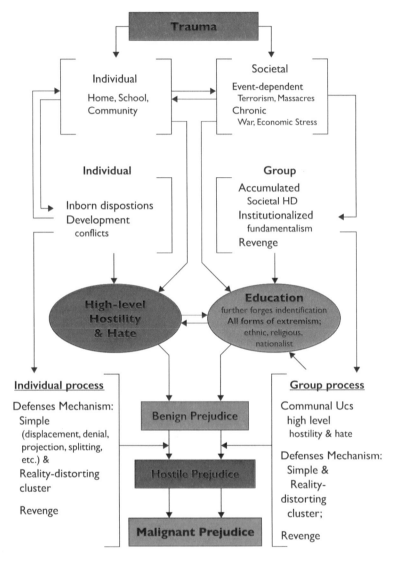

Figure 2. The complex psycho-genetics of malignant prejudice: from benign to malignant prejudice.

critical, *whether the event is perceived as intentional or accidental*; all these codetermine the degree to which we may become traumatised (Parens, 2008b). For example, abuse at the hands of one's own mother or father causes much more psychic pain than when the abuse is perpetrated by a stranger or "enemy" (Ornstein, 1985; Parens, 1999). Neglect or abuse by those we count on for love, nurture, and protection multiplies the degree of psychic pain experienced and is strongly correlated with delinquency and criminality by researchers in the humanities and the social sciences (see Aichhorn, 1944; Beebe, 2005; Bowlby, 1946; Brazelton, 1981; Gilligan, 1997; McCord, McCord, & Zola, 1959; Sroufe, Egeland, Carlson, & Collins, 2005; Werner & Smith, 1992).

I do not want to oversimplify what we encounter in the behaviours of traumatised humans. As these are amply documented, many cope with severe trauma with remarkable resilience that yields within them striking creativity and productivity. Neither do most who are traumatised become delinquents and criminals; many turn to depressive and masochistic character formations, as well as borderline and narcissistic adaptations. In addition, although many will erect the cluster of defences I have noted, these defences might not result in them developing malignant prejudice. They might not target a given group of "others" towards whom their hate is discharged, and they might not share their outrage with others; they act in solitude, sometimes with specified, sometimes with unspecified, target victims. Regrettably, many who are heavily traumatised develop a compelling need to discharge their hate in the form of "revenge" (Gilligan, 1997), which creates within them, as Volkan has proposed, *The Need to Have Enemies* (1988).

While high loads of accumulated hostile destructiveness may transform our benign prejudice into hostile and malignant prejudice, there is yet another path to its formation. Both hostile and malignant prejudice can be greatly facilitated within an individual whose hostile destructiveness is moderate and is not sufficient of itself to lead to the formation of hostile or malignant prejudice: it is through *education.*

The role of education and the "socialisation of identification"

As I have proposed (2007b), education that is programmed to socialise the child mandates and, indeed, tends to coerce the individual's identification with the group. Some aspect of education is committed just to this end, and can be a major contributor to the hostilification of prejudice by forging benign into hostile and even malignant prejudice.

Peter Riedesser, my friend from Hamburg, told me that when he was young, even though he knew no Jews, he had learnt to hate them, because he was taught that "the Jews" had killed Christ.

This teaching to hate a culture's established enemy is driven in large part by the demand that the child identify with his or her parents and the society they represent. It is an "identification demanded by the universe into which the child is born". This teaching of dogma often carries with it "malignant distortions" brought about by those "reality distorting defences" that rationalise and justify hostile and malignant prejudice. Here, education is put into service to compel the hostilification of benign prejudice.

The sum of the interacting forces detailed within this model of prejudice suggests pathways to the development of hostile and of malignant prejudice. In addition, the model reveals loci where we might fruitfully develop preventative interventions—some of which have already long been in place. While little is new in what I am showing here, some aspects of these genetic–dynamic factors, however, stand out as needing more attention than we have committed to them to date.

How can we intervene to lessen or even prevent malignant prejudice?

Let me first say that because benign prejudice is a normal phenomenon obligatory for the healthy development of self and love relationships, any effort to prevent benign prejudice would disturb their developments. It is the *hostilification* of *benign prejudice* that creates the problem.

As the malignant prejudice model shows, both "individual" and "group/societal" factors combine to produce it.

1. Individual factors include (a) inborn dispositions; (b) intense intrapsychic conflicts which are made more intense by traumatisation (familial and societal); and (c) the individual's psychic mechanisms set up to divert his accumulating HD and need for revenge, which easily attaches to communal calls for revenge.
2. Group factors play a large role in the organisation of hostile and malignant prejudice. Central are factors such as (a) societal

traumas, whether event-dependent or chronic, and (b) militant ethnic or militant religious fundamentalist education.

While this working model does not address all the factors that contribute to the development of malignant prejudice, I find it useful to work with.

As I said, two major pathways lead to the formation of malignant prejudice:

1. What I think is its centrepiece, high-level hostile destructiveness (HL-HD);
2. Ethno-fundamentalist education that fosters malignant prejudice.

Let's look at each in turn.

The centrepiece of malignant prejudice: high-level hostile destructiveness (HL-HD)

Here is a simple prejudice-pertinent spectrum of the role of hostile destructiveness:

1. Hostile destructiveness (HD) is the *sine qua non* of the wish to harm. It leads to the formation of hostile prejudice.
2. High-level hostile-destructiveness (HL-HD) is the *sine qua non* of *the hostile wish to destroy*. It contributes to the intensification of hostile prejudice into malignant prejudice.
3. Both HD and HL-HD attached to specified, selected others are forged by "defences specifically intended to distort reality about (these) others" and are, respectively, the *sine qua non* of hostile prejudice and of malignant prejudice.

How can we intervene to lessen the generation of hostile destructiveness (HD) in individuals?

Given its role in malignant prejudice, how can we intervene to lessen the generation of high-level hostile destructiveness within individuals? As I said earlier, research from disciplines within the humanities and social sciences hold that the generation of HD within individuals begins in their childhood, and that *the way we rear our children* primarily determines the level of hostile destructiveness they accumulate. In other words, families have the power to prevent the excessive generation of HD in their children, and, where such HD is generated, to actively reduce its accumulation within their children.

Let us not minimise the magnitude of trauma children experience. According to a UN-sponsored study led by Paulo Pinheiro, "an estimated *40 million children globally under the age of 15* suffer from violence, abuse, and neglect . . . [and UNICEF asks], what must [we do] to prevent and end the scourge" (UN News, 17 October 2005, my italics). Clinically, we find that children experience trauma within *their home*, but also *within their school* and *neighbourhood*.

How can society helpfully intervene?

At home: Given the information accumulated during the twentieth century concerning growth-promoting and growth-disturbing practices in rearing children, it is in the best interest of us all to avail ourselves of "formal parenting education". Since the 1970s, when the mental health community recognised the feasibility of optimising the way parents rear their children, a number of parent–child group programmes were developed, the aim of which was exactly that: optimising parenting in order to optimise their children's development (Parens, 1993). In fact, our own mother–child observational research evolved into groups for mothers and their infants to achieve this end, and these have been ongoing in our area to this day. Considering the question of prevention efforts towards reducing hostile and malignant prejudice, findings from our thirty-seven-year study (see Table 1) suggest that psychodynamically informed parenting education *can optimise parenting*, which, in turn, as I stated above, can reduce the generation and accumulation of excessive hostility within children, and bring with it a significant *reduction in their accumulating hostile destructiveness* (see Table 2). The line for implicating such a prevention effort is visibly illustrated on the left side of the malignant prejudice model (Figure 2). For example, the "Parenting for Emotional Growth" educational materials for students five to eighteen years of age (Parens, Scattergood, Duff, & Singletary, 1997a,b) have been shown to be capable of optimising parenting strategies.

Studies by Masterpasqua (1992) and Gulkus (1995) in the USA have documented the benefits to school students in preparation for parenting courses. Similarly, Brisch's (2007) *Das B.A.S.E. Babywatching* programme, which includes the training of teachers and mentors to help young children understand the experience-based dynamics of hostile destructiveness, has proved productive, and, according to Dr Brisch, was fortunately well received in Germany, New Zealand, Canada, and most recently in the UK (personal communications, 2008, 2012) and Austria (personal communication, Ursula Henzinger, 2011).

In school and neighbourhood: Some children experience much pain at the hands of sadistic and humiliating teachers, or sadistic and reject-ing peers. There are efforts to reduce this HD generating activity. For example, Twemlow and colleagues (Twemlow & Sacco, 2007; Twem-low, Fonagy, & Sacco, 2002) have reported strategies to deal with the fact that in many schools both staff and teacher–student relationships fail to contain intense interactive hostility, which, at times, have led to shocking reciprocal teacher–student sadism. In this, too many teachers try to get students to work by shaming them. The more they shame them, the greater the degree of HD generated within the child. Large demands can be made on students without abusing them. Also, the Safe Schools programmes of Twemlow and colleagues (2002, 2007), which focus on violence prevention and anti-bullying, are showing the potential for violence prevention among youth within school and community settings, all of which impact the individual's accumulated HD.

Societal, large group traumas often become key generators of malignant prejudice

A crucial parameter of trauma is whether the event occurs accidentally or intentionally. For example, accidental Chernobyl and intentional September 11 were experienced very differently, the first with fear and the call for greater safety measures, the second with outrage and the call for revenge and war.

For society, a trauma may be episodic, *event-dependent*, as in acts of terrorism, such as September 11, 2001, or the destruction of a shrine in India, or *chronic*, as in economic hard times with high-rate joblessness or massive food shortages, as occurred in Europe during the early

1930s. The world-wide economic situation today, with its current high rate of unemployment, while less devastating than that which preceded 1930, brings with it high levels of distress, which in turn leads to the increasing potential for crime and the activation of malignant prejudice: "It's got to be somebody's fault!"

Volkan observes that a societal trauma contributes to shaping the dynamics of that society and becomes inscribed in the history of that society as a "chosen trauma" (2004). This leads to the development of attitudes and rules of conduct towards the trauma perpetrators that forge a set of "sustainable malignant distortions" (Parens, 2007b), which, propagandised, lead to malignant prejudice.

Some of the group processes that foster malignant prejudice include:

1. *Communal accumulated HL-HD*, conscious and unconscious.
2. *Group process defence mechanisms*. While there is some difficulty in applying principles from individual to group psychology, there are group processes that operate similarly, or nearly so. For example, the more conscious cluster of "reality distorting defences about others", including reductionism, caricaturing, depreciation, and vilification seem usefully applicable to both individual and group psychology. In the 1930s, the Third Reich used them highly effectively. Currently in the USA, a less organised but painfully active process, Islamophobia, has developed since September 11.
3. *Brooding pre-conscious wishes for revenge*. Both Akhtar (1997) and Volkan (2004) have spoken of societal "historical narratives" that organise around "chosen traumas" and become valued historical memory. These narratives are fervently commemorated and, in those with extremist leanings, forge revenge into a driving force that is lauded. In the face of such extremist lauding of revenge, the moderation-inclined segment of society—the "silent majority"—seems not as determined to protect society from group processes that foster revenge. Nonetheless, moderating efforts are being made.

Education that fosters malignant prejudice

As I show in the right centre of the malignant prejudice model, another major factor, *education*, can directly convert benign into malignant prejudice. Here, rather than initiated by the individual, the individual takes on the collective societal HL-HD that is transmitted through education. Young children come to school already well educated in their religion, ethnicity, and nationality. At home, the line between identification and education fades; parents are their children's first and perhaps most determining teachers. In fact, the formal education a child receives in schools is *a continuation of the children's identifications with their parents*; indeed, society presents itself to the children for identification, and simply continues the task of the children's formation on behalf of their parents.

The role of militant extremism

In all extremism, distinctions between "us and them" are commonly emphasised, vigorously adhered to, and our own beliefs are proclaimed as more righteous than those of others (Strenger, 2009). This organises into a "militant prejudice". The risk in militant prejudice lies in that it too easily becomes hostilified into malignant prejudice.

What can society do to reduce militant extremism, of all kinds?

This question was of much concern during the past century to individuals and social groups, including governing bodies. I believe that since education has a large role in the formation of malignant prejudice, education can be, should be, and is implemented to lessen the development of malignant prejudice. Recent and ongoing efforts include:

1. Prevention efforts by the United Nations in combating racism. For example, in 2004–2007, Shashi Tharour, then United Nations' Under-Secretary-General for the Department of Public Information, initiated a series of seminars entitled "Unlearning Intolerance", which included topics on anti-Semitism and Islamophobia. A number of times, former UN Secretary-General Kofi Annan spoke out firmly against racism, following his declaration on 21 June 2004 that:

    No Muslim, no Jew, no Christian, no Hindu, no Buddhist – no one who is true to the principles of any of the world's faiths, no one who claims a cultural, national or religious identity based on values such as truth, decency and justice – can be neutral in the fight against intolerance (UN Chronicle, June 2004).

2.   Ethnic/religious group efforts toward peaceful coexistence have been set in motion within the USA and elsewhere by members of two, three, and more faiths, personally striving to know "the other"; interfaith gatherings and alliances seem to be gaining momentum.

3.   Prevention through educating children for peace and coexistence. For example, admirable efforts were made in the Middle East by collaborating Israeli, Arab, and Palestinian educators. According to Klang-Ma-oz:

> Indeed, during the 1980s and the beginning of the 1990s, tens of organizations, universities, teacher training colleges, institutes and NGOs in Israel have been engaged in implementing Jewish-Arab co-existence programmes. (cited in Parens, 2007b, p. 287)

Unfortunately, these decade-long "peace and co-existence" efforts were disrupted in 2000 by extremism-driven violence among these peoples. I believe that formal school curricula, secular, religious, and ethno-social, that educate children in peace and coexistence are probably among the widest avenues open to community efforts towards the prevention, or at least the lessening, of malignant prejudice.

Key obstacles that stand in our way

1.   *The Janus Dilemma*: Perhaps the largest problem is that, as with malignant prejudice, the terrorist's action, viewed by the victim as a crime against humanity, is seen by the perpetrator as an act of valour or honour. It is society that declares this valuation, not the individual.

It is, therefore, society's challenge to solve this group phenomenon, this Janus dilemma.

2.   *Changes are required within each of us*: Bar-on and colleagues (1997) as well as Eyad El-Sarraj, Director of the Gaza Community Mental Health Programme (National Public Radio, Morning Edition of August 23, 2005), on each side of the Palestinian–Israeli

conflict, have made this point. Bar-on struck at the heart of the matter: he holds that in order to make efforts at peace and coexistence work, it is important to recognise that "the peace process can bring about a severe crisis of identity. Who are we if there will be no enemy who tries to kill us?" (Bar-on, Sagy, Awwad, & Zak, 1997). As Bar-on and El-Saraj cogently note, peace and coexistence create a unique challenge to both Israelis and Palestinians, whose identity has long been forged by being reciprocal enemies. However, the world can achieve such peace and coexistence; Europe (Germany, Britain, and France), Japan, and the USA, after decades of wars and reciprocally inflicted catastrophes on one another have achieved such coexistence and even friendship! As Halperin (1997) notes, while such efforts encounter difficulties, results are sufficiently rewarding to continue making such efforts.

As Janusz Korczak[4] said, reminiscent of Schiller's "Ode to Joy",

> We are all brothers, sons of the same earth
> Generations of a joint fate, and trouble, and a long road together.
>
> The same sun shines on us, the same hail destroys our crops
> and the same dust covers the bones of our forefathers.
>
> If truth be told, we've had more tears than smiles
> and there is no sole blame in you nor in us.
>
> Let us begin working together.
>
> (quoted in Keich & Hourani, 1997, p. 95)

Notes

1. Much appreciation to Theodore Fallon, Jr., MD for his statistical analyses of our data.
2. Lorenz (1957) opened the path with his discovery of behaviour of geese and the conceptualisation of attachment through imprinting; Spitz (1946, 1965), and Bowlby (1953, 1969) followed.
3. Altricial organisms are immature at birth. Precocial organisms among mammals can stand on their legs and go to the mother's teats to nurse, for example, a calf or lamb. Altricial ones are less mature, cannot stand

on their legs at birth, and cannot go to the teat to nurse, for example, a kitten or pup. Homo sapiens are among the most immature among mammals.

4. While this stabilisation is progressive, Margaret Mahler (Mahler et al., 1975), in essence, suggested that when development is favourable, this stabilisation is securely achieved by about age three years, at which time the child attains object constancy.

5. Januscz Korczak (1878–1942), an innovative educator, physician, and author, held that "children [ought to be taught] about justice by treating them justly, and [that to cultivate] future leaders [one should give] them an opportunity to lead" (Weiss, 2001, p. 54).

References

Aichhorn, A. (1944). *Wayward Youth.* New York: Viking Press.

Akhtar, S. (1997). Hindu–Moslem conflict in India. Presented to Discussion Group #24: Psychoanalytic Perspectives of Prejudice and Beyond, A Mahfouz, Chair. Meetings, The American Psychoanalytic Assn., New York, December 17.

Akhtar, S. (2007). From unmentalized xenophobia to messianic sadism: some reflections on the phenomenology of prejudice. In: H. Parens, A. Mahfouz, S.W. Twemlow, & D. E. Scharff (Eds.), *The Future of Prejudice: Psychoanalysis and the Prevention of Prejudice* (pp. 7–19). Lanham, MD: Rowman & Littlefield.

Bar-on, D., Sagy, S., Awwad, E., & Zak, M. (1997). Recent research and intervention activities in the Palestinian-Israeli context: an overview. In: D.S. Halperin (Ed.), *To Live Together: Shaping New Attitudes to Peace through Education* (pp. 57–69). Paris: UNESCO: International Bureau of Education.

Beebe, B. (2005). Infant research and implications for adult treatment. Video presentation to the Psychoanalytic Center of Philadelphia Scientific Meeting, March 4, Philadelphia, PA.

Bowlby, J. (1946). *Forty-Four Juvenile Thieves.* London: Balliere, Tindall, & Cox.

Bowlby, J. (1953). Some pathological processes set in train by early mother–child separation. *Journal of Mental Science, 99*: 265–272.

Bowlby, J. (1969). *Attachment.* New York: Basic Books.

Brazelton, B. (1981). Affective reactivity in mother-child interaction. Presented to the Twelfth Annual M. S. Mahler Symposium on Child Development, Philadelphia, PA, May.

Brisch, K. H. (2007). *B. A. S. E. Babywatching*. DVD developed by PD Dr. med. Karl Heinz Brisch, Munich, Germany. Accessible at www.base-babywatching.de

Egeland, B., Yates, T., Appleyard, K., & van Dulman, M. (2001). The long-term consequences of maltreatment in the early years: a developmental pathway model to antisocial behavior. Paper presented to the American Psychological Association, San Francisco.

Eissler, K. R. (1949). *Searchlights on Delinquency*. New York: International Universities Press.

Freud, S. (1940a). *An Outline of Psycho-analysis. S.E.*, 23: 141–207. London: Hogarth.

Gilligan, J. (1997). *Violence: Reflections on a National Epidemic*. New York: Vintage Books.

Gulkus, S. P. (1995). Results: Mercer Junior/Senior H. S. Project Data. Reported by Research and Evaluation Associates, Wayne, PA, March 22 (unpublished).

Halperin, D. S. (Ed.) (1997). *To Live Together: Shaping New Attitudes to Peace through Education*. Paris: UNESCO: International Bureau of Education.

Hartmann, H., Kris, E., & Loewenstein, R. M. (1949). Notes on the theory of aggression. *Psychoanalytic Study of the Child*, 3/4: 9–36.

Keich, H., & Hourani, M. (1997). The Palestinian–Israeli co-education experience at a teachers college and its impact on encounters between Israeli Palestinian and Israeli Jewish kindergarten children. In: D. S. Halperin (Ed.), *To Live Together: Shaping New Attitudes to Peace through Education* (pp. 90–95). Paris: UNESCO: International Bureau of Education.

Kernberg, O. F. (1966). Structural derivatives of object relationships. *International Journal of Psychoanalysis*, 47: 236–253.

Klang-Ma-oz, I. (1997). A decade of structured educational encounters between Jews and Arabs in Israel. In: D. S. Halperin (Ed.), *To Live Together: Shaping New Attitudes to Peace through Education* (pp. 47–56). Paris: UNESCO: International Bureau of Education.

Lorenz, K. (1957). Companionship in bird life. In: C. H. Schiller (Ed.), *Instinctive Behavior* (pp. 83–175). New York: International Universities Press.

Mahler, M. S., Pine, F., & Bergman, A. (1975). *Psychological Birth of the Human Infant*. New York: Basic Books.

Masterpasqua, F. (1992). Evaluation of the "Learning About Parenting" curriculum. Report on Phase I, January 1992, for Educating Children for Parenting (unpublished).

McCord, W., McCord, J., & Zola, I. K. (1959). *Origins of Crime*. New York: Columbia University Press.

Ornstein, A. (1985). Survival and recovery. *Psychoanalytic Inquiry*, 5: 99–130.

Parens, H. (1973). Aggression: a reconsideration. *Journal of the American Psychoanalytic Association*, 21: 34–60.

Parens, H. (1979). *The Development of Aggression in Early Childhood*. New York: Jason Aronson [revised edition: Lanham, MD: Rowman & Littlefield (2008)].

Parens, H. (1993). Toward preventing experience-derived emotional disorders: education for parenting. In: H. Parens & S. Kramer (Eds.), *Prevention in Mental Health* (pp. 121–148). Northvale, NJ: Jason Aronson.

Parens, H. (1999). Toward the prevention of prejudice. In: M. R. Fort Brescia & M. Lemlij (Eds.), *At the Threshold of the Millennium: A Selection of the Proceeding of the Conference, Vol. II* (pp. 131–141). Prom Peru: SIDEA.

Parens, H. (2004). *Renewal of Life: Healing from the Holocaust*. Rockville, MD: Schreiber.

Parens, H. (2007a). Toward understanding prejudice—benign and malignant. In: H. Parens, A. Mahfouz, S. Twemlow, & D. Scharff (Eds.), *The Future of Prejudice: Psychoanalysis and the Prevention of Prejudice* (pp. 21–36). New York: Rowman & Littlefield.

Parens, H. (2007b). Malignant prejudice—guidelines toward its prevention. In: H. Parens, A. Mahfouz, S. Twemlow, & D. Scharff (Eds.), *The Future of Prejudice: Psychoanalysis and the Prevention of Prejudice* (pp. 269–289). New York: Rowman & Littlefield.

Parens, H. (2008a). *The Urgent Need for Universal Parenting Education—A Documentary*. Produced by Parens, H. & Gilligan, P., Director, Thomas Jefferson University, Medical School Media Division, Philadelphia, PA.

Parens, H. (2008b). An autobiographical study of resilience: healing from the Holocaust. In: H. Parens, H. P. Blum, & S. Akhtar, (Eds.), *The Unbroken Soul: Tragedy, Trauma, and Resilience* (pp. 85–116). Lanham, MD: Jason Aronson/Rowman & Littlefield.

Parens, H. (2011). *Handling Children's Aggression Constructively – Toward Taming Human Destructiveness*. Lanham, MD: Jason Aronson/Rowman & Littlefield.

Parens, H. (2012). Attachment, aggression, and the prevention of malignant prejudice. *Psychoanalytic Inquiry*, 32(2): 171–185.

Parens, H., & Rose-Itkoff, C. (1997). *Parenting for Emotional Growth: The Workshops Series*. Vol. 1: *On The Development of Self & Human Relationships*; Vol. 2: *On Aggression*; Vol. 3: *Conscience Formation*; Vol. 4: *Sexual Development in Children*. Philadelphia, PA: Parenting for Emotional Growth. © TXu 842 – 316 & 317.

Parens, H., Scattergood, E., Duff, A., & Singletary, W. (1997a). *Parenting for Emotional Growth: The Textbook*. Philadelphia: Parenting for Emotional Growth. © TXu 680–613.

Parens, H., Scattergood, E., Duff, A., & Singletary, W. (1997b). *Parenting for Emotional Growth: A Curriculum for Students in Grades K Thru 12*. Philadelphia: Parenting for Emotional Growth. © TXu 680–613.

Spitz, R. (1946). The smiling response: a contribution to the ontogenesis of social relations. *Genetic Psychology Monographs*, 34: 57–125.

Spitz, R. (1965). *The First Year of Life*. New York: International Universities Press.

Sroufe, A., Egeland, B., Carlson, E. A., & Collins, W. A. (2005). *The Development of the Person*. New York: The Guilford Press.

Strenger, C. (2009). The psychodynamics of self-righteousness and its impact on the Middle Eastern conflict. *International Journal of Applied Psychoanalytic Studies*, 6: 178–196.

Szekely, L. (1954). Biological remarks on fears originating in early childhood. *International Journal of Psychoanalysis*, 35(1): 57–67.

Twemlow, S. W., & Sacco, F. (2007). *Creating a Peaceful School Learning Environment*. Gawam, MA: T & S Publishers. Manual used in Menninger Child and Family Center's School Violence Reduction Research, www.backoffbully.com.

Twemlow, S. W., Fonagy, P., & Sacco, F. (2002). Feeling safe in school. *Smith Studies in Social Work*, 72(2). Also available at: www.backoff bully.com.

UN Chronicle (2004). @ www.un.org/chronicle. 25 June 2004.

UN News Centre (2005). @ www.un.org/news. 17 October 2005.

Volkan, V. D. (1988). *The Need to Have Enemies and Allies: From Clinical Practice to International Relationships*. Northvale, NJ: Jason Aronson.

Volkan, V. D. (2004). *Blind Trust, Large Groups and their Leaders in Times of Crisis*. Charlottesville, VA: Pitchstone Publishing.

Weiss, A. (2001). *The Last Album: Eyes from the Ashes of Auschwitz-Birkenau*. New York: W. W. Norton.

Werner, E. E., & Smith, R. S. (1992). *Overcoming the Odds: High Risk Children from Birth to Adulthood*. Ithaca, NY: Cornell University Press.

PART II
THEORY

CHAPTER TWO

Distinguishing between ordinary and criminal racism

Marcelo N. Viñar

A very valuable book published in 1981 gathers together a selected group of authors from the fields of natural and human sciences to approach the subject: *La Science Face au Racisme*. In this important work, Jacquard (1981, p. 21) sets out the methodological problem of natural and human sciences, as follows:

> So that our knowledge of the universe can progress, we need, given the limits of our spirit, to replace the infinite diversity of the real with a much more restricted number of categories or codes. To carry out that classification we constrict ourselves to retaining a fraction of the characteristics that we are capable of distinguishing in the objects, by which means we impoverish life. At this cost, we are capable of creating a certain order and of showing certain relationships amongst objects.
>
> This order belongs more to the outlook or representation we have of things than to the things themselves. The real that we talk about, the one that we look for so as to understand the relationship between the facts, and progressively elaborate a scientific discourse is only a caricature created by our spirit, having started in the real world which is perceived by the senses. In order that this caricature does not become false and keeps close to the facts, many precautions are needed. (translated for this edition)

The conceptual unity and coherence of the arguments and conclusions throughout the text are noteworthy. Biologists, geneticists, historians, and anthropologists, from diverse disciplinary fields, dismantle the supposed science underlying the concept of human races, and show the arbitrary and capricious nature of the statements justifying relevant performances of one ethnic group above others. The only constant feature that is found historically is the ethnocentric self-reference: the most elevated and superlative features belong to the group that makes the observation, sometimes as a simple solipsistic statement, at other times by appealing to more or less complex pseudo-evidentiary statistical demonstrations. As Michel de Montaigne cleverly pointed out centuries ago, we call all of those whose practices do not coincide with our habits, ways, models, and values, barbarian or savage.

Jacquard (1981, pp. 14–54), in his extensive and dense chapter, states that the need to classify is a common feature of our mind, so that we might introduce a certain order into the chaos that the complexity of reality imposes upon us. One consequence of classifying is the establishment of a hierarchy according to identifiable subgroups. It seems to be a spontaneous disposition of the mind, whereby the operation that is initiated as an innocent description results in an idealised, self-referential appraisal. This is what cultural anthropology calls ethnocentrism.

Race—as an operational concept—historically has had an enormous versatility in its references. It has used the patronymic (the race of aristocrats—by the grace of God—in contrast to the plebeians), and the ethno-cultural and linguistic diversity at the times of discoveries and voyages during the first globalisation (e.g., discovery of the Far East and America by Europe). However, since the nineteenth century, such observations have been obsessed with establishing (false) connections between biological features (phenotypes or genotypes) and cultural performances, not conceived as diversity, but, rather, superior or inferior hierarchy.

What I would like to underline is that "race", which seeks to be the conceptualisation of a fact that is both "natural" and observable by the senses, a result of a platonic universe's stability, is, instead, a mental construction made by a group to influence the actions of others. What presents itself as an innocent operation, using knowledge of a taxonomic character, is simultaneously a political operation for expression and occlusion.

*   *   *

As Guillaumin (1981, pp. 55–65) argues, the idea of race nowadays is violent and contradictory. It appears as the evidence of a primal truth that is perceived by the senses, while hiding the fact that it is a montage of a slow (and sinister) construction, always at the service of projects for exploitation, domination, or extermination. The slave trade and the debate between Hernán de Sepúlveda and Bartolomé de las Casas as to whether the natives of pre-Columbian America had a soul, and were, therefore, subject to being "evangelised", or, alternatively, did not have a soul and, therefore, could be exploited as animals are the more grotesque, strident, and criminal antecedents of the present situation. The passage of time allows us to reveal and condemn their absurdity and brutality.

What is paradoxical about the rigour of modern science, when denouncing and dismantling the fallacy of the biological foundation of superior races and showing the absurdity of its validity as an operational concept, is its own disregard of its justifying discourse by racists. It glosses over the fact that race is a crucial operator in approving genocide, as with apartheid in South Africa, the Balkans, or the genocidal outburst in the former Yugoslavia, known as ethnic cleansing, in the not too distant past.

It is necessary, but not sufficient, to expose the irrationality of the notion of superior races. There are no material facts that can justify it. But human beings can create realities with concepts. Words such as mother country, state, revolution, and sovereignty are built upon conceptual depth within the dominant consensus of each time and place; its semantic variation is always regional, transitory, and at the service of the dominant power. Ideas are never independent of their agents.

However, Freud taught us that there is another reality (a phantasmatic one) that exceeds the effective reality in force, and that it is possible that the reality of the phantom is not restricted to the territory of infantile sexuality alone.

Freud clearly and categorically stated that psychoanalysis should not be a conception of the world (*Weltanschauung*), but a scientific practice that is the application of an appropriate method to its object of study, which, in our case, is the functioning of the mind's unconscious processes, that he himself investigated and highlighted. The very wide diversity of psychoanalysis expressed within the spectrum of sensitivities, mentalities, preferences, and inclinations of the profession shares this premise and expectation.

Nevertheless, in other texts, Freud himself highlighted the difficulty in being impartial in certain extreme subjects relating to life or death. Neutrality and abstinence are, therefore, a motto in our work, with which it is impossible strictly to comply, but they mark the asymptotic direction of an unattainable ideal. The borders between science and ideology are less clear today than the rationalist school thought in the nineteenth century. Boundaries between ethics, ideology, and scientific practice are complex and less pure than our rationality would like. Boundaries between good and evil can be obscure and equivocal.

Luckily, this is not the case in the specific subject matter of hostile and malignant prejudice, and our motto and mandate is clear: no to racism, and no to anti-Semitism. All decent and responsible citizens— not only psychoanalysts—would subscribe to this position and align themselves in the fight against such arbitrary prejudice and discrimination. To this extent, psychoanalysts could and should act as citizens of the world, without privileges or objections. The true difficulty is the challenge that lies in the next step: in what way can psychoanalytical reflection throw some light on the genesis of racism? If the reflection is lucid, it could probably contribute to preventing it from arising with the appalling consequences that have laid waste to humanity throughout history, and continue to threaten today, and against which we should remain vigilant. This could be the "early warning" of which Hanna Arendt spoke.

However, this not only concerns what psychoanalytical theory can contribute to the understanding of the genesis of racism, but it also concerns posing the question to try to determine which ways the barbarity of racism affects our practice and reflection, as well as our models and our areas of concern. Without abandoning the primacy of the determinants deriving from infantile sexuality in our listening, by expanding our hearing horizon to a multi-causal one, we include other sources for the abject vicissitudes inherent in the human condition. Let us take the well-known example (an extreme caricature) of Melanie Klein interpreting the primal sadistic scene during the Nazi bombardment in London as reductionism. The psychoanalytical model that favours the vicissitudes of intimacy is likely to disregard the macro-social and political determinants that affect the organisation and dynamics of subjectivity. Even though the socio-anthropological axis of the Freudian texts, *Totem and Taboo* (1912–1913), *Group*

Psychology and the Analysis of the Ego (1921c), *Civilisation and Its Discontents* (1930a), and *Moses and Monotheism* (1939a), do not ignore this parameter of reflection, we are not in the habit of paying much attention to these matters in our routine clinical practice because we give almost exclusive emphasis to the vicissitudes of the oedipal constellation within the narration of the neurotic family romance. Perhaps—I am not certain of it—this is a minor sin under democratic conditions of pluralism and tolerance. However, the depressing memories of horror and its after-effects in the history of the twentieth century have taught us how quickly, and unexpectedly, the change towards tyranny and totalitarianism can take place, and that the utopian idea of civilised, linear, and uninterrupted progress is a fallacy. Freud himself used to say with irony that the civilised progress of the twentieth century could be recognised by the fact that the Nazi barbarity only resulted in setting fire to his books but not his person, as would have happened in previous centuries. Only five years later, he would have seen the error of his judgement and the reality of the horror of the Shoah.

For multiple and complex reasons, not least of which is the influence of the instantaneous transmission of information and the expansion of mass media, the frontier between what is public and what is intimate has faded away at a frantic pace, and the subject who comes to analysis is no longer a novelist telling of himself, inclined to long incursions into his internal labyrinths, but a subject immersed in the uproar of the city and its trends. As part of this cultural movement, the post Freudian studies with Lacan and the French school have made the findings of the internal world and psychosexual development more complex with the overriding notion of the "Priority of the Other". Put tersely: in the construction of the subject, the interchange of drives and identificatory constellations are not the only things to intervene (endopsychic and personological vicissitudes), but a dialogical thought emerges, where the mandate of language and culture create a "subject in relation", where something about the human condition is not in the essence (*esse*) or being of an individual, but rests, rather, within the community. The reproach that Elias Canetti made to Freud for having excessively favoured the subject of intimacy while underestimating the subject as a cell in the multitude, seems to have become an alarm signal on its way to being heard (by some). One should not look exclusively at the micro-cosmos of family intimacy, but accord space in the analytical process to those emerging from a world in convulsion.

* * *

I have long thought that Freudian conjecture regarding the beginnings and origins of psychic life constitute an excellent starting point for thought. In the opening lines of "Instincts and their vicissitudes", Freud (1915c) postulates that the most primitive psychism is constituted by incorporating what is one's own and, by extension, what belongs to his relations, his community, expelling or spitting out what is foreign or alien.

Hence, we must understand how this originary and founding xenophobia evolves and which endopsychic and cultural or educational factors help us to overcome it in the course of development. Furthermore, we ask how this initial point of phobia in relation to the stranger, the Other, which is almost universally observable in the second and third trimester of life, develops.

It is important to investigate how endopsychic and cultural factors interact to form the closed identity of the xenophobe, and the open and permeable identity that leads to the recognition and legitimation of difference. No doubt this requires long and slow psychic work. The combination of singular and collective logic seems unavoidable, and psychoanalysis and the social sciences should integrate to develop a discernible multi-factored approach.

* * *

The Other, the stranger, will always have an unknown side, and, therefore, appear hostile and thus likely to generate phobias. The stranger is an invincible otherness, for which we cannot find a name. However, his presence and his appeal are necessary, so as not to remain within a stagnant, inert, self-referenced sameness, which tends to disintegrate over time when repeated. The Other is vital in order to change through exchange—we know this from exogamic laws— and for the victor this is a risky path, but a more worthy one than genocide. Not only is it worthy in its ethical dimension, but in its practical effects as well, since the shame of one's own identity and the feelings this generates are, without a doubt, for the vanquished, one of the strongest roots that nourishes the world of terrorism.

* * *

Castoriadis (Viñar, 1998), following Freud, tells us that racism is not something limited to particular cultures, but is universal and is manifested in practically all human societies. He suggests further that we have not managed to construct our societies without excluding others whom we also diminish and come to hate. In this way, Castoriadis expresses—with remarkable accuracy—a trend which is thought as "natural" to the human spirit on account of its recurrence throughout history, and something which culture is supposed to work tirelessly to reverse. On the other hand, we could consider Hanna Arendt's axiom: diversity is perhaps the most characteristically human phenomenon and, I would add, the most sublime, the greatest asset of our species, a product achieved through culture and language.

How can the psychoanalyst contribute to this endless fight for plurality and the tolerance of diversity?

From the earliest of times, probably well before the development of conscience or memory ontogenetically, in those crucial early days without language or self-awareness, our spirit was being moulded and organised within an environment full of faces, glances, lights, colours, music, stories, legends, and traditions which shaped and modelled us before we knew what they meant. When I want to find meaning in what I am, I have already *been there* (*Dasein*) for some time and I am creating myself as I go along. The *Heimat* and the self are built simultaneously. This approach to the legend of origins that each people, group, and person ritualises to a greater or lesser extent, always doing so individually, is carried out with a regularity and continuity that is surprising throughout human history.

Human beings are soothed by the songs and legends which exist and mark them even before the appearance of the utopian and false idea that man is transparently conscious of himself and free to make his own determinations. For better or for worse, this is where we find the matrix of what is ours, what is sacred, and the collective spirit that precedes (chronologically and logically) individuality. This is where we need to look for the best aspects of our civilisation and where we will find everything that is so terrible about intolerance.

* * *

Since we began to recognise the value of language in the production of the human condition, the primacy of biology has given way in its causal explanations, so, today, we can consider "human nature" without the logical pre-eminence of biology over culture. (I prefer the expression "human condition" to underline its character as a cultural production.) This is why instinctivist, ethological explanations are as poor and invalid as the creationist ones, and why they are obsolete. Our minds are part of the world and not only part of our brain. We cannot treat culture and biology as sovereign and discontinuous realities, or as closed fields. Hence, we ought not to understand cruelty (and this includes war and racism) as traits of human nature, or consider it in the same way as the fact that we stand on two feet, or that the thumb is a flexible digit. There is no ethology for cruelty without a parallel understanding of the historical, political, and cultural space that produced it. There is no such thing as fixed, unchanging human nature, only collective and individual human processes that may encourage and foster culture, or lead to barbarism. There are spaces for cohabitation that are constructed or destroyed by interaction with commercial interests, through economic or ideological domination, where good people destroy the barbarians in the name of religion, or for the sake of civilisation.

*   *   *

From childhood to old age, we ask who we are, in the first person singular and plural: who am I, who are we? This self-theorising curiosity, which is so characteristic and definitive of our species, is with us from cradle to grave. Who are we, where do we come from? Where are we going? Our eagerness for answers to these questions, and their peremptory and insatiable nature, means that we suffer continuously. Only our repeated failing, throughout our personal lives and the history of humanity, teaches us that these questions are as essential as the answers are vain and ephemeral. The illusion of an imaginary fulfilment is only reached fleetingly, in the ideal of love or orgasm, or in a false way, through the pseudo-stability of a nationalist or religious ideal that exalts unity without faults and is transparent. However, this exaltation or rapture, disguised as success, only leads to mortifying paralysis, or to a binary world of "us", the men, and "the others", the scum.

It is necessary to promote an open, human mind capable of holding, supporting, and handling this internal experience of uncertainty that Derrida calls "the identity in disarray", to avoid the certainty— the core of fanaticism—where, as the Uruguayan writer Onetti suggests, a man with religious fervour can be considered to be as dangerous as a hungry animal.

* * *

We, as Freudians, have little to offer as an alternative to this faultless "all perfect unit". While not the only ones to offer an alternative, psychoanalysts can put forward the following proposal: to recognise and accept diversity along with its suffering. This work will involve a long path of frustration, and demand the relinquishment of the fetishistic allure of a unique ideal. Even the closest and most beloved person challenges us with their enigmatic and opaque zones.

Thus, identity in disarray is, and will always be, part of the human condition. It is the interminable effort to understand the enigma of our origins, which is always precariously uncertain and set in the context of anxiety. The symbolic debt of lineage weaves its way through the transmission between generations, using, as raw materials, the patronymic language and culture. This is, and will always be, a decisive core of any internal debate, where each generation must weave the continuity of its traditions while simultaneously creating its own originality. I believe that working through the symbolic debt with what is one's own is the task of the psychoanalytic subject, so as to prevent the violent splitting that racist hatred towards the Other creates.

From the most primitive functioning of the self, I integrate what is good; I introduce and assimilate it, and reject what is bad; I spit it out and discard it. In the construction of the world—the world which constitutes our social and mental reality—the psychological work with what is similar and comfortable, that with which we can develop a close relationship, because we have a certain affinity with it, is different from the psychological vicissitudes we undergo when assimilating what is strange and different. Fusional love is different from love that recognises otherness.

What surprises me is the coincidence of Freudian postulates with those of other disciplines, such as the definition of ethnocentrism in anthropology, and the processes of constructing identity in social psychology. Freudian definitions, which come from intimate and individual experiences, as well as from collective, social experiences, focus concomitantly on building what is ours and discerning what is foreign, by contrast. Opposite terms require one another reciprocally, like phonemes in a language: constructing the identity of what belongs to us by removing ourselves from what is different. That the exaltation of what is ours fosters affirmation, joy, and poetry is not surprising, but at least it does not cause any immediate or ostensible damage. What we have to become is more attentive to what is synthesised in patriotism and national symbols (such as the national anthem, flag, or coat of arms). It is to the unstable nature of what is different, to its development and psychological end, that we need to be more attentive. It is from these definitions, Freudian and sociological, that the vicissitudes of constructing identity come; it is the dialectic of what belongs to us (Philos) and what is different (Xenos).

The fundamentalists take only answers and, thus, acquire certainties. They are under the illusion of possessing "all" the answers, the point of arrival being God, such as the Alpha and Omega, or the ideal when it becomes a fanatical belief. The xenophobe is a taxonomist and that is why biological data that identify an ethnic group calm and complete the clearness of the difference. Gómez Mango (Viñar, 1998) writes about the open identity of democratic thought, and of the closed identity of the xenophobe. Simon Brainsky talks about inclusive narcissism (that accepts the Me and You) and of exclusive narcissism where the relationship is You–That. Naturalising the difference gives it an arbitrary value, and does not take into consideration the fact that what is ours and what is foreign is always a cultural construction.

From a Lacanian perspective, Didier-Weill (1987) suggests that the internal investigation and exploration of origins reach a point that cannot be taken further by speculation, which is a point of enigmatic opaqueness. At a point of pleasure and imaginary harmony between the world and me, at the delight in the mirror and the imaginary unit, we reach an idyllic relationship with our fellow man. But something always breaks down, and that is where Xenos, what is different, comes in, the limit between the known and what can be known, and the foreign, the worrisome foreigner, the unknown person without a name. The unsatisfied and peremptory search for a stable identity gradually fails, since the order in which it is sought fails and staggers the psyche.

*   *   *

Of course, such mechanisms, which we think are common to all individuals, only explain the ordinary racism we all carry hidden inside to differing degrees, and even the best of us only manage to contain it, maintaining it as though it were an internal conflict, without actually rejecting, mocking, attacking, or killing anyone.

However, how is it that under certain historical–political contexts, the same intimate and intrapsychical phenomena enter into social consonance, and, by hypnotic suggestion, acquire critical mass in a collective consensus to hurt the one who is different, who is seen as the (imaginary) cause of social gangrene, and whose amputation would achieve a return to equilibrium?

What are the psychological and social factors that unleash ordinary racism, and externalise these latent, primitive, universal, and cruel impulses? This happens regularly and repeatedly in history: ordinary racism becomes an ideological movement and a justification for genocide. When the agent is powerful, it takes on the form of extermination, like state-sponsored terrorism, and when the agents are militarily weaker, they go underground and form terrorist groups. Only dialogue between disciplines can shed light on such complex phenomena.

Castells (2009) talks about the resurgence of fundamentalist movements over the past decade, during which time the globalisation of the economy and information has increased. He points outs that economic expansion crushes many of the particularities of identity, which are essential to our psyche, just as food, air, and light are for the body.

Arendt's (1994) contribution (*Eichmann in Jerusalem: A Report on the Banality of Evil*), argues the position that extreme evil is committed by ordinary people, and rejects the hypothesis of the demonic monster and perverse personality. Her contribution constitutes a change of axis in terms of political action and research. Radical evil (*das radikale Böse*) has been discussed and, regarding Shakespeare's Richard III, Arendt argues, the search was orientated to the deeper levels of being, to study the demon or the devilishness by questioning the determinations that take place in the complexity of internal "motivations". Modern psychology and psychiatry have adopted this personalising and moralising approach in order to find in the maze of the human mind the profile of a perverse personality, whose baseness will lead them to commit monstrous acts. Arendt says, in *The Origins of Totalitarianism*:

> The simple but terrifying truth is that people who, in normal situations, could only have dreamt of crimes, without ever having the intention of

committing them, adopted scandalously criminal behaviour in a situation of complete tolerance by the law and society. (Revault d'Allonnes,
1997, p. 7)

The aim of finding causal explanations—which was dominant in
human science—is over. We are no longer looking to find the cause in
malicious intentions, but in the semiotics of politics, since we help to
create their texture and are, hence, co-responsible.

This shift in axis from the theory of diabolic agents to a more
ordinary, general kind of evil, produced by ordinary people, destroys
the oppositional paradox of good people and perverse people, and
looks for an explanation in the collectively created relational space at
the centre of politics. A renunciation of the explanation, based upon
the motivation of evil in individuals, and focusing responsibility on
belonging to the same space, implies that we have no radical otherness *vis-à-vis* the evil of each moment and each place for which we are
co-responsible.

As a Freudian, I think that Arendt's contribution on the banality of
evil helps to take us beyond the aporia of the intimate subject and
the political subject. Research, therefore, now looks for links and
convergences, given the new presentations of subjects in the modern
world. Arendt shows how totalitarianism and other forms of human
exclusion not only destroy the public sphere that is the juridico–
political sphere, but also penetrates the psyche (the ability to think
and to symbolise).

Human subjects are formed through their interactions and first
links with the Other. Human beings not only socialise their eroticism
and morality (as the first and basic Freudian ideas emphasised), but
are also formed by the internalised transmission of their history and
culture.

Arendt's brilliant observation in *Eichmann in Jerusalem* is that the
Nazi monster is an ordinary human being, a bureaucrat, stupid, like
any of us, and perhaps a good father, husband, or companion. This is
how Merle (1976) also describes Rudolf Hoess, the man responsible
for the death camps.

Radical evil, says Arendt, is not found in the motivational layer of
the human spirit, as in Shakespeare's *Richard III*. What we should ask
is how this type of leader comes into contact with the masses, and
how the masses allow themselves to become drawn into a dense and

monolithic message capable of dividing the world according to a binary system of pure and impious. We need to determine in greater detail when, how, and why this dormant ogre becomes active and predominant within the individual and collective conscience and behaviour.

In Dachau, on the fiftieth anniversary of the closure of the concentration camps, I heard Hermann Langbein, a survivor of Auschwitz, talk about the rise of Nazism in Austrian schools. I will always remember this message for its shrewdness and psychological finesse:

> Nazism begins in childhood under two conditions—when a child perceives his fellow man as being of inferior value, and when he is not able to acquire the capacity to say 'no' and withdraw from the hypnosis of a criminal majority.

References

Arendt, H. (1994). *Eichmann in Jerusalem: A Report on the Banality of Evil.* New York: Penguin.

Castells, M. (2009). *The Power of Identity: The Information Age: Economy, Society and Culture, Volume II (The Information Age)* (2nd edn). Malden, MA: Wiley-Blackwell.

Didier-Weill, A. (1987). Coloquio L'étranger. Paris: Psychoanalytical Event Federation.

Freud, S. (1912–1913). *Totem and Taboo. S.E.,* 13: 1–162. London: Hogarth.

Freud, S. (1915c). Instincts and their vicissitudes. *S.E., 14:* 111–140. London: Hogarth.

Freud, S. (1921c). *Group Psychology and the Analysis of the Ego. S.E., 18:* 69–143. London: Hogarth.

Freud, S. (1930a). *Civilization and Its Discontents. S.E., 21:* 57–145. London: Hogarth.

Freud, S. (1939a). *Moses and Monotheism. S.E.,* 23: 1–137. London: Hogarth.

Guillaumin, C. (1981). "Je sais bien mais quand meme" ou les avatars de la notion de race. In: *La Science Face au Racisme* (pp. 55–65). Paris: Seuil (Le Genre Humain).

Jacquard, A. (1981). Biologie et theories des 'elites'. In: *La Science Face au Racisme* (pp. 14–54). Paris: Seuil (Le Genre Humain).

Merle, R. (1976). *La mort est mon métier.* Paris: Gallimard.

Revault d'Allonnes, M. (1997). Paper presented to the Ginebra Collogquium, May.
Viñar, M. (1998). *"Similar or Enemy?" Col. Pertinences/Impertinen*ces. Montevideo, Uruguay: Ediciones Trilce.

CHAPTER THREE

Concerning prejudice: pragmatic utopias

Ignacio Gerber

"I once heard of a child who thought people were laughing at him, and began to cry, because when he asked where the eggs come from he was told 'from hens', and when he went on to ask where hens come from, he was told 'from eggs'. But they were not playing with words; on the contrary, they were telling him the truth"

(Freud, 1914, p. 57)

B ased upon his founding concept of psychoanalysis, the conscious–unconscious dualism, Freud sought to understand the human mind and its relations through other dualisms, through which the oppositions could lead to a comprehensive explanatory synthesis. The creation of psychoanalysis constituted a radical rupture in the heart of the Enlightenment, positivist, and Eurocentric science that dominated Vienna and other cultural centres within Europe at the end of the nineteenth and the beginning of the twentieth century. However, Freud was still a man of his place and time, grounded upon the rational logic tradition that extends back to Aristotle (384–322 BC) and his principle (or law) of the excluded third:

If a differs from b there cannot exist a third term, T, that is identical to a and b.

According to the principles of classical logic, which is bivalent, if someone claims they are simultaneously sleeping and awake, our immediate reaction is to point out a contradiction in their affirmation. This is the essence of the law of the excluded third: rational logic does not accept contradiction. It is interesting to remember that contemporary science—in particular, physics and mathematics—have decidedly broken with the principle of the excluded third. We are now in the included third era; the non-contradiction field has exponentially expanded, turning into the field of consented contradiction. An example of this is contradictory or paraconsistent mathematics, which consists today in one of the main lines of theoretical research in important universities around the world. What we call classical logical thinking is actually, or at least for the most part, the logic of our *conscious* way of being. This is the way in which the brilliant psychoanalyst, Ignacio Matte-Blanco (1908–1995), an author whom I consider to have anticipated the future of psychoanalysis in the present time, conceives the *conscious* and the *unconscious* systems: people have two ways of being; complementary opposites that constitute at once a dualism–monism (Matte-Blanco, 1975, 1981).

Another fundamental dualism was developed within the whole corpus of Freudian work: the one that opposes life instincts to death instincts. Basing itself on the initial concept of sexual instincts in opposition to instincts of self-preservation, this dualism was extended to its culmination in a final postulation, which is present in the texts of the 1930s (Freud, 1940a), expressing them in a more comprehensive and abstract sense: binding instinct (Eros) *vs.* unbinding instinct (Thanatos). In this last scheme of instinctive dualism, the binding instinct comprehends the loving instinct of life, Eros, whereas the death instinct loses its single and exclusively destructive character and now plays a role complementary to the life instinct in the eternal search for a healthy balance between binding things together and undoing connections.

When this balance is broken, and the tendency to undo connections surpasses that of its opposite, prejudices flourish; they manifest themselves either in the denial of differences—which seems to me the less harmful form—or in acting to eliminate differences. In this case, in which I believe the greater evil resides, the immediate product is racist thinking and action: "they are different from me; they belong to another species that does not deserve to be treated in the same fashion according to which I treat my equals". Exacerbating this kind of thinking, as we have seen so many times before in history, is the affirmation: "they don't have a soul" and, therefore, they may be legally and ethically enslaved, violated, or exterminated. Fortunately, contemporary science has come to our aid in this matter: present researches concerning DNA prove that, with regard to people, there is only one race: the *human* race. All human beings are "erotically" united within only one constitutive race, which contingent and circumstantial differences only help us to understand in its totality.

If we imagine a sample of human beings along the binding–unbinding axis, we will have, at one extreme, those that cannot tolerate differences, and, at the other, those who embrace differences. This gradation of attitudes, which we so often recognise in the day-to-day life of human relations, also determines our own attitude towards the facts. This goes beyond scientific neutrality. It is extremely tempting to find an infallible way to guide the practice of any subject, and it is even more the case in the practice of the always bewildering psychoanalysis. It is true that psychoanalysis constitutes a pioneering way of thinking that questions determinist causality, the division of knowledge, the classical non-contradictory logic inherited from Aristotle, and, finally, the certainties, even if they are temporary, of deductive–inductive reasoning. I quote David Bohm (1917–1992), the renowned physicist who collaborated with Einstein:

> Now, if we are not aware that our theories are ever-changing forms of insight, giving shape and form to experience in general, our vision will be limited. One could put it like this: experience with nature is much like experience with human beings. If one approaches another man with a fixed "theory" about him as an "enemy" against whom one must defend oneself, he will respond similarly, and thus one "theory" will apparently be confirmed by experience. (Bohm, 1980, p. 25)

As examples of mistakes provoked by the prejudiced use of the scientific method, we recall the large number of sociological articles and books with scientific pretensions that appeared in Europe after the defeat suffered by the libertarian ideals of 1848, which tried to demonstrate a presumed inequality between "human races". More specifically, this concerned the so-called superiority of the "European races" over the "inferior races", such as Jews, Africans, or Eastern peoples. Among those "scientific theories", we may cite: *The Races of Men*, by the Scottish author Robert Knox (1850); *Comparative Physiognomy or Resemblances Between Men and Animals*, written by the American author, James W. Redfield (1852); *Essai sur l'inégalité des races humaines*, by the French author, Joseph Arthur Gobineau[1] (1853).

The racist consequences of those publications, which tried to validate old prejudices through scientific explanations, had a direct impact on Freud and his Jewish community and they persist down to the present day in the form of anti-Semitism, Afrophobia, and aversion to Eastern peoples, among others; we shall consider the racial question further below.

Returning to the issue of different instincts, we approach a permanent controversy in the psychoanalytic movement through the following question: would there be an instinct of destruction, a congenital badness inherent in the human being, engraved in our archaic remnants, as Freud wrote, or in our collective unconscious, as it was understood by Jung? Another related question also occurs to me: what came first, the violence or the fear? This does not seem to me a sort of Byzantine question, or a moot point; on the contrary, it awakens in us an anxious uneasiness in the face of something that cannot be answered within the parameters of dualist and non-contradictory traditional logic.

This question reminds me of another one, the provoking, popular question with which I began this chapter: "what came first, the chicken or the egg?" It seems that each question (the other one being as stated above: "which came first, the violence or the fear?") can be seen as a *koan*. In the Zen tradition, a *koan* is a question proposed by the master to his disciple that escapes the non-contradictory logic, which dominates our mostly pragmatic conscious system. We know that pragmatism is necessary to the survival of the individual; in order to survive, he must react to a threat with a specific, non-contradictory action. Maybe that is the origin of the aversion we feel—or, better said, which is presented to us by our conscious system—towards contradictory situations; in general, we prefer clear assertions, such as "in this situation, I have to do this", or "this is right, this is wrong". In this way, our conscious thinking may plan an action, basing itself upon prior experiences and, thereby, limit the infinite number of possible reactions in the face of a dangerous situation.

Our deeper unconscious, in its turn, is mainly the field of emotions, and these are essentially contradictory; they are guided by another logical field, which is not limited by the principle of non-contradiction: everything may associate in a way to everything else; in other words, the unconscious logic expands possibilities up to the unthinkable infinite. The function of the *koan*, in this context, is to awaken a human essence that lies beyond rational logic to which we are habituated (conscious logic). It is to empty our heads of the usual logic and deliver ourselves to mental emptiness, an absence of thoughts saturated by memory, getting closer, and in a less defensive way, to this other way of being. It is like welcoming (or being welcomed by) this Unconscious, which only manifests itself within the rational logic absences and silences. The *koan*, in its way of posing questions that puzzle conventional logic, opens possibilities to the unthinkable unknown, a dive into the infinite. For example, a classical *koan*: "What is the sound of one hand clapping?"

This problem belongs not only to the psychoanalytic realm or to therapists in general; contemporary science itself is daring to confront questions that go beyond classical, Aristotelian logic. The theories and practices of complex thinking (see Gerber, 2003a) institute another way of thinking about our cosmos and ourselves. We have to remember, though, that psychoanalysis was pioneering in proposing a new way of being, with another, different, symbolic logic, another level of reality (see unconscious logic as another level of reality in Gerber (2003b, 2004)): this is the realm of the Unconscious that constitutes us as much or even more than our usual conscious mind.

Complex thinking is an essentially human characteristic; it is enough to think about the complexity of a spontaneous thought or the chain of free associations. We may quote Morin (1994, p. 157), a French thinker born in 1921 who helped found the contemporary trans-disciplinary approach: "The most vertiginous computation is still less complex than a minimal tenderness".

Today, as it incorporates psychoanalysis's contributions and the eastern philosophical tradition, among others, science tends to consider that a possible synthesis of a contradiction takes place at another level of reality, which accepts what was considered contradictory at an otherwise less complex level: a *transcendent dialogical vision*. Dialogic reasoning is an expansion of the dialectic concept; at this second, transcendent level, synthesis occurs a little later—even if only a little—and at the same level of reality. In the dialogic view, on the other hand, synthesis occurs simultaneously, but in another level of reality, in another logical field. The postulation of quantum mechanics itself implies that it can only act in another level of reality, with its own physical, logical, and mathematical rules, which cannot be reconciled, at least for the moment, with the physics of our common sense material universe. The concordance that I propose between those two levels of reality that constitute the physical universe—represented by classical and quantum physics—and between the two levels that constitute the psychic universe—represented by conscious and unconscious processes—goes beyond a mere poetic metaphor; I approach this concordance with analogical reasoning, usually applied in the present day by contemporary science.

Returning now to the question of fear and violence, but going beyond logical conceptions, we see that the posing of this question certainly brings out ideological contents, *prejudices*, which are found in every one of us. For example, the eternal question: is man born violent or does he become violent through the circumstances of life? I personally subscribe to the idea that as a human being develops from its embryonic state, it is expecting, even as a potentiality, the humankind to which it *a priori* belongs (a preconception as Bion would say); it already awaits the loving welcome of its equals. The mother's body represents Gaia, or the Earth and the Cosmos that contain us. In other words, there is a hope of love in the baby, love being the primordial quality that constitutes us, and that is exactly the grounds for the fear of losing love, the fear of exclusion, and the fear of losing the bond with another within the human hive, which means destitution and death.

I propose that at the core of the fear of death lies the fear of exclusion. The possibility of a meteor hitting and destroying Earth would be accepted with calmer resignation than the solitary individual death of any one of us. In the first case, the "party" would end for us all; in the second, the party would continue, and only one of us is left out by death. Those who pick up their teenagers at parties and discos know that the youth go much more willingly when the party is truly over than when the music continues to play loudly in the background.

I consider that hate and violence are derived from fear. Thus, the genetic chain *love → fear → hate → violence* tends to repeat the most varied emotional experiences. According to the basic principles of complexity theory, there is no longer any room for linear reasoning and one-dimensional simplifications; the relations between the basic emotions—love, fear, and hate—are complex, almost as complex as the mutant configurations of the quantum level of reality. This way, the love, fear, hate module manifests in itself infinite fractal variations, from an almost instant scintillation of the emotional experience during a psychoanalytic session to the establishment of a permanent rigid pattern that is capable of turning a whole life neurotic or psychotic. In *Attention and Interpretation*, Bion (1970, p. 66) writes, ". . . these fundamental characteristics, love, hate, and dread, are sharpened to a point that . . . [we] may feel them to be almost unbearable".

The actions of Eros, the instinct that binds and unites, and Thanatos, which unbinds and separates, determine those diverse subjective configurations that may render feelings bearable or unbearable.

Furthermore, the ideological attitude that is implicit within the model proposed above presumes that the feeling of excessive and disproportional fear, the nameless dread, as Bion (1962) would say, defensively changes into hate in anticipation of the violent act. This takes into account the more specific context of the violent act as an attenuating factor and enables us to look at the author of the violence with more tolerant eyes, but, nonetheless, no less active and worried: a more generous look upon our imperfect humanity. A genetic question arises at this point: considering that our basic instincts are the products of a phylogenetic chain (the archaic remnants, as Freud would say, or the collective unconscious, as defined by Jung), is it possible to imagine that historical fears, the ones that appeared throughout the evolution of homo sapiens, might have changed into instinctive, congenital hates in subsequent generations?

Moreover, I think that we can see in this violence that originates from fear a certain utilitarian function that, in a way, makes sense to us. As unreasonable as a crime of passion might seem to us, be it political torture, a terrorist act, or genocide, those acts of force seek to achieve a practical gain, even if they are incapable of obtaining that goal. There is, however, a more intolerable sort of violence, the violence that is cold, psychopathic, non-functional, and devoid of sense; we are talking here about acts based upon hate for hate's sake, and violence for violence's sake, that are attempted by someone who has cut himself off—or who is cut off—from all the affective bonds of humanity. Acts of this order, apart from other possible reasons, result from the most absolute and terrifying solitude, to be radically alone on a planet which one experiences as completely hostile. At the opposite extreme to this feeling of absolute loneliness there is the feeling of belonging, the feeling of being part of a totality, part of humanity; in Bionian terms, a feeling expressive of the pre-conception of humankind. This is humanity thought of as one and only one planetary human race.

As a practical suggestion, I propose we consider fear as a primary cause of the violence, and, in turn, violence as the immediate cause of fear, and so on, in an insane geometric progression. To take into account the love and fear present within the origin of hate and violence can help us better understand the emotional reasons (and unreasons) of the violent being.

Surely, I cannot ignore the importance of fear in psychoanalytic texts from the time of Freud. It is interesting to say, in search of terminological precision, that it appears in the most varied forms, such as: terror, dread, fright, apprehension, insecurity, anxiety, denial, or manic defences; thus, other discriminative scientific terminologies are created, and are rapidly absorbed by the usages of colloquial language. This is why I consider it important not to lose sight of the *fear*—singular, total, without any nuances or alibis.

Malignant prejudice: the strength of these two words, brought together in Henri Parens' beautiful chapter, is deeply touching. In his text, Parens proposes a temporal genetic trajectory for the installation of prejudice into the human being. He builds upon the reactions of three- or four-month-old children being confronted by persons foreign to their known circle of relations. Parens calls this stranger anxiety reaction *benign prejudice*. From this, passing through *hostile prejudice* (negative beliefs about others), we arrive at manifestations of *malignant prejudice* (the advocacy and support for actions of exclusion, expulsion, and genocide).

This interesting proposition made me think of a parallel version to this development, emphasising the fear described above. To think of fear as an intermediary transitional state—between a feeling of being well received by known persons who are trustworthy and a nascent hatred towards the menacing unknown—might lead us to an alternative in understanding the relationship between a precocious infantile attitude and the genesis of prejudice. Indeed, it is interesting to remember, in passing, that the usual translation of *prejudice* in Portuguese is *preconceito*, but it is also commonly translated as *prejuízo*, which connotes *damage*. Both senses of the term, although different, similarly imply a pre-established concept or judgement that obscures the liberty to think. In other words, it obscures the capacity to live the transformation from unknown to known.

This idea may stimulate an interesting discussion regarding the validity of applying the term "prejudice" to the precocious infantile reaction. I ask myself if the reaction of pure strangeness, when faced with the unknown, may be characterised by prejudice, or if it should merely deserve this name after the phase of hostile prejudice. Of course, this is a matter of semantics; we are all describing a similar phenomenon. However, simply to promote dialogue with Parens' highly substantial idea, we may think of the matter in a different way: as a sort of index of malignancy of prejudice. It would vary from very small indices, which would not conduce directly to violent or destructive actions, to very high indices, such as those pertaining to the emblematic example of Nazism.

I do know that we refer to similar experiences using different words, but it worries me to think that the association of *prejudice* with *benign* might reduce the virulence implied by the word prejudice, even when considering it within the specific and limited sense of perfectly justified psychological research.

It seems important to me that, increasingly, the word prejudice may produce, by free association, a connotation of malignancy in the mind of the man on the street. This is to say: All prejudice is, in principle, malignant, yet only its malignancy index will vary. We know that the variation range of this hypothetical index is ample. This makes it difficult to identify prejudice when indices are small. In the film *The Serpent's Egg*, by Ingmar Bergman (1977), we observe an apparently inoffensive egg, characterised by few prejudices, which, left unperceived and unrestricted, develops into the terrible serpent of Nazism.

Thus, I iterate the importance of the expression coined by Henri Parens: "malignant prejudice".

We may now venture a provisional conclusion, a first pragmatic utopia that is so simple that it seems naïve: if we can reduce the threats that hover over a human being, there will be a reduction—probably disproportional and inexact—in the rate of violence.

As you can see, I have allocated to myself the task of producing a pragmatic utopia. A pragmatic utopia can be defined as a *viable* utopia in the future, even without a specific timetable, because proposing it will provoke tenacious resistance from those who fear change, irrespective of its substance. However, as we do in psychoanalysis, we can use those resistances to help us understand and better elaborate utopias themselves, constantly considering and reconsidering them; for once established, thoughts are generally watered down. On the other hand, if the proposed utopia is absorbed with ease and without major resistance, then we ought to worry that its absorption might sterilise it, thus minimising its disruptive effect. A new idea, when it is really new, forces us to think, evaluate; it forces us to look at our assumptions in a critical way, and face uncertainties and possible radical changes in an otherwise comfortably established scheme. We fear the unknown or we simply do not understand it, but only the unknown is, in fact, new. To face the new truth—including here the little quotidian truths of each emotional experience—it is necessary to tolerate the potential frustration of having our personal truths refuted.

I propose a second pragmatic utopia—which is a paradox for a utopia—that is rigorously grounded on absolutely concrete statistical data, both factual and reliable. What is it about? It is enough to look at the crime sections of any newspaper to conclude, before turning to scientific statistics, that the percentage of violent physical acts, such as murder, or torture, committed by women represent less than 10% of those committed by men; I do not include herein acts of war ("officially recognised violence"), in which men constitute effectively all the combatants, but only "civil" crimes. The argument that females have less physical strength or stamina does not stand up in face of the easy access to, and handling of, light but deadly weapons: their use by small children and teenagers is current these days, and, by the way, here as well there is a predominance of boys. To sum up, it is the general consensus that women tend to be less physically violent, but when it comes to verbal or psychological violence, the difference between genders becomes relativised.

Once that is said, our second pragmatic utopia seems obvious: *the search for a new human social contract in which the feminine spirit prevails;* I speak here about an essential feminine spirit that is mostly unconscious, and not of the "men in skirts" variety, such as Margaret Thatcher[2] or Condoleezza Rice.[3] What is, in fact, suggested here is an increase of the feminine portion in the desirable balance of the psychological and ethical genders of the human being.

This proposal is, to a certain degree, similar to the one of getting closer to our unconscious emotional processes. Women are closer to the unconscious; they more easily admit to contradiction, incorporating it into their usual reasoning; they deal with paradoxes with such tranquillity that it exasperates their male interlocutors. In a practical discussion, men tend to direct their arguments to a determined non-contradictory action, but this is possibly a reductionist one; women, on the other hand, expand associations not inherent to the question in mind, with more or less pertinence, and it is undeniable that they continuously open the field of discussion towards wider solutions, even if less immediate. Of course, here I generalise by appeal to the average, but I find them recognisable in our day-to-day life. The female capacity to welcome contradictory situations is parallel to female biology, which is orientated to maternal care and, prior to that, to welcoming the man that penetrates her.

It is important to say that there is no point in using value judgements in the masculine or feminine hierarchy, simply because they only exist as complementary opposites, like Yin and Yang. In Chinese philosophy, Yin and Yang are complementary forces that put everything together; it is from the dynamic balance that exists between them that all movement and mutation come. Yin could be understood as a more feminine, passive, nocturnal, and dark principle; Yang would be the more masculine, active, daily, and luminous principle. The Taiji diagram, a well-known symbol, represents the integration between Yin (black) and Yang (white). It is important to remember, however, that the Yang is only more Yang than Yin, and the Yin is only more Yin than Yang, and that neither of them exists without the other.

To a certain extent, I propose an ego that is closer to the non-contradictory, rational masculine, in complementary opposition— yes, opposites complement each other, as proposed by Heraclitus (ca. 535–475 BC) and by the Danish physicist Niels Bohr (1885–1962)—to an id that is closer to the contradictory emotional feminine, that can deal with greater ease with the contradictions that are inherent in the "lived reality" without appealing to physical violence. When I talk about a more masculine ego and more feminine id, I refer only to the prevailing configurations of both ways of being, which are combinations with different proportions of conscious and uncon-scious logic—a strange but creative marriage.

Sometimes I meditate—playfully or not—on the idea of two human races: women and men, the feminine added to the masculine, the two complementing each other in an indispensable way, unaware of hierarchic disputes. Within this context, I will tell of a recent experience: among many publications, writings, and images that fall into my hands, surprising me and helping me to think, the cover of a recent issue of the magazine *Psicoanálisis Internacional*, produced by the International Psychoanalytic Association to celebrate its centennial anniversary (1910–2010), is composed of pictures of all its presidents, during these past hundred years. The fact that all of them were men, without exception, caught my attention: the psychoanalytic associa-tion has an equal number of men and women members, and today women have even come to outnumber the men; both have also made similar contributions to psychoanalytic theory and clinical practice. I asked myself, was this a random occurrence? It is difficult to accept this under the investigative lens of psychoanalysis.

In the face of such undeniable factual evidence, I imagine two possible reactions: the first is to consider the fact as something natural or a matter of pure coincidence, but, in any event, a fact that deserves no further attention; the second reaction is a strange feeling, one that would entice us to think and try to understand the fact. This seems to me a good example of how any one of us might react to a "symptom" that conceals or reveals a possible personal prejudice. To admit a prejudice is always the first step in transforming it. A prejudice that is admitted is no longer entirely a prejudice, because it is already the object of reflection.

I conclude with an ancient Jewish parable:

> An old and wise rabbi, with a disciple by his side, receives a quarrel-some couple. The man is the first to present his version of the disagree-ment and, in the end, the rabbi says: "You are right". Then it's the woman's turn to present her version, totally different from the one told by her husband, and the rabbi says: "You are right". When the couple leaves, the disciple, who is confused, asks, "But, rabbi how is it possible that, in face of such contradictory accounts, you can tell that they are both right?" And the rabbi calmly answers, "You know, you are right too!"

Notes

1. Gobineau did not consider the Jews to be an inferior race.
2. Margaret Thatcher (1925–2013): British politician and Prime Minister (1979–1990).
3. Condoleezza Rice (born in 1954): Secretary of State of the United States who served during the George W. Bush government (2005–2009).

References

Bion, W. R. (1962). A theory of thinking. In: *Second Thoughts* (pp. 110–119). London: Karnac, 1967.

Bion, W. R. (1970). *Attention and Interpretation.* London: Karnac.

Bohm, D. (1980). *A totalidade e a ordem implicada.* São Paulo: Cultrix.

Freud, S. (1914d). On the history of the psycho-analytic movement. *S.E., 14*: 3–66. London: Hogarth.

Freud, S. (1940a). *An Outline of Psycho-Analysis. S.E., 23*: 141–207. London: Hogarth.

Gerber, I. (2003a). E depois de Bion? Pensamento complexo e atitude clínica em psicanálise. *Panorama*: 155–178. São Paulo: Sociedade Brasileira de Psicanálise de São Paula.

Gerber, I. (2003b). A Segunda Inocência: psicanalise e artes. *Revista Brasileira de Psicanálise, 37*(2/3): 777–784.

Gerber, I. (2004). O Inconsciente Infinito segundo Bion e Matte-Blanco. *Revista Brasileira de Psicanálise, 38*(1): 39–57.

Gobineau, J. A., comte de (1853). *Essai sur l'inégalité des races humaines.* Paris: Librairie de Firmin Didot.

Knox, R. (1850). *The Races of Men.* Philadelphia: Lea & Blanchard.

Matte-Blanco, I. (1975). *The Unconscious as Infinite Sets.* London: Duckworth.

Matte-Blanco, I. (1981). Reflecting with Bion. In: J. S. Grotstein (Ed.), *Do I Dare Disturb the Universe?* (pp. 489–528). Beverly Hills, CA: Caesura Press.

Morin, E. (1994). *La complexité humaine.* Paris: Flammarion.

Redfield, J. W. (1852). *Comparative Physiognomy or Resemblances Between Men and Animals.* New York: Redfield.

CHAPTER FOUR

International relations and psychoanalysis*

Vamık D. Volkan

This chapter examines some aspects of large-group identity issues, prejudices, and the need to have enemies and allies. To illustrate how I became interested in these topics, I will start with a few stories from my childhood.

I was born on the Mediterranean island of Cyprus when it was a British colony, seven years before the beginning of the Second World War. I was raised in a good home, but grew up during a time of impending danger coming from the outside world that, as a child, my mind could not fully comprehend. After the Nazis' 1941 airborne invasion of another Mediterranean island, Crete, it was expected that they would next invade Cyprus. We dug a bomb shelter in our garden and took refuge there on many occasions, sometimes in the middle of rainy nights when sirens woke us. Food was rationed and we were forced to eat dark, tasteless bread, and taught how to wear gas masks. I began seeing Indian Sikh soldiers with long beards and turbans walking around the streets of my neighbourhood in Nicosia, the

---

* Keynote speech delivered to the American Psychoanalytic Annual Meeting, Washington, DC, June 11, 2010.

capital city. I witnessed a British Spitfire shooting down an Italian warplane just above my elementary schoolyard, where I was playing with other children. This must have been a frightening experience for me, as I had kept a small piece of glass from the plane's wreckage among my valuable objects until I came to the USA as an adult in early 1957. I suspect that this piece of glass was a kind of linking object (Volkan, 1981) to this terrible event and, by keeping it and, in a sense, controlling it, I might have been attempting to master my childhood anxiety that I might lose my life.

Anticipating an invasion by the Nazis, my mother, two sisters, grandmother, and I left Nicosia and went to live in a village some twenty miles away because we thought we were safer there. My father remained in Nicosia to carry out his duties as a schoolteacher. I recall German warplanes, flying very low, passing over the village to bomb military installations near Nicosia. In my mind's eye, I still see a German pilot waving down at me while flying over the village. I would hear the bombs drop, and I did not know if my father was killed or not. I would remain anxious until I saw him during his weekend trips with us, as in those days there were no telephones or electricity in this village. To the women in my family, I was the little prince while my father was away. Consider this, combined with my fear that my father could be killed by German bombs, and you can imagine how this environment influenced my oedipal strivings. In my childhood, my internal wars were intertwined with external wars.

The Germans never did invade Cyprus, but continuous fear that they might made me keenly aware of what is called large-group identity. As a Turkish child, I wondered why I should be exposed to dangers because of "others'" war. Being "British" to me meant the governor and other rulers of the island, for whom I was only a "native". Most of my people, the Turks, lived in another location, the Turkish mainland, separated from the island. The mainland Turks were not involved in the war. At home, sometimes I would hear stories about Cyprus when it was an Ottoman territory and about my long-gone relatives on my mother's side, who were high-level Turkish administrators of the island. The British, who, by coming to the island, had ruined my mother's family's fortunes, seemed very foreign to me. As a child, I never met a German or an Italian, but learnt that there were persons belonging to these identities that I should be afraid of. I heard about Jews being in danger in Germany, but I had never met a Jewish person.

In Nicosia, we lived in a house situated just where a Turkish section of the city ended, and the Greek section began. In fact, a nice Greek family lived next door to us. However, we could not be intimate with them; they had another large-group identity. I did not know their language, their prophet, or their God. My family members, like most Cypriot Turks at that time, were followers of cultural revolutions in the new mainland Turkey, and our daily lives did not involve religion. I never went to a mosque or learnt even one prayer. We were cultural Muslim people. We felt no "bad" prejudice against Cypriot Greeks. Simply, they were different. There were also those soldiers from India who were supposed to protect us, but they did not seem friendly.

What is large-group identity?

Freud seldom referred to the term "identity". One well-known reference to identity is found in a speech he wrote that was delivered on his behalf at B'nai B'rith. In the course of his paper, Freud wondered why he was bound to Jewry, since, as a non-believer, he was never instilled with ethno-national pride or religious faith. Nevertheless, Freud noted a "safe privacy of a common mental construction", and a clear consciousness of his "inner identity" (as a Jew) (Freud, 1941e, p. 274). It is interesting that Freud's remarks linked his individual identity with his large-group identity.

Although there was no clear description of "identity", in specific psychoanalytic terms, until Erikson's (1956) interest in this topic, there is a consensus that it refers to a subjective experience. Revising Erikson's description of individual identity, I define large-group identity—whether it refers to tribes, ethnicity, nationality, religion, or political ideology, such as "We are Apache", "We are Kurds", "We are French", "We are Muslims", or "We are Communists"—as the subjective experience of thousands or millions of people. These people are linked by a persistent sense of sameness from childhood on, although they share some characteristics with others who belong to foreign groups. Under the umbrella of large-group identity there are sub-group identities, such as professional identities. A person can change a subgroup identity without much anxiety, unless such a change unconsciously becomes connected with an intrapsychic danger, such as losing an internalised mother image, or external danger, such as losing environmental security. But for all practical purposes, an in-dividual cannot change his or her large-group identity, especially after the adolescence passage (Blos, 1979), just as the person cannot change the individual core identity (Volkan, 1988). Think of a man—let us say he is Italian—who is a photographer. If he decides to stop practising photography and take up carpentry, he may call himself a carpenter instead of a photographer, but he cannot stop being an Italian and become an Englishman. His Italian-ness is part of his core large-group identity.

Each large-group identity includes "identity markers", or what Mack (1979) called "cultural amplifiers", which are concrete or abstract symbols, signs, and actions ranging from physical body characteristics, language, nursery rhymes, food, dances, religious or magical beliefs, cultural traditions, myths, or flags, to images of histor-ical events and past heroes. In places such as the USA and Israel, which Loewenberg (1995) describes as "synthetic" nations, identity markers are variable and some of them are not shared. This is not so in other nations, such as Greece, where one ethnic group comprises the majority. Although there may be dissenters in a large group, they do not modify the basic elements of a large-group identity, unless they have huge followings that then start an influential subgroup and become involved in a new large-group identity. In a large-group setting, a "normal" degree of shared narcissism attaches itself to a large-group identity and creates a sense of uniqueness in identity markers and usually makes them a source of pride.

A letter from Albert Einstein: resistance to studying wars and war-like situations

In the year I was born, 1932, Albert Einstein was fifty-three years old and Sigmund Freud was seventy-six. That year, Einstein wrote to Freud, asking if the new science called psychoanalysis could offer insights that might deliver humankind from the menace of war. In his response to Einstein, Freud (1933b) expressed little hope for an end to war and violence, or the role of psychoanalysis in changing human behaviour beyond the individual level.

In 2006, when it was Austria's turn to lead the European Union, Austria declared that year the Year of Mozart and the Year of Freud. I had the honour to be the Fulbright-Sigmund Freud Privatstiftung Professor of Psychoanalysis in Vienna. At this time, I taught political psychology at the University of Vienna for a semester, and had an office at nineteen Berggasse. While working in Freud's house for four months, trying to organise an international meeting between psychoanalysts and diplomats to celebrate Freud's 150th birthday, I pictured him at this same location in 1932 and wondered about his response to Einstein. Anti-Semitism surrounded Freud at that time, and a year later Adolf Hitler became Germany's dictator. Was Freud's response to Einstein an attempt to deny the impending danger to himself, his family, and Jewish neighbours? I came to a conclusion that this might be true, even though, of course, he was conscious of what was happening in Europe. As Loewenberg (1991) and Rangell (2003) remind us, some aspects of a large-group history induce anxiety.

Even though some analysts, such as Arlow (1973), have found indications of cautious optimism in some of Freud's writings, Freud's general pessimism about the role of psychoanalysis in large-group issues and international relations was mirrored by many of his followers. This, I think, has played a key role in limiting, for a long time, the contributions psychoanalysis has made to the understanding of what exists within specific large groups and international relations, even though some analysts, such as Glower (1947), Fornari (1966), Waelder (1971), Alexander Mitscherlich, and Margarete Mitscherlich (Mitscherlich, A. 1971; Mitscherlich & Mitscherlich, 1975) tried to open doors to such investigations.

There was another factor that played a role until relatively recently in limiting psychoanalytic contributions to international relations. Freud's (1921c) large-group psychology reflects a theme that mainly focuses on the understanding of the individual: the members of the group sublimate their aggression towards the leader and turn it into loyalty, in a process that is similar to that of a son turning his negative feelings toward his oedipal father to an identification with the father. The members of a large group idealise the leader, identify with each other, and rally around the leader. As Waelder (1971) would remark later, Freud described only regressed groups. Much later, others (Anzieu, 1984; Chasseguet-Smirgel, 1984; Kernberg, 1980) wrote about fantasies shared by members of a large group. They suggested that large groups represent idealised mothers (breast mothers) who repair narcissistic injuries. It is assumed that external processes that threaten the group members' image of an idealised mother can initiate political processes and influence international affairs. However, these theories primarily focused on individuals' perceptions, and they did not offer specificity concerning what exists within a large-group psychology itself, and what might be useful in a diplomatic or political strategy to tame malignant prejudice and avoid massive aggression.

A third factor that prevented psychoanalysis from playing a significant role in contributing to international relations again goes back to Freud. In his early efforts to develop psychoanalytic theories, Freud introduced the important role of drives, wishes, and fantasies. While acknowledging that real sexual abuse was traumatic, he focused on the stimuli that come from the child's own drives, wishes, and fantasies for the formation of psychopathology. Influenced by Freud's interest in the child's internal world, early psychoanalysis paid less attention to the role of actual seduction coming from the external world, and generalised it so as to de-emphasise the role of other types of traumatic external events, including international events.

Freud was aware of widespread "war neurosis". He attended the first meeting of the "International", the psychoanalytic organisation, in The Hague after the First World War. He noted that Englishmen and Germans sat at the same table "for the friendly discussion of scientific interests", which focused on "war neurosis", "gain from illness", and "flight from illness". He seemed upset with his "opponents", who declared that "The war neurosis . . . had proved that sexual factors were unnecessary to the aetiology of neurotic disorders". But he added that his opponents' "triumph was frivolous and premature" (Freud, 1925d, p. 54). For, on the one hand, at that time no one had fully analysed a person with war neurosis, while, on the other hand, "psycho-analysis had long before arrived at the concept of narcissism and the narcissistic neurosis, in which the subject's libido is attached to his own ego instead of to an object" (Freud, 1925d, p. 55). He returned to this topic in *Inhibitions, Symptoms and Anxiety* (Freud 1926d) and repeated his arguments against his opponents. His focus was on understanding the internal worlds of traumatised individuals.

Decades ago, as today, there were multiple psychoanalytic schools. All the schools seemed to bypass, to a great extent, the influence of traumatising external historical events. Only a relative emphasis was given to patients' experiences in wars, war-like conditions, drastic political changes, and reactivations of ancestors' historical events. For example, Klein (1961) did not pay attention to the war when she treated a ten-year-old boy named Richard in 1941. During Richard's analysis, the terror of the Blitz under which Melanie Klein and Richard lived was not examined. We will never know for sure why Klein avoided the influence of the war while analysing Richard. There are other occasions when analysts' failure to pay attention to dangerous current, chronic, or past historical events was clearly connected with their own resistance to recalling or re-experiencing troublesome affects, and with the analyst's own resistance dovetailing with the patient's resistance. Blum's (1985) description of a Jewish patient, who came to him for re-analysis, illustrates the extent to which mutual resistances may prevail when both analyst and patient belong to the same large group, which was massively traumatised by an external historical event. Blum's patient's first analyst, who was also Jewish, failed to "hear" their large group's shared trauma at the hands of the Nazis in his patient's material; as a consequence, mutually sanctioned silence and denial pervaded the entire analytic experience, leaving unanalysed residues of the Holocaust in the patient's symptoms. German-speaking psychoanalysts have also explored the difficulties of "hearing" Nazi-related influences in their German and Jewish patients (Eckstaedt, 1989; Grubrich-Simitis, 1979; Jokl, 1997; Streeck-Fischer, 1999; Volkan, Ast, & Greer, 2002).

As time went on, however, psychoanalytic studies on the Holocaust-related psychic processes, especially on transgenerational transmissions, were deepened. There are too many such studies to list here (see Kestenberg & Brenner, 1996; Kogan, 1995; Volkan, Ast, & Greer, 2002 for reviews of such studies). These studies, however, mostly focused on traumatised individuals and only dealt with large-group psychology primarily when its influence on individual psychology was examined.

Before referring to others' work as well as my own that more directly pertains to large-group psychology and international relations, I return to 1933 and refer to another letter by Einstein, this one to the Turkish government. Indirectly, this letter played a role in my becoming a psychoanalyst, and my interest in international relations. It also illustrates, once again, how personal internal issues become interconnected with historical events.

Another letter by Einstein:
its indirect influence on me

In 1933, Einstein lived in France and was the honorary president of the Organisation for the Protection of Jewish Population (OZE). In a letter of 17 September 1933, Einstein asks the President of the Turkish Cabinet of Ministers,

> ... to allow forty professors and doctors from Germany to continue their scientific and medical work in Turkey. The above mentioned cannot practice further in Germany on account of the laws governing there now. The majority of these men possess vast experience, knowledge and scientific merits and could prove very useful when settling in a new country.

OZE would pay their salaries during the first year of their stay in Turkey. The letter ends as follows:

> In supporting this application, I take the liberty to express my hope, that in granting this request your Government will not only perform an act of high humanity, but will also bring profit to your own country.[1]

Einstein's request was sent to the Turkish Ministry of Education, which rejected this proposal on the grounds that there were no existing conditions to accept such an unusual request. However, Einstein's request was accepted when the leader of the new Turkey, Mustafa Kemal, who became better known as Atatürk, intervened. At that time, the Turkish Republic, born from the ashes of the Ottoman Empire, was only ten years old and extremely poor. We know that Turkey had accepted some German-Jewish scholars, even before Einstein's request (Günergün, 2006). Following Einstein's letter, in 1933, thirty German-Jewish scholars and their families came to Turkey, and eventually 190 other intellectuals and their families arrived. Thus, ultimately, over 1000 lives were saved (Reisman, 2006).

Among the German-Jewish intellectuals who fled to Turkey was Professor Oscar Weigert. He eventually became a consultant to Atatürk in changing the attitude of Turkish people towards labour, by bringing labour out of its feudal state and introducing such ideas as the eight-hour day, regular vacations for workers, workers' compensation, and the idea of organising Turkish labour unions (Weigert, 1937). Professor Weigert's wife was an ethnic German psychoanalyst, Edith Vowinckel Weigert. She accompanied her husband to Turkey in 1935 and spent over three years in Ankara, before she and her husband went to the USA (Usak-Sahin, 2009; Volkan & Itzkowitz, 1984).

As per Atatürk's instructions, Edith Weigert was given a licence to practise psychoanalysis in Turkey. She worked mostly with foreigners assigned to different embassies, but she had one Turkish patient who began publishing papers and books on psychoanalysis. Known to the Turkish authorities and diplomats mainly due to her husband's position, Edith Weigert's discussion of psychoanalysis at private parties encouraged interest in Freud's writings. In any case, after the Turkish Republic was born, the Turkish Ministry of Education began to translate, one by one, all major works of Western philosophers, thinkers, and novelists. Thus, Freud's papers and books became available in Turkish.

My father, who was the only educated child of a farming family in Cyprus, apparently became interested in Freud's writings and bought some of his books in Turkish. The books were kept in a huge black wooden box in my parents' bedroom. As a youngster, whose oedipal strivings were kept alive due to external historical circumstances, as I described above, I was greatly interested in what he kept in this locked box. Only later would I learn why the wooden box was kept locked. Due to a shared belief that the Nazis would invade Cyprus, some intellectuals obtained German dictionaries so that they could communicate with the invading Germans and protect their families. However, this was a forbidden act, so my father had to hide his German dictionary. One day, when I could open the box, I found Freud's book, titled *Three Essays on the Theory of Sexuality* (Freud, 1905d) in Turkish next to his German dictionary. You can imagine the symbolism of the black box in my parent's bedroom, and how once more my oedipal strivings were influenced by historical circumstances. Years later, I became a medical student at the University of Ankara, where some of the German-Jewish professors who had escaped to Turkey after Einstein's letter was written were still teaching, and very early in my studies, I knew that I wanted to become a psychoanalyst.

Developing survival guilt and sublimations connected with ethnic violence

During the Second World War, an estimated 35,000 Cypriot volunteers, both Greek and Turkish, served side-by-side in the British armed forces—650 died, and 2,500 were taken prisoner. When I was in medical school, new trends within the international arena turned the island's "natives", as the British used to call them, against the colonising powers. Greeks wanted union with Greece, and to achieve this aim they used terrorism. Within a few decades, reliance on terrorism became a routine and very deadly tool for violence connected with ethnic, ideological, and, most recently, religious large-group identities. Cypriot Greek terrorism against the British spread and turned the Greek and Turkish communities in Cyprus against each other. As my medical studies continued into the 1950s, the large-group violence on the island steadily increased.

During my last two years of medical school, I shared a rented room with Erol, another Cypriot Turkish medical student, who was two years younger than I, and he became the brother I never had. I graduated from medical school in 1956, and six months later took part in a process called a "brain drain", and came to the USA. Three months after my arrival in the USA, I received a letter from my father. In the envelope there was a newspaper article with Erol's picture, describing how my friend had gone to Cyprus from Ankara to visit his ailing mother. While trying to purchase medicine for her at a pharmacy, he was shot seven times by Cypriot Greek terrorists.

These people killed Erol, a bright young man with a promising future, in order to terrorise the ethnic group to which he belonged. He was killed in the name of large-group identity. I was an intern in a Chicago hospital, in a new environment, in a new culture with no friends. I could not mourn Erol's death or even realise my own survival guilt.

A few years later, I was in my training analysis. At that time, the Cypriot Turks back home were forced to live under subhuman conditions, within horrible enclaves that were confined to only three per cent of the island. They would remain as such, prisoners, for eleven years. One day when I was still in analysis, on an American television news broadcast, I saw my mother and one of my sisters running away from my sister's house, which was under enemy fire. We all know that we repress memories of our personal analyses. Nevertheless, I am certain that what was happening to my family, my people on the island, my inability to mourn Erol's death, and my survival guilt were not much of a focus during my personal analysis.

Years later, I wondered if my Jewish analyst's Holocaust-related problems might have prevented him from opening up war-related issues while I was on the couch. Years later again, I also noticed that I had made many sublimations. I wrote a book on Cyprus (Volkan, 1979) and I studied different aspects of complicated mourning, especially perennial mourning, and wrote books on this topic as well (Volkan, 1981; Volkan & Zintl, 1993). I became aware of my special relationship with the late psychoanalyst William Niederland, who coined the term "survival guilt" (Niederland, 1968). I also realised that I had chosen Greek colleagues as partners in important professional activities.

In 1979, I had a real opportunity to study large-group prejudices, wars, war-like situations, and the role of large-group identity in these situations. There are many other psychoanalytic colleagues who, for their own personal motivations, were examining similar topics.

Noticing large-group interactions and large-group psychology

Happenings in the Middle East, Latin America, India, Africa, the Soviet Union, Yugoslavia, Rwanda, and elsewhere during recent decades have motivated psychoanalysts to write about shared malignant prejudice about the "Other", wars, war-like situations, terrorism, and international relations, by referring not only to traumatised individuals and individual psychology; they are also interested in aspects of large-group psychology and societal processes. Here are some examples.

Moses (1982) examined the Arab-Israeli conflict from a psychoanalytic point of view. Michael Šebek (1992, 1994) examined societal responses to living under communism in Europe. Loewenberg (1995) went back to the history of the Weimar Republic, and emphasised its humiliation and economic collapse as major factors in creating shared personality characteristics among the German youth and their embrace of Nazi ideology. Kakar (1996) explored the effects of Hindu–Muslim religious conflict in Hyderabad, India. Apprey (1993, 1998) focused on the influence of transgenerational transmission of trauma on African-Americans and their culture. Hollander (1997) explored events in South America and later (Hollander, 2010) in the USA after September 11, 2001. Elliott, Bishop, and Stokes (2004), and Alderdice (2007, 2010) examined the situation in Northern Ireland. After September 11, 2001 the International Psychoanalytic Association (IPA) formed the Terror and Terrorism Study Group. Norwegian analyst Sverre Varvin chaired this study group that lasted for several years (Varvin & Volkan, 2003). Also, the IPA established a committee on the United Nations that still functions under the chairmanship of Affaf Mahfouz, a member of the American Psychoanalytic Association. The theme of the 44th Annual Meeting of the IPA in Rio de Janeiro, in the summer of 2005, was "trauma", including trauma due to historical events.

Clearly, psychoanalytic studies covering prejudicial large-group process in many parts of the world have begun. There are serious efforts to study psychoanalytically large-group processes and large-group psychology, alongside those of traumatised individuals. Back in 1979, I wrote about two ethnic groups in conflict within Cyprus. Since then, I have published books and papers on the human need to have large-group enemies and allies, the Arab-Israeli conflict, Communism, the psychological process in the Baltic Republics after independence following the collapse of the Soviet Union, the Serbian group psychology after the collapse of the former Yugoslavia, the psychology of Albanians following the death of dictator Enver Hodxa, Kuwaiti responses to the invasion by Saddam Hussein's forces, the Georgian–South Ossetian conflict, the Turkish-Greek as well as Turkish-Armenian relationships, the psychology of extreme religious fundamentalism, and the psychology of suicide bombers (Volkan, 1988, 1997, 2004, 2006; Volkan & Kayatekin, 2006; Volkan & Itzkowitz, 1994).

The time has come to expand a psychodynamic large-group psychology in its own right, one that explains patterns of large-group interaction in times of peace and war. I am making some efforts towards this.

Focus on large-group identity

Some background on the concept of large-group identity and related issues might be helpful in explaining what I mean by large-group psychology *in its own right* and why it is important. An opportunity for me to study large-group identity in earnest occurred in 1979, when Egyptian president Anwar Sadat made a historic trip to Israel. During his speech at the Knesset, he declared that 70% of the problems between Arabs and Israelis are psychological. Following Sadat's visit to Israel, with the blessing of the American, Egyptian, and Israeli governments, the Committee of Psychiatry and Foreign Affairs of the American Psychiatric Association began bringing together influential Egyptians and Israelis, every six months or so, for three–four days of unofficial dialogue. I was a member, and then the Chairperson, of this committee. This project lasted for six and a half years. During the third year of this dialogue series, we included Palestinian representatives.

The Palestinians joined us for the first time in Switzerland. By that time, we had learnt that by dividing the participants and facilitators into small groups, we could obtain better results. I was in charge of one small group. A young Palestinian physician from Gaza happened to sit next to retired Israeli Major-General Shlomo Gazit. General Gazit was an Israeli hero due to his participation in the Six-day War, and Defence Minister Moshe Dayan gave him the authority to run the political, security, and economic affairs of the newly captured territories. I noticed that the Palestinian physician was nervous. I could understand how difficult it was for him to sit next to a former Israeli general, as an equal within a neutral country. He turned to General Gazit and said that he did not like living under Israeli occupation. He then explained that General Gazit, who was the first Israeli General assigned to run the Gaza strip, was a man with high integrity. For this reason, the Palestinian physician respected Gazit. He continued by saying that after General Gazit, all other Israeli generals who were assigned to Gaza were "bad" administrators who had caused increased shame, humiliation, and helplessness among Palestinians in Gaza.

As he was talking, I noticed that the Palestinian physician put his right hand into the right pocket of his trousers. I could see the frantic movements of his fingers under the cloth. I thought that sitting next to General Gazit had induced castration anxiety in him, and that he was touching his penis in order to confirm that it was not castrated. However, the Palestinian physician, almost screaming, then declared, "As long as I have this, you cannot take my Palestinian identity from me." When I enquired what "this" was, I learnt that he had a little stone in his pocket painted with Palestinian colours. We learnt that Palestinians in Gaza at that time carried little stones such as this in their pockets. Whenever they saw Israeli soldiers or felt humiliated and threatened by Israelis, they would put their fingers in their pockets and touch the stones. This way, they would know that their Palestinian identity still existed.

After working with Arab and Israeli representatives for six and a half years, I became involved, as the leader of an interdisciplinary team, in bringing together other groups in conflict for years-long unofficial dialogues: representatives from the USA and the Soviet Union, Russia and Estonia, Serbia and Croatia, Georgia and South Ossetia, and others. I noticed that this abstract thing called large-group identity occupies the central role in international relations. Large groups, usually with the guidance or manipulation of political leaders, will do anything to protect, maintain, and repair their large-group identities, even if such activities include massive extreme sadism, as well as extreme masochism. When large-group identities are threatened, the political leader's personality organisation, even in democracies, becomes a major factor in providing adaptive or maladaptive direction to large groups' movements. When the large-group identity is threatened, subgroups and dissenters within a large group do not substantially change how large groups react and deal with "others" who are foreign to them.

Large-group psychology in its own right

Large groups do not have one brain to think with, or two eyes to cry. When thousands or millions of members of a large group share a defence mechanism or a psychological journey, what we see are societal, cultural, and political processes that are specific to the large group under study. Large-group psychology *in its own right* can be examined and theories about it can be developed by finding the shared mental phenomena that initiate such specific societal, cultural, and political processes. In order to illustrate and explain this, I will focus on three areas: large-group regression, large-group externalisations, or projections, and large-group mourning. All three areas are connected with the concept of large-group identity. A large group regresses when there is a shared threat or harm done to its large-group identity, it utilises massive externalisations or projections in order to strengthen the large-group identity, and it mourns when various types of losses are associated with harm to the large-group identity.

Large-group regression and the reactivation of a chosen trauma

In our daily clinical practice, we see behaviour patterns in our patients that can be explained by the concept of regression. We should ask how large-group regression exhibits itself. Kernberg (2003a,b) explains that regressed large groups experience narcissistic or paranoid reorganisation. If we plan to develop strategies to deal with a specific large-group's regression and share them with diplomats and others, we need to be more specific. Elsewhere, I came up with twenty tell-tale signs and symptoms of societal regression that a group can exhibit (Volkan, 1988, 1997), ranging from rallying around a leader to preoccupation with certain identity markers, to exaggerating the significance of minor differences, or being involved in magical thinking. In this chapter, I focus on one sign of large-group regression: the reactivation and inflaming of the mental representation of a past historical event.

When individuals regress, they "go back" and repeat their childhood experiences contaminated with unconscious fantasies, mental defences, and childhood ways of dealing with conflicts. The things they repeat are specific to them. When a large group regresses, it also "goes back", reactivates and inflames certain mental representations of its ancestors' history, events that might have occurred decades or centuries ago. I name such shared mental representations of history "chosen traumas" and "chosen glories". They are "chosen" to become key large-group identity markers, as sentiments about chosen glories and chosen traumas are often mixed.

Chosen glories refer to shared mental representations of a historical event, and heroic persons attached to them that are heavily mythologised over time. Chosen glories are passed on to succeeding generations, through transgenerational transmissions made in parent– or teacher–child interactions, and through participation in ritualistic ceremonies recalling past successful events. Chosen glories link children of a large group with each other and their large group, and the children experience increased self-esteem through association with such glories.

While no complicated psychological processes are involved, when chosen glories are reactivated, the reactivation of chosen traumas, in supporting large-group identity and its cohesiveness, is more complex. Chosen traumas—shared mental representations of ancestors' traumas at the hands of "others"—are more complicated, and stronger, large-group amplifiers.

After a massive trauma at the hands of others who have a different large-group identity, members of a large group experience a combination of the following shared experiences (Volkan, 2006, 2009):

1. Sense of shame and humiliation for being helpless.
2. Sense of victimisation and feeling dehumanised.
3. Sense of guilt for surviving while others perished.
4. Inability to be assertive.
5. Increase in externalisations/projections.
6. Exaggeration of "bad" prejudice.
7. Increase in narcissistic investment in large-group identity.
8. Envy toward the victimiser and (defensive) identification with the oppressor.
9. Difficulty, or often inability, to mourn losses.
    When such shared psychological experiences continue, and the members of a large group cannot find adaptive solutions for them, they become involved in the next shared experience:
10. Shared transgenerational transmission of psychological tasks to deal with the influence of the trauma.

Massive trauma after natural disasters such as earthquakes—unless they directly or indirectly become connected with harm by others who belong to another large-group identity—do not induce shame, humiliation, or dehumanisation, and its consequences have different shared psychology. Attempts to complete unfinished psychological tasks, associated with the ancestor's trauma at the hands of others, are handed down from generation to generation. All these tasks are associated with the shared mental representation of the same event, and, eventually, this mental representation evolves as the most significant large-group identity marker, a chosen trauma.

Not all past massive tragedies at the hands of others evolve as chosen traumas. We see the mythologising of victimised heroes and hear moving stories associated with a trauma popularised in songs and poetry, and we see political leaders of later times create a preoccupation with a past trauma and related events, turning this historic event into a chosen trauma. Polish President Lech Kaczynski and others were killed in an aeroplane crash, on their way to a ceremony marking the anniversary of the Katyn Forest massacre of Polish nationals by Russians that occurred in April–May, 1940. I believe that this plane crash will play a role in turning the Katyn massacre into a chosen trauma.

More than a child's identification with traumatised adults, the concept of "depositing" self and object images into the self-representation of a child explains how transgenerational transmission of trauma occurs in chosen traumas (Volkan, 1987; Volkan, Ast, & Greer, 2002). Depositing is closely related to "identification" in childhood, but it is in some ways significantly different from identification. In identification, the child is the primary active partner in taking in and assimilating object images and related ego and superego functions from another person. In depositing, the other, the adult person, more actively pushes his or her specific self and internalised object images into the developing self-representation of the child. In other words, the other person uses the child (mostly unconsciously) as a permanent reservoir for certain self and object images belonging to that adult. The experiences that created these mental images in the adult are not accessible to the child, yet those mental images are pushed into the child, without the experiential or contextual framework that created them. Memories belonging to one person cannot be transmitted to another person, but adults can deposit their traumatised self and object images into a child's self-representation, and assign ego tasks to such internal images. Kestenberg's term (1982) "transgenerational transportation", I believe, refers to depositing traumatised images. It is related to a well-known concept in individual psychology called "projective identification" (Klein, 1946). Depositing in the large-group psychology, however, refers to a process shared by thousands or millions, starts in childhood, and becomes like a "psychological DNA", creating a sense of belonging.

Tasks that are assigned to deposited self and object images change into functions (Waelder, 1930) that connect members of the new generation with one another, and chosen glories and traumas evolve as key large-group identity markers. Each chosen trauma or chosen glory belongs to only one specific group. These identity markers continue to exist for centuries. In "normal" times, they can be ritualistically recalled at the anniversary of the original event. Greeks link themselves when they share the "memory" of the fall of Constantinople (Istanbul) to the Turks in 1453; Russians recall the "memory" of the Tatar invasion centuries ago; Czechs commemorate the 1620 battle of Bila Hora, which led to their subjugation under the Hapsburg Empire for nearly 300 years; Scots keep alive the story of the 1746 battle of Culloden, and the failure of Bonnie Prince Charlie to restore a Stuart to the British throne; the Dakota people of the USA recall the anniversary of the massacre at Wounded Knee in 1890; and Crimean Tatars define themselves by the collective suffering of their deportation from Crimea in 1944. Israelis and Jews around the globe, including those not personally affected by the Holocaust, to some degree define their large-group identity by direct or indirect reference to the Holocaust. The Holocaust is still too "hot" to be considered a truly established chosen trauma, but it has already become an ethnic marker, even though Orthodox Jews still refer to the 586 BC destruction of the Jewish temple in Jerusalem, by Nebuchadnezzar II of Babylonia, as the chosen trauma of the Jews. Some chosen traumas are difficult to detect because they are not simply connected to one well-recognised historical event. For example, the Estonians' chosen trauma is not related to one specific event, but to the fact that they had lived under almost constant dominance (Swedes, Germans, and Russians) for thousands of years.

When enemy representatives get together for unofficial diplomatic dialogues, they become spokespersons for their large groups. When one side feels humiliated, they reactivate their chosen traumas, usually contaminated with chosen glories. For example, while discussing current international affairs, Russians might start focusing on the Tatar invasion, while Greeks might refer to the loss of Constantinople. When such images of past historical events are reactivated within a large group, a "time collapse" occurs. Shared perceptions, feelings, and thoughts about a past historical image become intertwined with perceptions, feelings, and thoughts about current events. This magnifies the present danger. Unless a way is found to deal with the time collapse, routine diplomatic efforts will most probably fail. Today's extreme Muslim religious fundamentalists have reactivated numerous chosen traumas and glories. We need to study and understand them, in order to develop new and, one hopes, more effective strategies for a peaceful world.

Large-group externalisations or projections as purifications

We are familiar with a person's externalising his or her unacceptable self and object images, or projecting unacceptable thoughts or affects on to another person. This creates a personal negative prejudice. If we want to develop a large-group psychology in its own right, and understand at least one key aspect of societal prejudice, we must try to understand what happens when a large-group uses externalisation and projection. When a large group finds itself asking questions such as "Who are we now?", or "How do we define our large-group identity now?", usually following a revolution, a war, freedom after a long oppression by "others", or even after economic trauma for which others are blamed, it purifies its large-group identity from unwanted elements. Such purifications stand for large-group externalisations and projections.

After the Greek struggle for independence, Greeks purified their language of all Turkish words. After Latvia gained its independence from the Soviet Union, its people wanted to get rid of some twenty "Russian" bodies in their national cemetery. There are non-dangerous as well as genocidal purifications. Understanding the meaning and psychological necessity of purifications can help to develop strategies to keep shared prejudices within "normal" limits and from becoming destructive.

Large-group mourning

Large groups, like some individuals, also exhibit complicated and perennial mourning (Volkan, 1981) after losses caused by the actions of others belonging to another large-group identity. Mourning in large groups connects itself with losing "normal" narcissistic investment in large-group identity. As a response, large-group narcissism can be defensively exaggerated. Exaggerated large-group narcissism describes a process within a large group when people within it become preoccupied and obsessed with the superiority of almost anything connected with their large-group identity, even when such perceptions and beliefs are not realistic. A society's assimilation of chronic victimhood and utilisation of a sense of suffering in order secretly to feel superior, or at least entitled to attention, represent the existence of masochistic large-group narcissism. Malignant large-group narcissism explains the initiation of a process in a large group, when members of that large group wish to oppress or kill "others" either within or outside their legal boundaries, a process motivated by a shared spoken or unspoken notion that contamination by the devalued "others" is threatening their superiority.

As the narcissistic investment in the large-group identity is modified, the large group may develop what I call political entitlement ideologies—a shared sense of entitlement to recover what is lost in reality and fantasy. Holding on to such an ideology reflects a complication in large-group mourning, an attempt both to deny losses and a wish to recover them, and a narcissistic reorganisation. Each large group's entitlement ideology is specific. Some entitlement ideologies are known by specific names in diplomatic literature. What Italians call irredentism (related to *Italia Irredenta*), what Greeks call the "Megali Idea" (Great Idea), what Turks call Pan-Turanism, what extreme religious Islamists of today call "the return of an Islamic Empire", and what Hollander (2010) called "American exceptionalism" after September 11, 2001 are examples of entitlement ideologies. Such ideologies might last for centuries, and may disappear and reappear when historical circumstances change and chosen traumas are activated. They contaminate diplomatic negotiations. They could result in changing the world map in peaceful or, unfortunately too often, dreadful ways.

Making a formulation about what exists within a large-group psychology

What I have said above about large-group regression, externalisation, or projection mechanisms that lead to negative prejudice and mourning is summarised in the following schema (Figure 4.1).

Using this schema, we can make a formulation about what exists within a large group's psychology, just as we make a formulation about the internal world of a patient who comes to us for analysis. Making a formulation about a patient's internal world is necessary for good analysis, because it gives us direction about what we will be treating. Similarly, making a formulation about what exists in the psychology of a large group can give us directions to help those dealing with that large group to develop helpful strategies.

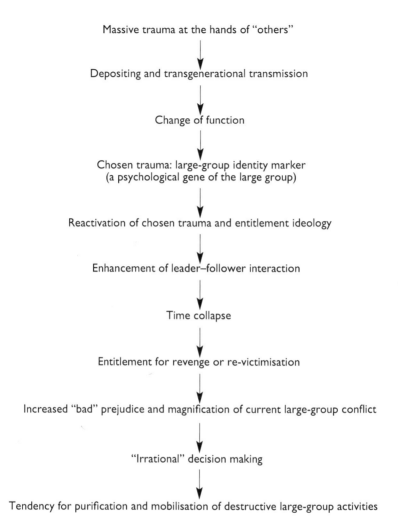

Massive trauma at the hands of "others"

Depositing and transgenerational transmission

Change of function

Chosen trauma: large-group identity marker
(a psychological gene of the large group)

Reactivation of chosen trauma and entitlement ideology

Enhancement of leader–follower interaction

Time collapse

Entitlement for revenge or re-victimisation

Increased "bad" prejudice and magnification of current large-group conflict

"Irrational" decision making

Tendency for purification and mobilisation of destructive large-group activities

Figure 4.1.

Following the above schema, we can understand a significant
aspect of what happened after the former Yugoslavia collapsed. The
shared mental representation of the Battle of Kosovo, which occurred
more than 600 years ago, is the Serbian chosen trauma, a key Serbian
ethnic identity marker. It was reactivated by Slobodan Milošević and
persons around him associated with the Serbian church and Serbian
universities. It enhanced the leader–followers relationship and was

contaminated with the inflammation of the Serbian entitlement ideology, known by political scientists as Christoslavism (Sells, 2002). This resulted in a time collapse, and the Bosnians (Muslims) in the former Yugoslavia were perceived as the Ottoman Turks who were the Serbians' enemies during the Battle of Kosovo. The result was genocidal purification. I told the story of these events in detail elsewhere (Volkan, 1997).

Conclusion

Besides the issues that are originally connected with chosen traumas, "bad" prejudice, entitlement ideologies, and their reactivations, other specific psychological processes are present within a large group. These processes, such as circumstances that increase the need to have enemies or allies, shared transference expectations from a political leader, a political leader's utilisation of the large-group arena for finding solutions for personal conflicts, also require formulations. Because of the reality that many factors in large-group psychology stand side by side and complicate the situation, any attempt to understand large groups or societies is very difficult (Shapiro & Carr, 2006). However, like Alderdice (2010), I am convinced that our psychoanalytical perspective can make a contribution. Such studies will expand our knowledge, in both clinical and international affairs.

On the clinical level, as we analyse individuals, psychoanalytic work on international relations expands our clinical knowledge about the intertwining of external and internal wars, the connections between individual and large-group prejudices, and intergenerational transmissions of shared massive traumas. Analysts need to learn and examine their "foreign" patients' or immigrants' large-group histories, and the psychological processes that such histories might initiate.

In the international relations arena, the same studies raise the following basic question: can psychoanalysis offer serious information about international relations and help develop strategies for peace in areas where attempts are made to utilise it? My answer is "yes". Elsewhere, I have described what my interdisciplinary colleagues and I have done over the past three decades in this area, such as finding ways to create a "time expansion" between current conditions and mental representations of past historical events, in order to help the enemies in a dialogue have more realistic discussions (Volkan, 1987, 1988, 1997, 2006). Enemies are both real and fantasised (Stein, 1988). When the fantasy aspect of the enemy is removed, real dangers can be dealt with more effectively.

Wars or war-like situations do not start because of large-group psychology. But after they begin, especially after they become chronic, large-group psychology contaminates economic, legal, military, and other "real world" issues. Over the past three years, every six months, John Alderdice, Edward Shapiro, Gerard Fromm, and I, as psychoanalysts, have brought together interdisciplinary representatives from Israel, Iran, Turkey, Arab Emirates, Jordan, Egypt, Russia, Germany, the UK, Russia, and the USA in order to understand our present globalised and turbulent world (see: www.internationaldialogue initiative.com).

Two years ago, we celebrated the 100th year of the founding of the International Psychoanalytic Association (IPA). Despite our professional anxieties regarding the future of psychoanalysis, the teaching and practice of our profession under the umbrella of the IPA is now reaching new countries such as Korea, Turkey, and China. This suggests that we will be required to understand different cultures, and specific aspects of their large-group psychologies. With this chapter, I strove to share my view that if we choose to collaborate with professionals from different disciplines, such as diplomats, and be involved in international relations, such efforts will bring new excitement to psychoanalysis and make it, as a scientific field, more accessible and helpful in human affairs.

Note

1. This letter was never published. I obtained a copy from the Turkish government.

References

Alderdice, J. (2007). The individual, the group and the psychology of terrorism. *International Review of Psychiatry*, *19*: 201–209.

Alderdice, J. (2010). Off the couch and round the conference table. In: A. Lemma & M. Patrick (Eds.), *Off the Couch: Contemporary Psychoanalytic Approaches* (pp. 15–32). London: Routledge.

Anzieu, D. (1984). *The Group and the Unconscious*. London: Routledge & Kegan Paul.

Apprey, M. (1993). The African-American experience: forced immigration and transgenerational trauma. *Mind and Human Interaction, 4*: 70–75.

Apprey, M. (1998). Reinventing the self in the face of received transgenerational hatred in the African American community. *Mind and Human Interaction, 9*: 30–37.

Arlow, J. (1973). Motivations for peace. In: H. Z. Winnik, R. Moses, & M. Ostow (Eds.), *Psychological Basis of War* (pp. 193–204). Jerusalem: Jerusalem Academic Press.

Blos, P. (1979). *The Adolescent Passage: Developmental Issues*. New York: International Universities Press.

Blum, H. P. (1985). Super-ego formation, adolescent transformation and the adult neurosis. *Journal of the American Psychoanalytic Association, 4*: 887–909.

Chasseguet-Smirgel, J. (1984). *The Ego Ideal*. New York: W. W. Norton.

Eckstaedt, A. (1989). *Nationalsozialismus in der "zweiten Generation": Psychoanalyse von Hörigkeitsverhältnissen* (National Socialism in the Second Generation: Psychoanalysis of Master–Slave Relationships). Frankfurt: Suhrkamp.

Elliott, M., Bishop, K., & Stokes, P. (2004). Societal PTSD? Historic shock in Northern Ireland. *Psychotherapy and Politics International, 2*: 1–16.

Erikson, E. H. (1956). The problem of ego identification. *Journal of the American Psychoanalytic Association, 4*: 56–121.

Fornari, F. (1975). *The Psychoanalysis of War*, A. Pfeifer (Trans.). Bloomington, IN: University of Indiana Press.

Freud, S. (1905d). *Three Essays on the Theory of Sexuality. S.E., 7*: 123–243. London: Hogarth.

Freud, S. (1921c). *Group Psychology and the Analysis of the Ego. S.E., 18*: 65–143. London: Hogarth.

Freud, S. (1925d). An autobiographical study. *S.E., 20*: 1–74. London: Hogarth.

Freud, S. (1926d). *Inhibitions, Symptoms and Anxiety. S.E., 20*: 87–156. London: Hogarth.

Freud, S. (1933b). Why war? *S.E., 22*: 197–215. London: Hogarth.

Freud, S. (1941e). Address to the Society of B'nai B'rith. *S.E., 20*: 271–274. London: Hogarth.

Glower, E. (1947). *War, Sadism, and Pacifism: Further Essays on Group Psychology and War*. London: G. Allen and Unwin.

Grubrich-Simitis, I. (1979). Extremtraumatisierung als kumulatives Trauma. Psychoanalytische Studien über seelische Nachwirkungen der Konzentrationslagerhaft bei Überlebenden und ihren Kindern (Extreme traumatisation as a cumulative trauma. Psychoanalytic studies on the mental effects of imprisonment in concentration camps on survivors and their children). *Psyche: Zeitschrift Für Psychoanalyse Und Ihre Anwendungen, 33*(11): 991–1023.

Günergün, F. (2006). Cumhuriyet gazetesi. *Science and Technology Supplement*, November 3..

Hollander, N. (1997). *Love in a Time of Hate: Liberation Psychology in Latin America*. New York: Other Press.

Hollander, N. (2010). *Uprooted Minds: Surviving the Political Terror in the Americas*. New York: Taylor & Francis.

Jokl, A. M. (1997). Zwei Fälle zum Thema "Bewältigung der Vergangenheit" (Two Cases Referring to the Theme of "Mastering the Past"). Frankfurt: Jüdischer.

Kakar, S. (1996). *The Colors of Violence: Cultural Identities, Religion, and Conflict*. Chicago, IL: University of Chicago Press.

Kernberg, O. F. (1980). *Internal World and External Reality: Object Relations Theory Applied*. New York: Jason Aronson.

Kernberg, O. F. (2003a). Sanctioned political violence: a psychoanalytic view—Part 1. *International Journal of Psychoanalysis, 84*: 683–698.

Kernberg, O. F. (2003b). Sanctioned political violence: a psychoanalytic view—Part 2. *International Journal of Psychoanalysis, 84*: 953–968.

Kestenberg, J. S. (1982). A psychological assessment based on analysis of a survivor's child. In: M. S. Bergman, & M. E. Jucovy (Eds.), *Generations of the Holocaust* (pp. 158–177). New York: Columbia University Press.

Kestenberg, J. S., & Brenner, I. (1996). *The Last Witness*. Washington, DC: American Psychiatric Press.

Klein, M. (1946). Notes on some schizoid mechanisms. In: J. Riviere (Ed.), *Development of Psychoanalysis* (pp. 292–320). London: Hogarth Press.

Klein, M. (1961). *Narrative of a Child Analysis: The Conduct of the Psychoanalysis of Children as Seen in the Treatment of a Ten-Year-Old Boy*. London: Hogarth Press, 1975.

Kogan, I. (1995). *The Cry of Mute Children: A Psychoanalytic Perspective of the Second Generation of the Holocaust*. London: Free Association Books.

Loewenberg, P. (1991). Uses of anxiety. *Partisan Review*, 3: 514–525.

Loewenberg, P. (1995). *Fantasy and Reality in History*. London: Oxford University Press.

Mack, J. E. (1979). Foreword. In: V. D. Volkan, *Cyprus: War and Adaptation* (pp. ix–xxi). Charlottesville, VA: University of Virginia Press.

Mitscherlich, A. (1971). Psychoanalysis and aggression of large groups. *International Journal of Psychoanalysis, 52*: 161–167.

Mitscherlich, A., & Mitscherlich, M. (1975). *The Inability to Mourn: Principals of Collective Behavior*, B. R. Placzek (Trans.). New York: Grove Press.

Moses, R. (1982). The group-self and the Arab–Israeli conflict. *International Review of Psychoanalysis, 9*: 55–65.

Niederland, W. C. (1968). Clinical observations on the "survivor syndrome". *International Journal of Psychoanalysis, 49*: 313–315.

Rangell, L. (2003). Affects: in an individual and a nation. First Annual Volkan Lecture, November 15, University of Virginia, Charlottesville, VA.

Reisman, A. (2006). *Turkey's Modernization: Refugees from Nazism and Atatürk's Vision*. Washington DC: New Academia.

Šebek, M. (1992). Anality in the totalitarian system and the psychology of post-totalitarian society. *Mind and Human Interaction, 4*: 52–59.

Šebek, M. (1994). Psychopathology of everyday life in the post-totalitarian society. *Mind and Human Interaction, 5*: 104–109.

Sells, M. A. (2002). The construction of Islam in Serbian religious mythology and its consequences. In: M. Shatzmiller (Ed.), *Islam and Bosnia* (pp. 56–85). Montreal: McGill University Press.

Shapiro, E., & Carr, W. (2006). Those people were some kind of solution: can society in any sense be understood? *Organisational & Social Dynamics, 6*: 241–257.

Stein, J. (1988). Building politics into psychology: the misperceptions of threat. *Political Psychology, 9*: 245–271.

Streeck-Fischer, A. (1999). Naziskins in Germany: how traumatization deals with the past. *Mind and Human Interaction, 10*: 84–97.

Usak-Sahin, H. (2009). Perspectives on Freudian Psychoanalysis from Central Europe, Turkey and the United States. Paper presented to the symposium "After Freud Left: Centennial Reflections on his 1909 Visit to the United States". New York Academy of Medicine, New York, October 4.

Varvin, S., & Volkan, V. D., (Eds.) (2003). *Violence or Dialogue: Psychoanalytic Insights on Terror and Terrorism*. London: International Psychoanalytical Association.

Volkan, V. D. (1979). *Cyprus: War and Adaptation: A Psychoanalytic History of Two Ethnic Groups in Conflict*. Charlottesville, VA: University of Virginia Press.

Volkan, V. D. (1981). *Linking Objects and Linking Phenomena: A Study of the Forms, Symptoms, Metapsychology and Therapy of Complicated Mourning.* New York: International Universities Press.

Volkan, V. D. (1987). Psychological concepts useful in the building of political foundations between nations: Track II Diplomacy. *Journal of the American Psychoanalytic Association, 35*: 903–935.

Volkan, V. D. (1988). *The Need to have Enemies and Allies: From Clinical Practice to International Relationships.* Northvale, NJ: Jason Aronson.

Volkan, V. D. (1997). *Bloodlines: From Ethnic Pride to Ethnic Terrorism.* New York: Farrar, Straus, and Giroux.

Volkan, V. D. (2004). *Blind Trust: Large Groups and Their Leaders in Times of Crisis and Terror.* Charlottesville, VA: Pitchstone.

Volkan, V. D. (2006). *Killing in the Name of Identity: A Study of Bloody Conflicts.* Charlottesville, VA: Pitchstone.

Volkan, V. D. (2009). The next chapter: consequences of societal trauma. In: P. Gobodo-Madikizela & C. van der Merve (Eds.), *Memory, Narrative and Forgiveness: Perspectives of the Unfinished Journeys of the Past* (pp. 1–26). Cambridge: Cambridge Scholars.

Volkan, V. D., & Itzkowitz, N. (1984). *The Immortal Atatürk: A Psycho-biography.* Chicago, IL: University of Chicago Press.

Volkan, V. D., & Itzkowitz, N. (1994). *Turks and Greeks: Neighbours in Conflict.* Huntingdon: Eothen Press.

Volkan, V. D., & Kayatekin, S. (2006). Extreme religious fundamentalism and violence: some psychoanalytic and psychopolitical thoughts. *Psyche & Geloof, 17*: 71–91.

Volkan, V. D., & Zintl, E. (1993). *Life after Loss: Lessons of Grief.* New York: C. Scribner's Sons.

Volkan, V. D., Ast, G., & Greer, W. F. (2002). *The Third Reich in the Unconscious: Transgenerational Transmission and its Consequences.* New York: Brunner-Routledge.

Waelder, R. (1930). The principle of multiple function: observations on over-determination. *Psychoanalytic Quarterly, 5*: 45–62.

Waelder, R. (1971). Psychoanalysis and history. In: B. B. Wolman (Ed.), *The Psychoanalytic Interpretation of History* (pp. 3–22). New York: Basic Books.

Weigert, O. (1937). New Turkish Labour Code. *International Labor Review, 35*: 753–774.

PART III
APPLICATIONS

CHAPTER FIVE

Secrecy and the denial of trauma

Susann Heenen-Wolff and Adeline Fohn

Introduction

I n this chapter, we attempt to highlight the extent to which the lack of acknowledgement of traumatic events, and the secrecy surrounding them, can be prejudicial to the individuals and groups who were subjected to them. The seemingly endless struggle of the Armenians, almost a century after that genocide,[1] for some acknowledgement of the trauma they suffered, is an eloquent example of the enduring distress caused by attempts to deny historical reality and its traumatic impact.

Using as our example what happened to the Jewish children who were taken into hiding during the Second World War, we shall highlight the manner in which silence and secrecy have given rise to the denial of traumatism, as well as the extent to which that denial lay at the origin of psychical distress. In our view, what happened to the Jewish "hidden children" is paradigmatic of other situations, such as the genocide in Rwanda, in which the need to construct some form of social cohesion brings in its wake a denial of the trauma to which some people were subjected.

Is such a denial necessary, or even inevitable, in order to enable some form of individual and collective reconstruction to take place?

We do not in any way see ourselves as being in a position to answer that question, but we shall underline the potential long-term psychological effects, and show just how those Jewish children were victims of prejudice, coming both from other people and themselves.

Different kinds of prejudice

Generally speaking, any kind of prejudice or negative bias may prove dangerous, both for individuals and the society in which they live. Prejudice always lasts longer than the circumstances that gave birth to it. Collective prejudice usually arises when there is an urgent need for social cohesion or survival, depending upon how that need is perceived in the given historical context. It is then passed on and tends to merge into the group's cultural background in such a way that it becomes difficult to break free of it, as we shall see with respect to the experience of those hidden Jewish children. Building up various kinds of prejudice also has the effect of diminishing the ability to adapt to changing circumstances; often it leads to a weakening of self-esteem and undermining the feeling of belonging to the group that is subjected to such discrimination.

Prejudice is not always a universal phenomenon—indeed, far from it. Each individual constructs his or her own system of prejudice through experience and learning within a given cultural context. Subsequent encounters between individuals or social groups who have their own different and incompatible sets of prejudicial assumptions might lead to conflicts, some of which might well be serious. From that point of view, prejudice—which initially was felt to promote cohesion within a given society—can in the end lead to exclusion.

Our research project

The observations that we present here are taken from a research project that we undertook between 2007 and 2011 in Belgium[2] to determine the present mental state of those who were hidden Jewish children in Belgium during the Second World War. The results are based upon the analysis of sixty autobiographical narratives and psychoanalytically orientated group work. At our request, sixty Jews who, as children, were hidden during the Second World War agreed to testify to their experience. When they were separated from their parents they were between just a few months and twelve years old. When we began to record their autobiographical narratives, they were all between sixty-six and seventy-nine years old.

The interviews—two or three, lasting from sixty to ninety minutes each—were conducted between March and June 2007. They were then transcribed and analysed. This kind of testimony represents a meaningful way to recount one's past and create a narrative identity.

We observed that the "deferred effect", or *après-coup* dimension (Freud, 1895, 1918b; Green, 2002), played a significant role in their lives, a feature the importance of which no other contemporary research has highlighted in the context of collective trauma, and which seems crucial to us in order to understand the long-term effects of trauma (Fohn & Heenen-Wolff, 2011). The idea of *après-coup*[3] is crucial to the psychoanalytic conception of psychical temporality: it relates to the manner in which mental processes become organised over time. *Après-coup* involves the complex relationship between a significant event and the new meaning that it takes on later, one that can attribute "psychic effectiveness" to the initial event, which, until that moment, had apparently no impact (Laplanche, 2004). When it actually occurred, that initial event might not have been experienced as traumatic; it becomes so only later when some other event gives it new meaning. Thus, there are two phases in psychological trauma: that of the event as such, and that of its subsequent resurgence. Laplanche (2006) makes use of a powerful image to illustrate this phenomenon: the first memory is like a "time bomb" which is triggered when it is set off at a later time—a delayed action. For an *après-coup* to exist, to weave a link between the first and second events, the memory of that initial experience must not be neutral: it has to be "emotionally charged" (Oliner, 2000, p. 46). Unlike a genetic approach, the earliest events that have taken place within an individual's past are not necessarily the most crucial for the mind.

What happened to those Jewish children?

Between 4,500 and 6,000 Jewish children managed to survive the Nazi occupation of Belgium: they were hidden away, lived under false identities, and, in most cases, were separated from their parents. They had learnt how to lie, to hide their true identity, and keep a low profile (Richman, 2006). They had to cope with major changes in their young lives: they were separated from their parents and had to live far away from them, often without any news of them, and cut off from their cultural background; they had to adapt to a strange new life and say nothing about where they came from, their real names, and even, at times, the very existence of their parents. Many of them realised just how precarious their situation was (Kestenberg & Brenner, 1996).

From 1942 onwards, they were placed in the care of foster families, or in institutional environments (convents, orphanages, or children's homes). Some were "visible", obliged to lead a double life in the outside world under a false identity, while others remained apart and sheltered from the eyes of others (Dwork, 1991). Some children suffered from malnutrition, while others did not attend school during that period; in addition, some were exploited or abused.

The post-war period gave rise to even more traumatic situations (Keilson, 1992). Many children, having lost one or both of their parents, then learnt what had happened to them: hiding followed by captivity, deportation, and, finally, extermination. When one or both parents survived, life in the concentration camps or in hiding and the loss of those near and dear to them transformed them so much that they were unrecognisable.

At that time, the children experienced another potentially traumatic separation, when they were taken out of foster care. Fogelman (1993) has shown that it was when a "perfect stranger" (the parents whom the child did not recognise, another relative, or a representative from a Jewish organisation) came to take them away that the trauma of the hidden children really began. Often, they felt that their foster parents had abandoned them; also, it was difficult for them to see themselves as Jewish, as they were torn between, on the one hand, their foster parents and the religion that they had perhaps adopted during the war and, on the other, their origins.

Nowadays, it goes almost without saying that the Jewish children hidden during the war experienced "traumatic sequences", as Keilson (1992) puts it. In order to survive, they had to develop strategies, which they were still using even after the war ended (Cohen, 2005). Suspicion, extreme precautions, and mistrust—strategies that during the war were appropriate for survival—might have proved detrimental in times of peace, because of their ongoing impact on relationships with other people (Fogelman, 1993). When those children were very young, they had to cope with different kinds of loss, and after the war they grew up in a world devastated by the Holocaust. As Sossin (2007) has shown, the cumulative effect of so many traumas made it difficult for the children who survived to integrate and "mentalize" those events.

For many long years, those hidden children were thought to have been "lucky", when compared to what had happened to those imprisoned in the concentration camps (Frydman, 2002); in addition, it was assumed they were too young to remember what had happened to them (Sternberg & Rosenbloom, 2000). The specific nature of what they went through was thought of, in and beyond the Jewish community, as being "trivial in the extreme" (Frydman, 2002, p. 33). That lack of acknowledgement is now looked upon as one of the factors that explains the extraordinarily long latency period that occurred before those Jewish children were themselves able to accept that they had indeed gone through a traumatic experience. For almost forty years—and, in some cases, for almost sixty years—most of them said nothing about what had happened to them. They themselves often wanted to forget the past, and build a new life for themselves.

Until the 1980s, the voices of those hidden Jewish children were relatively absent from the great narrative accounts of the Holocaust.[4] It was in 1991, during the first international meeting in New York that brought together 1,600 of those Jews who, as children, were "hidden", that some awareness of the situation at last became possible; scientific studies of the psychical trauma that the hidden children experienced were then undertaken. (See Feldman, 2003, 2006; Fogelman, 1993; Fogelman & Bass-Wichelhaus, 2002; Fohn, 2010, 2011; Fohn & Heenen-Wolff, 2011; Fohn & Luminet, 2011; Fohn, Grynberg, & Luminet, 2012; Heenen-Wolff, 2009; Kestenberg & Brenner, 1996; Kestenberg & Fogelman, 1994; Mouchenik, 2006.) It would seem that it was only thanks to the social acknowledgement of what they had undergone and the sharing of their narrative accounts that many of those hidden Jewish children were thereafter able to see themselves as survivors of the Holocaust.

Those who have worked with them described the symptoms that they presented: anxiety, a tendency to self-depreciation, disorders of memory, psychosomatic disorders, amnesia, and recurrent nightmares (Feldman, Mouchenik, & Moro, 2008). There were probably four elements that played a part in that symptomatology: the psycho-logical intrusion that they were subjected to as children, the fact that they had survived and the guilt experienced as a consequence of this, the attacks on their ties of filiation and belonging to which they were subjected, and the difficulty in mourning significant losses (Feldman & Moro, 2008).

Although most of those formerly hidden children may indeed present some specific symptoms, we would agree with Oliner's (2000, p. 59) argument, according to which "[a]nalysts cannot treat trauma; they treat the individual, with all the complexities that this entails, respectful of all there is yet to learn about the integration of trauma". Even though much of what occurred was common to all of those hidden Jewish children, they do not constitute a diagnostic entity as such. Terry (1984) and, more recently, Kahn (2005) have challenged the validity of an indiscriminate diagnosis derived from experienced events, even extremely traumatic ones such as those of the Holocaust survivors. According to Terry (1984, p. 135), the so-called "survivor syndrome" of those imprisoned in concentration camps in fact deprives them of their individuality: "When a survivor comes for treatment, the syndrome is presumed to exist and often insisted upon".

Nevertheless, there is no doubt that those formerly hidden Jewish children shared comparable experiences, the long-term effects of which are similar. Given how young they were at the time, they had to cope with situations that were often difficult to understand and to process (the round-up, deportation and death of relatives, and the need to hide in order to survive).

Their understanding of the situation varies according to their age. The very young children had difficulties comprehending the situation. It is often years later that they are able to recognise what they went through, an understanding that awakens a trauma in *après-coup* years later, while for the older ones, the better understanding of the danger during wartime induced a powerful trauma that created a mental paralysis, as far as their emotions and representations were concerned.

The silence, the over-adaptation of those hidden children to the demands of their new environment during the war, and the absence of any social acknowledgement of what they went through did noth-ing to facilitate the mental processing of those events. The traumatism then emerged without any possibility for the kind of psychic figura-bility (Botella & Botella, 1990) that would have enabled a better integration of their experience.

Our observations have led us to suggest that a further trauma—that of the *après-coup* dimension—took place when those who were hidden as children began to talk about their experiences in the 1990s. That subsequent processing, facilitated either by the international meeting that brought together many of those who were in hiding as children, or through psychotherapy, seems to have given new mean-ing to past events, although, somewhat paradoxically, this has had a traumatic impact on them in their present-day life.

Clinical examples help us to illustrate in those hidden Jewish children the *après-coup* phenomenon, resulting from prejudice and secrecy, relating to separation and the moment at which they—both personally and as a group—became aware of it, at a time when the wider community was also beginning to acknowledge what they had gone through.

The impact of secrecy

We began to think about the possible consequences of prejudice, of being driven to secrecy at such an early stage in development, and of having to remain silent as a result. We shall see how the secrecy to which the hidden Jewish children were subjected gradually led to a very specific kind of psychical functioning. We shall discuss the psychological consequences of secrecy in terms of splitting, feelings of guilt, and shame. We pay particular attention to the moment when the secret was at last lifted, thus giving rise to a deferred retroactive (*après-coup*) impact.

Those children were taken away from their family and friends, at a very early stage in their development. They had to deal with the absence of those closest to them—and that of their parents was the most difficult of all—while at the same time adapting as best they could to a new environment, often completely unfamiliar, in order to survive. They then set up a "survival mechanism", as described by Feldman (2006, p. 71). They had to do this because of all the terror that they were going through, a response, as it were, to the absolute neces-sity to be "transformed" in order to escape the many round-ups and exterminations. They simply *had* to become "someone else", to make other people "forget" that they were Jews—but without forgetting it themselves—and internalise it silently. As Feldman, Mouchenik, and Moro (2008) argued, secrecy was the keystone of the mechanism thanks to which the hidden Jewish children could survive; silence was part of its very nature. In our view, it was also a psychological defence mechanism, the aim of which was to protect the individual against prejudice, persecution, and the threat of annihilation.

We have chosen extracts that highlight this element in particular.[5]

> The nun who took me in said: "Listen, we'll work all that out. To start with, you won't be called Esther[6] any more. Forget your name. Forget your name, forget your address, forget your parents, and forget your brother. From now on, you will be called—she told me what my new name was—you were born in such-and-such a place, you're an orphan, and now you live here with us. And above all, don't say anything to anybody." Those were my instructions, and I followed them. At first, it seemed like a game: above all, I mustn't forget that I'm not called Esther any more, but it very quickly turned into some-thing else.

As soon as they were separated from their parents, the Jewish children were bound to secrecy. They learned to keep silent and not to disclose their identity to anyone else. In changing their names, they had to remove themselves from their line of descent, eradicating any link to their birth family and its cultural background. Separated as they were from their original environment at such an early age, most of those children could not understand what belonging to a particular group meant—but often they very quickly came to understand that they were different.

> I wasn't really aware of it, but somehow I knew that the Germans didn't like little girls like me because of my race, but I didn't really know why.

Some Jewish children found themselves being referred to in a demeaning and anti-Semitic way, and this only strengthened their resolve to keep silent.

> They would say to me: "Dirty Jew, go back to your own country."
>
> They said that it was the Jews who killed Jesus.

They transferred me elsewhere, to another family. Those people were very unpleasant, they said wicked things to me and I didn't understand why. I hadn't done anything to them. They said all sorts of things to me: "You people, we know you're like this, like that . . ."

Under such circumstances, given such important threats to their sense of identity and narcissism, how could those children succeed in constructing their own individuality, other than by withdrawing into themselves and hiding their sense of belonging? Their Jewish identity a source of disgrace, and the secrecy surrounding their "former" life and origins meant that their psyche was split. This is what Tisseron (2004, p. 60) calls secrecy as a psychical phenomenon,[7] in other words "a kind of mental organisation (sometimes partly conscious, at others completely unconscious) corresponding to the work of a secret within the individual's mind" (translated for this edition). We would argue that a kind of mental structure typical of secrecy was set up in the minds of those hidden Jewish children: the secret created a split within their personality. It brought about an "uncanny" feeling (Freud, 1919h), an upheaval in the construction of their ego, a break in their feeling of continuity, and some degree of fragmentation within their mind.

When the war came, I had to deny my own self—it wasn't my name any more, I was somebody else.

I adapted very well; I wore clogs like everybody else, I spoke their language without any difficulty like a real little Flemish girl,[8] but it wasn't really me . . .

Guilt feelings

In these hidden Jewish children, secrecy gave rise to the unfolding of imaginary scenarios (Tisseron, 1996), because the mind must fill in what is left unsaid. Faced with silence, and the meaninglessness of their situation, they tried to find answers to the agonising questions that came into their mind ("Where are my parents? Why are they not here with me?"). However, the meaning that they gave to themselves was often misinterpreted, and had to do with a feeling of having been abandoned by their parents:

I said to myself that I must have been a very naughty child, and that was why my parents left me behind.

Guilt feelings are a frequent theme of the narratives that we recorded; such feelings also affect the individual's self-esteem, and most of the time were impossible to put into words—all the more so, since after the war, those children were thought of as having been "lucky".

> At first, I would say to myself: "I've survived, I was not . . . I was lucky to be hidden; I survived, while others . . ." Some girls in my class had been deported and were dead. But I was still here, because I was lucky enough to be hidden. So there was a kind of guilt feeling that tormented me for quite some time.

> I carried a lot of guilt within myself, and for a long time, because my sister was the one who died, not me . . . So . . . it's something . . . well . . . I worked on that for . . . [laughs] a very long time, but I'm still . . . very, very sensitive about it.

Nowadays, we are all well aware of the fact that feelings of guilt and shame can be obstacles to social sharing, that is, to the sharing with other people of an emotional experience (Rimé, 2005).

The development of feelings of shame

In these hidden Jewish children, leaving things unsaid and stigmatising them facilitated the development of psychical representations that gave rise to distortions in the process of symbolisation.

> Having to hide and tell lies all day long, being unable to say who you were . . . We must have done something really awful . . .

Feelings of shame, whether clearly expressed or not, are very much a part of what those hidden Jewish children tell us. As de Gaulejac (1996) pointed out, such feelings often occur in a context of secrecy and humiliation. They go all the way back to childhood and become stronger as the child grows older. According to de Gaulejac, shame has a twofold impact on the sense of identity. On the one hand, it affects the individual's sense of identity, because it disorganises the construction of the personality and is an obstacle to self-confidence. On the other hand, it poses a challenge to family and social identity, because of the doubts, dissimulation, and stigmatisation that are part of it. Shame, therefore, attacks narcissism and the affection that we feel for those near and dear to us, and undermines our feeling of belonging to a community that accepts us (Tisseron, 2007). Long after the war was over, many of those hidden children—by now adults—were still concealing their Jewishness.

> During the war, I was told that my name would be Simon, because it was better that way. And I still sign my name "Simon" because that's what I've always been called. "Samuel", that's the name on my identity card. I've always preferred to be called Simon, because after the war "Samuel" sounded Jewish and I wanted to wipe out everything that seemed Jewish. My professional environment was completely non-Jewish; I wanted to be part of a non-Jewish society. That's why I wanted people to call me Simon.

Even nowadays, some of those hidden Jewish children still use their assumed name, the name that they were given during the war years, in order to continue concealing their Jewishness. Concealing their identity is also what those Tutsis who sought refuge in Belgium do, because they are afraid of being discovered and once again assaulted by Hutus. This survival strategy is due to the fact that survivors are afraid that similar atrocities could occur again. Although this means of adapting enables people to feel more secure, thinking that they will gradually become less anxious, nevertheless it imprisons them in the idea that they will never escape the deadly grip of trauma.

In the case of the hidden Jewish children, feelings of shame also reinforced their silence, and their tendency to conceal the fact that they belonged to a particular group. That sense of belonging was either played down or experienced as something shameful, so, as a consequence, some of them did not want to be identified with it.

> For me, it's nothing more than one's origins.

> I've never had anything to do with religion, but the fact of being Jewish did matter to me—and for a long time there was something shameful about it. I didn't feel that way during the war years, but once I learnt about what occurred inside the concentration camps, I really felt ashamed—as an adolescent, I just couldn't stand the idea that six million people just let themselves be led like lambs to slaughter.

A Jew is always guilty of something. He is someone who "arranges" things, makes money illicitly ... In the long run that's what people think.

In order to counter the threat of psychical destruction, some of them created a kind of splitting mechanism, and, from time to time, internalised what was said about Jews at that time. Sometimes, there also occurred a movement away from their identity as Jews (de M'Uzan, 2001), ranging from ambivalence to rejecting the feeling of belonging.

I felt quite ashamed of being a Jew, and I never really felt myself to be Jewish ... I always took comfort from the fact that I wasn't Jewish. So, I was rather negative compared to those who show clearly where they come from.

For a long time, there was this paradox—I no longer wanted to be Jewish. I can't say how or why, but ... well, why, yes, because of all we went through; I just didn't want to be a Jew any more. Yet at the same time, I was attending meetings of a Jewish youth organisation.

In the case of those hidden Jewish children, feelings of shame and concealment of their identity sometimes gave rise to guilt feelings ("By continuing to hide, I am betraying my people"; "What would my parents think if they saw me acting in that way, hiding my origins?"). As we shall see, that reaction is very much a part of the case studies that we shall now discuss in detail. However, we must acknowledge that some hidden Jewish children always tried to keep a positive sense of self, in terms of Jewish identity, during and after the war. Those who were able to do so were old enough and had already developed a sense of belonging before the separation occurred. Furthermore, this positive reaction concerning the Jewish identity is more commonly seen when parents survived the war and maintained a positive sense of belonging after the war.

Lifting the veil of secrecy and après-coup trauma. Two case studies

Case study 1. Remembering via a psychotic breakdown

Mrs S was born into a Jewish family in Vienna in 1929. She remembered that she was happy as a child, surrounded by her loving parents and grandparents. This situation came to an abrupt end with the annexation of Austria by Germany in 1938. In her autobiographical narrative, this is what she said.

> Very abruptly—I would even say from one day to the next—my parents and I were excluded from the neighbourhood, from everything. I didn't understand anything that was happening. I knew that many people didn't like Jews, but I didn't know why.

Mrs S witnessed scenes of extreme brutality.

> The cruelty was unimaginable, the Orthodox Jews who had long beards and "paiyes" . . . I saw them being dragged out of their houses by their beards, and these beards were cut off by also cutting pieces of their chin; that was, really that was . . . I don't like to speak of all that, it was the darkest moment of my childhood.

In the presence of Mrs S and her mother, her father was beaten up in the street by a neighbour. Only in our final conversation did Mrs S tell us that she had also witnessed a particularly agonising and humiliating scene: an anti-Semitic and excited crowd jeered as her mother was forced to scrub the pavements of Vienna on her knees with a toothbrush.

Several months after the German invasion, the family left Austria and fled to Belgium. They managed to get there in spite of all the dangers, and, when the situation became more settled, Mrs S was able to go back to school and follow the lessons, even though at first she had no knowledge of French.

In 1940, when she was eleven years old, she was sent by the National Children's Health Organisation to a children's camp by the seaside. During this same period, Belgium was invaded by German troops, and she was evacuated with other children to a school in the north of France, without any possibility of contacting her parents. It was several months later that she returned to Belgium to join her mother, and then her father was arrested for the first time.

In 1942, the round-ups became more and more frequent. Mrs S's father was arrested again, deported, and killed. As the risks became greater, Mrs S was placed into the care of a Catholic convent in the suburbs of Brussels.

I felt abandoned. And I was mad at my mother. I was mad at her because I didn't understand why she had "left me there" all alone (today I understand better, of course!). She did not know if I would be safe; after all, it was a dangerous situation. For many years I felt like I had been abandoned . . .

She then learnt from her uncle that her mother had fled to Switzerland, probably hoping that her daughter could join her later. At her uncle's request, she was forced to keep that information secret.

"Don't tell the nuns in Brussels, it will make a bad impression." So I had to keep everything to myself. The nuns noticed that something was wrong with me and I told them: "Mummy has been arrested". I lied.

A week later, she was informed by her uncle that her mother had been arrested. This time she had to keep her suffering to herself.

I could no longer tell anyone about that, because I had lied. I could not even cry any more . . . I had to keep everything to myself.

Here, the scale of guilt feelings become quite clear, and it is probable that there was some "magical" link that this young adolescent made between her "lying" and the actual arrest of her mother. In the years following, overwhelmed by feelings of shame, she withdrew more and more into herself.

During her lengthy stay in the convent, Mrs S converted of her own accord to Catholicism.

There was this little church, with flowers and singing. I loved to sing, and there I could sing in the choir. I was enthusiastic and very sincere in my conversion to Catholicism.

In her narrative, she told us that she was very affected by all the weird things that she had heard as a child about the Jews, and she thought,

I only knew the Good Friday prayer. I don't know if you realise it but the prayer says: "Let us pray for the perfidious Jews" [pro perfidis judaeis] and that was really very hurtful. However, at the same time, I was privileged because I had received this Grace and was saved!

The humiliation of being a Jew, induced by the prejudice with which she was confronted, gave her the impression that the Jews must have done something wrong and generated feelings of guilt that might perhaps explain her conversion to Roman Catholicism. She tried to make some sense of such destructive hatred:

> We must have done something bad; otherwise we would not be treated in this way! I said to myself: "We must have done something wrong! Something wrong must have happened."

According to Hogman (1988), their Catholic experience helped those children to cope with separation from their parents, and gave them feelings of acceptance and salvation that could protect them from fear and the humiliation of being a Jew. This was the case with Mrs S, who wanted to convince her parents, as well as other Jews, to convert to Catholicism.

> My idea was to convert others, those who had not experienced Grace, and I was told that it was my task to give others what I had benefited from, and I was very keen on this task.

Since her mother had been deported and murdered in Auschwitz, Mrs S stayed in the convent until 1949. Unaware that she was now an orphan, she kept hoping that her mother would come back. She also attributed her conversion to Catholicism to her loneliness and the loss of her parents:

> I don't think that I was forced to convert, because there were many children who didn't convert and were still well respected. Nothing was forced, nothing at all. I only said to myself that the moment was suitable for it. I was all alone. My parents had not come back. So it was quite a favourable situation for conversion. I was lost, and in this convent I felt sheltered. I had known nothing but hate for a couple of years, and here I felt really protected. I could be like everyone else and I felt good about it.

When Mrs S was nineteen years old, she went to visit one of her uncles, who lived in Austria. That was in 1948. Suddenly, she was confronted with unexpected criticism.

> He said to me: "Are you aware of what your grandparents and parents would have thought, if they had known that you rejected your

origins?" These words caused me such guilty feelings! So, so, so much guilt! I had converted, and at the time it had been very soothing for me, but afterwards, it really threw me into confusion.

Mrs S's contacts with the Jewish community once again cast a new light on her conversion during puberty. What had been a shelter for her became transformed into a betrayal of her family. We can see here the deferred retroactive (*après-coup*) effect of trauma:

> I had so many guilt feelings that it was no longer possible to think of my parents and grandparents without saying to myself that I had betrayed them. So from one second to the other I became really upset and I said to myself: "No, I can't do that to my parents and grandparents, [and] I can't do that to the Jewish people, I can't!"

Here, we can see the psychical effect of this new awareness for Mrs S in a deferred retroactive dimension. What was a kind of refuge, a protective shield for her when she was an adolescent, during a period of uncertainty and loneliness, was transformed after the war into a traumatic experience that created guilt feelings. Conversion to Catholicism felt like a betrayal to her family and the Jewish people. One can measure the importance of her guilt feelings, by considering her understanding in adulthood of the scope of the catastrophe, the *Shoah*, which killed her parents and her people.

In 1949, she left the convent to live with her godmother, her sponsor at her baptism during her years in the convent, and a year later moved to live on her own. Her situation was difficult: she had no family any more, she hardly knew anyone, and she had no formal education. She tried to get in touch with the Jewish community, and met her future husband, who had been deported. Together they had three children.

Her feelings of shame about being Jewish have continued up until now. In her autobiographical narrative, recorded in 2007, she said,

> I think that I remained a hidden child until today, and it was just last week that my friends made me aware of it. I went to the seaside with two friends. We were talking, discussing. At one moment, I was saying something and I used the word "Jew". I said it in a very low voice. At that point, one of my friends asked me: "Why are you suddenly talking in a low voice?" I realised that I didn't want people around me to know that I was Jewish.

Mrs S rarely spoke about her past, which seemed insignificant in comparison to what her husband had gone through inside concentration camps. Furthermore, it was only ten years after their marriage that Mrs S dared to tell her husband that she had been baptised. Since the death of her husband in 1996, Mrs S feels freer to speak of her own story, and to take care of herself.

Mrs S told us that between 1955 and 1992, family life went on without any major conflicts. There was no indication that could have predicted the very impressive mental breakdown with acoustic hallucinations that occurred when Mrs S was sixty-three years old. Concerning this quite unexpected episode, she said, "It was as if the lid had blown off!"

During her psychoanalytic group sessions, Mrs S told us that she could situate the beginning of her breakdown at a very precise moment: when her name—which has a German-Jewish connotation—was pronounced loudly in public.

> It was when we had a local election here. I have a rather German name and that really bothered me, because I was anxious about my neighbours knowing that I was a foreigner. Nobody knew that I was Jewish.

We shall see how this breakdown reflects her trauma in an *après-coup* kind of phenomenon. Mrs S made a link between the rise of the extreme right-wing party in Austria and an inner bewilderment, preceding the psychotic episode in 1992. Without a doubt, this made her old anxieties become reality.

> It was the rise of the far right in many countries, especially in Austria. It affected me so much that I had to go to hospital because I had acoustic hallucinations. From one minute to the other, I also remembered monuments, for example, which existed in Vienna and which I had forgotten for many long years. That was perhaps the nice side of all this, but on the other hand, it was really torture. With these hallucinations, I was no longer able to turn on a tap without hearing insults come out! I was at a point where . . .

> There were voices that told me to jump out the window. Sometimes, these voices told me: "If you do not denounce all the Jews you know, you will be irradiated." I was in a complete state of hallucination. I had problems with my nice neighbours because I would bang on the ceiling with a broom, because I thought I heard them shout: "Dirty

Jews!" In reality, they hadn't said or done anything. Later on, I explained to them what had happened. I didn't want to stay overnight any more in my place. So in the evening, my daughter came with her car to fetch me. In the car, these voices told me: "If you go to your daughter's, you will contaminate her with your bad radiation." So, at that point, I understood that I couldn't get out of this on my own. Finally, I recovered because I got the medication that I needed, and because I was surrounded by my children, who were very supportive. So I managed to come out of it.

Mrs S made a link between the beginning of her psychotic episode and the pronunciation of her German-Jewish name, a name that referred back to her traumatic experiences in Austria. Moreover, the voices she heard during the psychotic episode spoke in German, her mother tongue, which she had not spoken since she was thirteen years old (when she was placed in the convent). Neither had she spoken German to her own children. We can see here a first direct link with her past and the return of what was split off, which, in this case, was the language that was banned by many Jews after, and because of, the *Shoah*.

In the theme of her psychotic breakdown, we can see the return of more or less disguised events from the past related to the prejudice that she had suffered in her childhood: (a) she was insulted as a "dirty Jew", as in the past; (b) she thought that she had "done wrong", exactly as she had thought she had done by talking to the nuns and thus "betraying" her mother; (c) she had the idea that she had to denounce or betray all of the Jews, and also had to convert the Jews around her because they were "perfidious" and had made the "mistake" of crucifying Jesus Christ.

Mrs S's psychotic breakdown brought earlier traumatic conflicts to the surface. This made a new formulation of her past possible, and led to a better understanding and integration of her life as a Jewish child hidden during the war. She remained in hospital for two weeks, at the time of her psychotic episode. For the past sixteen years, she has not suffered from any further psychiatric symptoms. Her psychical functioning is again quite normal.

As we have seen, the psychotic breakdown took place in 1992. The 1990s were also a period during which many of the formerly hidden Jewish children from different countries expressed themselves publicly, and gathered together in conferences and associations for the first time in their lives. Not only for Mrs S, but also for others, an extraordinarily long period of silence relating to their trauma finally came to an end. It seems it was due to social sharing that the majority of the formerly hidden Jewish children were able finally to see themselves as Holocaust survivors. We would argue that this new consciousness was, for many of them, the first opportunity to experience and symbolise their trauma, which they had held back for so many years through defence mechanisms, such as keeping secret, repression, and splitting. Here, we see a clear deferred action movement, an *après-coup*, because, for many of them, the trauma "hit them"[9] only then, in the 1990s. In the case of Mrs S, we can see the convergence and the cumulative effect of her traumatic experience within social sharing. Mrs S succeeded in working out an intelligible story, but she paid a price. She was confronted once again with her old anxieties and internal conflicts, which, for a short period, overwhelmed her and caused the total collapse of her ego. This difficult period, however, enabled Mrs S to work through her past and construct the core of her ego identity, that of a Jewish child hidden in Belgium during the Second World War, who had to come to terms with the extent of the disaster that had struck her family, herself, and the Jewish people. Moreover, with the beginning of social sharing, it became possible to overcome shame, feelings of guilt, and the subsequent silence in order to speak about experiences related to the war.

Even if not many of those Jewish children who were hidden away experienced such an impressive retraumatisation, the phenomena of trauma in *après-coup* were present for most of them as they became older. In our view, if there is an initial trauma, the "time-bomb" (Laplanche, 2006) can always be triggered later in time, in a delayed action, *après-coup* dimension.

Case study 2. Remembering as a result of a claim for compensation

Ms G was born in Brussels in 1939. Her mother was Jewish, of Hungarian origin, and her father a Jew from Lithuania. She was the eldest of their three children. Her younger sister was born in 1940, and her brother in 1942. During the war, the children were put into a childcare centre run by nuns. Ms G's mother, who was worried about her own future and that of her children, asked the nuns to take care of them if she herself was deported. In 1942, their father was arrested in the course of a round-up, and about six months later their mother, probably denounced to the authorities, was deported to Auschwitz in 1943. Both parents died during the Holocaust.

Throughout the war years, Ms G and her sister were kept hidden in that child-care unit. Their names were changed, and they were both baptised in order to survive. Their brother could not stay with them because he had been circumcised—he was put into the care of a foster family. Given her age at the time, Ms G has no memory of her parents, her brother, or of the various separations that took place. Separated from her parents when she was three years old, she says,

> We were so lucky during our childhood because we didn't feel we were missing our parents—that's what people think! But I must say that we didn't really feel they were missing, because we were very well looked after.

Ms G does remember, all the same, that she was already more or less aware of the danger that surrounded her. During the war, the Gestapo came several times to inspect the children's home, because they suspected that Jewish children were being hidden there. She escaped being rounded up by hiding in a cupboard.

At the end of the war, no one from their family turned up to take the girls home. As orphans, they stayed in that Catholic home, just as Mrs S had done. All through her childhood, Ms G was brought up as a Catholic, and she was very successful in her schoolwork. In 1953, the Jewish organisation[10] set up to find Jewish orphans still being brought up in Catholic institutions discovered where they were. When she was given the opportunity, at thirteen years of age, of going to the USA to live with one of her uncles, she was delighted at the prospect—but things did not quite turn out that way.

> The very next day, I left Brussels for Tournai[11] because the nuns didn't want us to be taken away . . . and that must have been terribly traumatic.

Once again, she had to hide and change her name. "At that time, we were given another name, because the nuns were well aware of the fact that they were searching mainly for orphans." She was then abruptly separated from her sister and the nuns, after staying eleven years in that home. That second abrupt separation represented the second phase of a deferred retroactive trauma (*après-coup/ Nachträglichkeit*—Freud, 1895).

Throughout her childhood, Ms G had no contact at all with the Jewish community. She knew that she was Jewish, but she was forced by the nuns to keep quiet. In spite of her young age, we can see that the prejudice and negative assumptions concerning Jews, communicated through Roman Catholicism, struck her head-on and, thereby, undermined the construction of her narcissism.

> The boarders could not talk about the Jewish problem, because it would have been too confrontational for me, so it was never mentioned. I pushed the whole thing to one side, all through my childhood and adolescence. I remember that, in religious instruction class, they said that it was the Jews who killed Jesus Christ. With my dual nature, being both Catholic and Jewish, I would go all red in the face— I would have liked to hide beneath the desk. It gave me terrible feelings of guilt.

As with Mrs S, we can see here the guilt and shame that Ms G felt. For a considerable length of time, Ms G kept her Jewishness at arm's length, and integrated with her Catholic environment.

> I think that I hid it above all, because I wouldn't have been able to stand the harassment and racist remarks. I think that it was mainly to protect myself. It was above all a form of self-defence—I didn't want to say that I was Jewish, but given my name it would have been difficult to hide the fact.

Ms G therefore set up considerable psychical defence mechanisms, in order to protect herself against prejudice and the traumatic impact of losing her parents. When, as an adult, she left Europe to live in the USA, she thought that she could leave her painful past behind her.

> I think that it was also, perhaps, a way of breaking off all contact with a childhood that I had never thought about as being dramatic, but which, in the end, psychologically speaking, must have been terribly traumatising [she starts to cry, and goes off into the kitchen by herself for a while]. I think that's why I left for the United States, perhaps also to hide what I was . . . and also to become someone.

Ms G never married; she has no children. All through her life she tried to repress her pain.

I have always kept quiet about my private life, never telling anybody that I was an orphan and that my parents had been deported. At times, that became very painful. . . . I have always wanted to believe that I was someone who had a happy childhood, a normal childhood with nothing to be sad about.

In order to survive psychologically, she had built her sense of self on the basis of a past that did not correspond to reality. Having denied reality and transformed it, she was able to function psychologically and construct a narrative that was personally and socially more acceptable.

I pretended that I had been adopted, not raised by nuns, so in a way I was like my brother, who was adopted into a family. I never admitted that nuns had raised me, so in fact I actually made up my own past history. Yes, if you like, if I had been adopted that would perhaps have been less shameful than being brought up in an orphanage. It was that above all [she cries]. Yes, I think it was the fact of being an orph . . . [she cannot finish her sentence, and bursts into tears]. But many orphans were not as lucky as we were, because we were indeed very lucky [she cries]. I think that's . . . that's what I built up, I built it up mentally and had to demolish it in order to experience something; well, it's true, that's part of what I am, but . . . it's very hard. And all these sessions for the compensation claim . . .

Approximately ten years ago, with the help of her sister, Ms G decided to instigate proceedings with a view to claiming compensation for what she had gone through during the Holocaust. In the course of her application, she had about ten meetings with a psychiatrist, in order to undergo a psychiatric examination. Her claim for compensation was rejected, because she lived in the USA. She appealed against that decision, and, in 2011, was still in the process of seeking indemnification. That whole process reactivated, in a deferred and retroactive way, all the suffering that she had gone through. It was only then, it seems, that she fully managed to face the reality of losing her parents. The claim for compensation led to the resurgence of depressive feelings and the outbreak of a traumatic neurosis.

That stirred up so many things inside me . . . I really did have to work on it, I had to show photos of me as a child, and return to that childhood of mine. It was awful [she cries]. I'd always managed to hide it away, I'd always wanted to hide it away—that's why I left for the United States. But having to do all that work again, it was really too difficult. . . . And, each time, I have to go through my whole past once again, from the beginning, it's killing me, it's very traumatising. Everything that was buried comes back again sooner or later, and re-emerges in quite a drama . . . [her sobbing covers her words] . . . a dramatic way.

Before her claim for compensation, that state of psychical fragility was latent but had never surfaced. "I knew about my past, but it didn't make me suffer," she said. From that point on, she had recurrent nightmares linked to her traumatic experience.

The nightmares are about trains. I myself was never in any of those trains, but I've been told so much about them and they've shown films of them on TV so many times. So there are trains going past and I'm afraid of them. And then I get lost in some town or other and have no idea where I am. I feel completely lost, and terribly anxious.

For Ms G, it is clear that the claim for compensation brought about a weakening of her psychical structure and a breakdown in her defence mechanisms. Ms G's experience leads us to think deeply about the impact of narrative. What Ms G did not have was the opportunity of being accompanied when recalling her terrifying experience—the support that is necessary if a traumatic experience is to be transformed and integrated within a collective and symbolic history (Gampel, 2005). Her claim for compensation led to an aware-ness of the reality of the traumatism, that is, what Lacan (1953) called the Real, but she was not helped to process it; she was left all alone to deal with her feelings of solitude, helplessness, and meaninglessness. In such a situation, the hidden Jewish child is confronted with the return of something that had been split off, without having any operational defences at his or her disposal.

Conclusion

As we have seen, prejudice against Jewishness and persecution has had a major impact, both from an individual and social point of view. They were led to silence, a concealment of identity that lasted for many years, a weakening of self-esteem, feelings of guilt and shame, and an attack on the very idea of belonging to a specific group. Carried to its extreme, when prejudice is a characteristic feature within a group of people, this can lead to the destruction and annihilation of a whole section of society or of another social group. Genocide—of Armenians, Jews, and, more recently, Tutsis—bears witness to the destructiveness that consists in denying and eliminating any trace of what was carried out.

In what happened to the hidden Jewish children, a close link was set up between prejudice, secrecy, and what was left unsaid—particularly since it was thanks to silence that they managed to stay alive. The secret was not kept deliberately; it was the result of a traumatic past. It was a means of self-protection, a defence mechanism of the ego. They learnt to say nothing about their true identity, and they continued in that vein long after the war ended. When they reached adulthood, the whole point of saying nothing about the group to which they belong was to avoid stirring up any negative behaviour in other people, based upon whatever prejudice they might harbour. In this way, some of them were able to pursue their work of assimilation, and win social and professional success. However, the price to pay was a heavy one; in particular, it brought about a kind of splitting as well as significant feelings of guilt and shame. Secrecy, shame, and guilt affected their psychical structure as growing children, and help us to understand why those hidden Jewish children went through such a long latency period before they were able to "talk about themselves".

The narratives have also shown that those who were able to assert their identity as Jews, after the war, were encouraged to do so either by those surviving members of their family who valued their Jewishness, or by the fact that the Jewish centres which took in orphans of the Holocaust also valued their Jewishness. That reconstruction of their sense of identity, which, for the survivors, was highly supportive, enabled many of them to overcome the trauma to which they had been subjected. All the same, for decades in fact, most of the hidden Jewish children kept quiet about whom they were. As we have seen, both Mrs S and Ms G, the two women whose autobiographical narratives we presented in some detail, belong to that category. These case studies show that silence, keeping quiet about one's Jewishness, and finding it difficult to reappropriate a sense of belonging simply kept alive—and perhaps even facilitated—the deadly impact of inter-nalised prejudice. Children who lost one or both of their parents during the Holocaust were often the most affected in the long term. The *après-coup* impact of their memories was often extremely violent and devastating, more so perhaps than in other victims, but they were thereafter often able to open themselves up towards some kind of working through. The psychoanalytic concept of deferred retroactive effect (*après-coup*, *Nachträglichkeit*) helps us to understand that, in so far as any form of prejudice has a traumatic impact, it can have an effect on the mind in the medium or long term.

We have shown that society's acknowledgement of the traumatism to which those hidden Jewish children were subjected, was the *sine qua non* condition for them to experience retroactively the pain and suffering they had gone through. It could, perhaps, be said that it might have been better not to open up such a traumatic period in their past, one that for such a long time had remained little known and, therefore, kept silent. Would it not have been better to spare them that *après-coup* traumatism? Would not Mrs S and Ms G—and many others—have been happier if they had not needed to undergo such severe mental breakdowns?

That is not our view. Many of the people to whom we talked in the context of our research project told us how important it was for them to share their past history. Several of them, indeed, made that quite clear when we reached the end of their narrative, saying, for example, "I think I must have been waiting all my life for you to come along so that I could tell my story!" Yes, the trauma was kept silent, but was awaiting acknowledgement and processing, even though this was often a painful step. It would seem that the narrative identity that those who took part in our research were able to construct for them-selves, through our meetings with them, did, in fact, comfort them and set them free from the loneliness in which they found themselves when what they had gone through was never acknowledged as such.

As we have seen, the mistaken idea that they were "lucky" prevented them from developing their subjectivity. The feelings of relief and of pride that many of them spoke about, at the end of the research project, bear witness to an enhancement of their self-esteem, thanks to sharing their story with others. In addition, social acknowledgement gave support to various individual and group-based processes, such as speaking out, bearing witness, as well as undertaking research in order to find some trace of their past history, thereby leading to a reappropriation of their own past, both as individuals and as members of a specific group. Furthermore, society's acknowledgement encouraged those Jewish children to reveal their hidden identity; this enabled them to live in a less split-off manner, to draw closer to the Jewish community, and to take their own past on board, given that once it was shared with others it felt less threatening.

The Jewish children hidden during the war are certainly not the only ones who have had to deal with ignorance and absence of acknowledgement with regard to what they went through. As we have shown, acknowledgement of trauma through a social kind of sharing is a necessary condition for activating the healing process.

Notes

1. Even now, the Turkish government disputes the term "genocide" as applied to the killing of 1,200,000 Armenians in 1915–1916.
2. That research project led to the publication of a doctoral thesis (Fohn, 2011), with the help of a grant from the special research fund provided by the University of Louvain, UCL (Belgium). The authors have gone on to publish several papers based on that research project (see Fohn and Heenen-Wolff, 2011, 2012, 2012 in the References section).
3. Strachey's translation of *Nachträglichkeit* in the *Standard Edition* is "deferred action", a term that fails to give sufficient importance to the retroactive and proactive movements that the term *après-coup* in French implies.
4. Keilson (1992), Vegh (1979), Hogman (1983, 1988), Fogelman (1988), and Kestenberg (1982) were among the first to give a voice to those formerly-hidden children and to highlight their past and present suffering.
5. All extracts cited in this chapter are taken from transcripts of unpublished interviews with formerly hidden children.
6. The names of the participants were changed in order to protect the confidentiality of their identity.
7. Tisseron makes a distinction between secrecy (with a lower-case "s") as a relation-based phenomenon and Secrecy (with a capital "S") as a psychical fact.
8. As a young girl, she spoke French, but she learned to speak Flemish, the other official language of Belgium, which closely resembles Dutch.

9. The French term *après-coup* includes the idea of *coup*, that is, of a blow, of being struck.
10. L'Aide aux Israelites Victimes de la Guerre (AIVG)—Aid for Israelite Victims of the War.
11. A town in Belgium, near the frontier with France.

References

Botella, C., & Botella, S. (1990). La problématique de la régression formelle de la pensée et de l'hallucinatoire. *Monographie de la Revue française de psychanalyse*, 63–90.

Cohen, S. K. (2005). The silence of hidden child survivors of the Holocaust. *Yad Vashem Studies, 33*: 171–202.

De Gaulejac, V. (1996). *Les sources de la honte*. Paris: Desclée de Brouwer.

Dwork, D. (1991). *Children with a Star. Jewish Youth in Nazi Europe*. New Haven, CT: Yale University Press.

Feldman, M. (2003). Enfants juifs cachés (1940–1944): quelle aide psychologique leur apporter aujourd'hui ? *Stress et Trauma, 3*(2): 111–118.

Feldman, M. (2006). Survie et destin psychique des enfants juifs cachés en France pendant la Deuxième Guerre Mondiale. *L'autre; clinique, cultures et sociétés, 7*(1): 61–77.

Feldman, M., & Moro, M. R. (2008). "Enfants cachés : 1940-1944" : un vécu traumatique qui se poursuit. *Neuropsychiatrie de l'enfance et de l'adolescence, 56*: 215–222.

Feldman, M., Mouchenik, Y., & Moro, M. R. (2008). Les enfants juifs cachés en France pendant la Seconde Guerre Mondiale: des traces du traumatisme repérables plus de soixante ans après. *La Psychiatrie de l'enfant, 51*(2): 481–513.

Fogelman, E. (1988). Intergenerational group therapy: child survivors of the Holocaust and offspring of survivors. *Psychoanalytic Review, 75*(4): 619–640.

Fogelman, E. (1993). The psychology behind being a hidden child. In: J. Marks (Ed.), *The Hidden Children. The Secret Survivors of the Holocaust* (pp. 292–307). New York: Ballantine Books.

Fogelman, E., & Bass-Wichelhaus, H. (2002). The role of group experiences in the healing process of massive childhood Holocaust trauma. *Journal of Applied Psychoanalytic Studies, 4*(1): 31–47.

Fohn, A. (2010). Secret et traumatisme: l'expérience des enfants juifs cachés en Belgique. (Secret and trauma: The experience of hidden Jewish children in Belgium). *L'autre: Clinique, Culture et Sociétés, 11*(2): 189–198.

Fohn, A. (2011). Traumatismes, souvenirs et après-coup: l'expérience des enfants juifs cachés en Belgique [Trauma, memories and "après-coup": the experience of hidden Jewish children in Belgium]. PhD thesis, Université catholique de Louvain, Belgium.

Fohn, A., & Heenen-Wolff, S. (2011). The destiny of an unacknowledged trauma: the deferred retroactive effect of *après-coup* in the hidden Jewish children of wartime Belgium. *International Journal of Psychoanalysis, 92*: 5–20.

Fohn, A., & Heenen-Wolff, S. (2012). Das Schicksal eines nicht anerkannten Traumas: Die Dimension der Nachträglichkeit bei während des Krieges in Belgien versteckten jüdischen Kindern [The fate of an unrecognised trauma: the dimension of deferred action in the hidden Jewish children during wartime in Belgium]. In: A. Mauss-Hanke (Ed.), *Internationale Psychoanalyse 2012: Ausgewählte Beiträge aus dem International Journal of Psychoanalysis, 7*: 187–207.

Fohn, A., & Heenen-Wolff, S. (2013). Coup et après-coup: le destin d'un traumatisme infantile chez un ancien enfant juif caché [Coup and "après-coup": The destiny of an infantile trauma in a hidden Jewish child]. *Psychiatrie De L'enfant, 56* no. 1: 245–265.

Fohn, A., & Luminet, O. (2011). Souvenirs d'une enfance douloureuse: l'expérience des enfants juifs cachés en Belgique [Memories of a painful childhood: the experience of hidden Jewish children in Belgium]. *Les Cahiers de la Mémoire Contemporaine, 10*: 319–352.

Fohn, A., Grynberg, D., & Luminet, O. (2012). Post-traumatic severity and thought control strategies in a group of Jewish children who survived the Holocaust by hiding in Belgium. *Journal of Loss and Trauma, 17*(1): 38–55.

Freud, S. (1895). *Project for a Scientific Psychology. S.E., 1*: 295–394.

Freud, S. (1918b). *From the History of an Infantile Neurosis. S.E., 14*: 7–66. London: Hogarth

Freud, S. (1919h). The "uncanny". *S.E., 17*: 219–256. London: Hogarth.

Frydman, M. (2002). *Le traumatisme de l'enfant caché. Répercussions psychologiques à court et à long termes.* Paris: Harmattan.

Gampel, Y. (2005). *Ces parents qui vivent à travers moi. Les enfants de la guerre.* Paris: Fayard.

Green, A. (2002). *Time in Psychoanalysis: Some Contradictory Aspects,* A. Weller (Trans.). London: Free Association Books.

Heenen-Wolff, S. (2009). Die Reminiszenz in der Halluzination. Der Fall eines vormals versteckten jüdischen Kindes. *Psyche. Zeitschrift für Psychoanalyse und ihre Anwendungen, 63*(1): 73–85.

Hogman, F. (1983). Displaced Jewish children during World War II: how they coped. *Journal of Humanistic Psychology, 23*(1): 51–66.

Hogman, F. (1988). The experience of Catholicism for Jewish children during World War II. *Psychoanalytic Review, 75*(4): 511–532.

Kahn, L. (2005). Quand la Shoah est un trauma et que le père disparaît de la théorie analytique. *Penser/Rêver, 7:* 281–308.

Keilson, H. A. (1992). *Sequential Traumatization in Children.* Jerusalem: Magnes Press.

Kestenberg, J. (1982). A metapsychological assessment based on an analysis of a survivor's child. In: M. Bergmann & M. E. Jucovy (Eds.), *Generations of the Holocaust* (pp. 137–158). New York: Basic Books.

Kestenberg, J. S., & Brenner, I. (1996). *The Last Witness: The Child Survivor of the Holocaust.* Washington: American Psychiatric Press.

Kestenberg, J. S., & Fogelman, E. (1994). *Children During the Nazi Reign: Psychological Perspective on the Interview Process.* Westport, CT: Praeger.

Lacan, J. (1953). Le Symbolique, l'Imaginaire et le Réel, Conférence à la Société Française de Psychanalyse. *Bulletin de l'Association Freudienne, 1982:* 4–13.

Laplanche, J. (2004). *International Dictionary of Psychoanalysis.* London: Macmillan.

Laplanche, J. (2006). L'après-coup. In: *Problématiques VI (Problematics, vol. VI).* Paris: PUF.

Mouchenik, Y. (2006). *Ce n'est qu'un nom sur une liste, mais c'est mon cimetière. Traumas, deuils et transmission chez les enfants juifs cachés en France pendant l'Occupation.* Grenoble: Pensée sauvage.

M'Uzan de, M. (2001). Séparation et identité. *Revue Française de Psychanalyse, 65*(1): 355–360.

Oliner, M. (2000). The unsolved puzzle of trauma. *Psychoanalytic Quarterly, 69:* 41–62.

Richman, S. (2006). Finding one's voice. transforming trauma into auto-biographical narrative. *Contemporary Psychoanalysis, 42*(4): 639–650.

Rimé, B. (2005). *Le partage social des émotions.* Paris: PUF.

Sossin, K. M. (2007). Nonmentalizing states in early-childhood survivors of the Holocaust: developmental considerations regarding treatment of child survivors of genocidal atrocities. *American Journal of Psychoanalysis, 67:* 68–81.

Sternberg, M., & Rosenbloom, M. (2000). "Lost childhood": lessons from the Holocaust: implications for adult adjustment. *Child and Adolescent Social Work Journal*, *17*(1): 5–17.

Terry, J. (1984). The damaging effects of the "survivor syndrome". In: S. A. Luel & P. Marcus (Eds.), *Psychoanalytic Reflections on the Holocaust: Selected Essays* (pp. 135–148). Denver: Holocaust Awareness Institute, Center for Judaic Studies, University of Denver.

Tisseron, S. (1996). *Secret de famille: mode d'emploi. Quand et comment faut-il en parler?* Paris: Marabout.

Tisseron, S. (2004). Le secret ne s'oppose pas à la vérité, mais à la communication. *Cahiers critiques de thérapie familiale et de pratiques de réseaux*, *33*(2): 55–67.

Tisseron, S. (2007). *La honte. Psychanalyse d'un lien social.* Paris: Dunod.

CHAPTER SIX

Collective mourning: who or what frees a collective to mourn?*

Concerning the first step out of the most malignant collective prejudice

Hermann Beland

An approach to the grief of loss of collective goodness

The question, indeed, is whether individually or as a collective, people can work on the current past, grieving, understanding, and reflecting. Many Germans would like to mourn the Holocaust, the loss of the infinite value of the many individuals who were annihilated as persons, and the loss of their goodness as Germans. If the pain of loss can dissolve in tears, the mourner can then give himself up to the work of mourning; he knows that the process will continue, by its nature, even in the case of a collective, sometimes lasting forever.

In this chapter, I concentrate on that particular kind of pain that is felt in mourning the loss of one's own normality and goodness, the grief of a collective which has murdered innocent people in a paranoid delusion. Germans feel themselves to be the heirs of the

---

* Translated by Mitch Cohen. Revised version of: Kollektive Trauer – Wer oder was befreit ein Kollektiv zu seiner Trauer? Annäherung an die Trauer des Selbstverlustes über den Vergleich mit Freuds Empirie und Theoriegeschichte des Trauerns. In: Franz Wellendorf/Thomas Wesle (Hrsg.): *Über die (Un)Möglichkeit zu trauern* (pp. 243–262). Stuttgart: Klett Cotta, 2009.

genocide committed by Germans, and feel that the peoples of the world see them that way, as well. Can this heritage be mourned? I am convinced that, in our, the German, case, the pain about the loss of our own collective humanity must first be accepted and endured; otherwise we cannot devote ourselves to grieving the lost victims.

Here, I approach grief as the loss of one's own valued identity, as a form of narcissistic grief through the comparison with grieving for the lost object, and will use Freud as an example. He found some aspects of the pain of mourning enigmatic, as is well known. I have the impression that what he meant was a theoretical conundrum. However, his descriptions of his pain are imperishable testimony. In the letter to Katja and Lajos Levy (11 June 1923) after the death of his grandson, Heinerle, he wrote,

> He was a charming guy, and I myself knew that I have hardly ever loved a person, certainly never a child, as much as him. . . . I endure this loss so poorly; I think I have never experienced anything more severe, perhaps the shock of my own disease is part of the effect. I carry on my work by necessity, but basically everything has lost its value to me. (Freud, 1968, p. 361)

Six years later, in a letter dated 11 April 1929, he returned to the death of his daughter Sophie to console Binswanger, who had just told him of the death of his twenty-year-old son.

> One knows that the acute mourning after such a loss will run its course, but one will remain unconsoled and never find a substitute. Everything that takes its place, even if it should fill that place entirely, remains something else. And actually, it's good that way. It is the only way to continue the love, which after all one does not want to give up. (Freud, 1968, pp. 222–223)

Freud's grief was grief for the lost object. The intention to continue a love that one does not want to give up fails, initially, if one must give up one's own goodness as part of narcissistic grief and the pain is judged unbearable.

Grief work includes, above all, the anchoring of the self and the object in time, space, and in symbolic thinking, including all dreams from birth onwards, coming to terms with loss and conflict. Separating the index of living time from the lost object is, therefore, a central piece of psychological work: a person who has died no longer has a future or memory. There is no new shared fate with him. One can no longer make real amends. The recognition of reality leads to a crucial questioning of all self-determinations that are connected with the object, and that were valid in the same way for the self and the object. This requires a decision as to whether one wants to die as well, or endure the privations of a lonely life. The pain of disruption is related to a real psychological disruption. The person so necessary to life no longer exists and is present only in memory. Such persons remain lovable and loved, after grief work has already buried them, as real existents. What happens, psychologically, if the object lost is one's own goodness?

Laplanche and Pontalis (1973, p. 484) elucidate the Freudian term "work of mourning" in greater detail when they write, "The concept of the work of mourning should be seen in its kinship with the more general one of psychical working out, understood as a necessity for the psychical apparatus *to bind traumatic impressions*" (my italics).

If we add Freud's other two work terms, dream work, whose original counter-term was analytic work (interpretation work), we can say that in all three modes of work we strive for the same psychological goal, "to bind the traumatising impressions". This might be the heading for narcissistic grief work, as well.

Can the grief reaction, whether object related or narcissistic, be halted, inhibited, or derailed? Yes, it can very easily, as we know. Defence mechanisms hinder the work of mourning when the loss is not yet imaginable and, therefore, not yet recognisable; that is, if the pain is unbearable, the entry to grief work is thereby hindered, as long as it is felt as a life-threatening condition. During the process there are also several obstacles, in the face of which the mourner wants to break off the work. In particular, in ambivalence conflicts, as we know, a sense of guilt can refuse us the internal right to grief, and the transformation of pain into tears. In such cases, the rule of emptiness remains and the grief work does not continue. It stagnates as pathological grief or worsens.

"The fear that the inner void will spread threatens, because it could become the actual core of the personality and damage it or render it superficial" (Durban, 2007, p. 64).

Something like this was the Mitscherlichs' (1967) diagnosis of the German inability to mourn.

The mutual dependence between
individual and collective mourning

Continuing to feel my way into the interrelationship between object related and narcissistic, individual and collective grief, I remind the reader of the three eras of Germans dealing with German war crimes, as Rüsen (2001) formulated them in "Holocaust-Erfahrung und deutsche Identität" (Holocaust experience and German identity), by providing a sociological survey of public discourse concerning the Holocaust. In the context of what he calls the third phase, I situate the grief content that today seems the most important work requirement for the individual and for German groups: the grief content of the loss of one's own goodness.[1] In my opinion, without recognising this loss there can be no collective pain regarding the murder of our Jewish neighbours and their loss to Germany, about the rule of the most malignant prejudice the world has met.

According to Rüsen, the first attitude of the Germans after the war (1945–1968) was the maintenance of collective silence and an exterritorialisation, as he called it, an outward projection of Nazi crimes and the Holocaust on to the large "not-us" groups of perpetrators and their victims. One turned oneself into a victim of Hitler and a small group of his fanatic adherents and perpetrators. One's own war dead, prisoners, expellees, refugees, and homeland and property losses were seen as offsetting those of the Holocaust victims. The destructive core of annihilating everything humane was not yet recognised as the essence of the Third Reich, in the public discussion. The destruction of national identity was not yet felt, so it could not be psychologically accepted. Maintaining silence regarding the knowledge of the genocide made it possible, as a counter-movement, to integrate the larger part of the Nazi system's elite into leading functionaries in the emerging Federal Republic. The historian Herbert (1992; cited in Rüsen, 2001, p. 99) wrote,

> . . . considering the millions of victims of National Socialist policy, that the majority of the perpetrators should get off scot-free was a process so fundamentally contradicting all ideas of morality that it was impossible for it to remain without serious consequences for society. (translated for this edition)

The second approach to dealing with the Nazi era (1968–1989) was moulded by the book by Alexander and Margarethe Mitscherlich

(1967): *Die Unfähigkeit zu Trauern* [The Inability to Mourn]. In this era, moralising and dissociating themselves, people brought the Nazi era to the forefront, questioning and distancing themselves from guilty fathers, and identifying with the genealogical victims, the children of the Holocaust victims. "In the eyes of the children, the fathers more or less fell under suspicion of being perpetrators. In opposition and counter-identification, the children turned to the victims of this generation of fathers and perpetrators" (Bohleber, 2007, p. 346).

The third way of dealing with the Nazi era (1989–present) finally—according to Rüsen—could be characterised by the start of the closing of the generational gap. Rüsen heard many public voices stressing the intergenerational "We" as the inescapable task of the immediate future. Von Dohnanyi makes sense when he formulates the task that I believe lies before us:

> He who in these days truly wants to belong to this country with its tragedy and its whole history, he who really understands his Germanness seriously and sincerely must be able to say: we took racism to the point of genocide, we committed the Holocaust, we waged a war of annihilation in Russia. To speak with Martin Walser, these crimes are therefore our own personal disgrace. Not Germany, the abstract nation; not the German Reich, the state organization; not the other Germans; no, it was we ourselves. . . . German identity today is defined by nothing else as clearly as our common descent from this disgraceful period . . . (von Dohnanyi, 1998; quoted in Rüsen, 2001, p. 103, translated for this edition)

The grief over the loss of the collective normal good identity

In my opinion, the grief over belonging to a genocidal nation has three aspects that must be first accepted then repeatedly worked through.

1. The first aspect is the loss of one's own average good normality, through the awareness of the real murderous actions. The shadow of eliminatory anti-Semitism, of the genocide, lies upon us as a collective, and will remain unforgotten by the world's nations as long as our nation exists. (Cf. how the nations have preserved the memory of the senseless destruction of culture by the Huns and,

after the Vandals plundered Rome, eternalised them in the word "vandalism".)

2.   The second aspect is investigating the historical reasons that led to delusional anti-Semitism, which must be acknowledged and understood. The point here is to grasp a collective history of the mentality that ended in genocide. The current grappling with historically and actually existing Christianity, along with the anti-Semitism it collectively induced over a period of two millennia, can lead the individual to the painful loss of Christianity as the central good object of the European nations' historical identity.

3.   The third aspect is the loss of the prior German identity and pertains to the grasping, acknowledging, and penetrating of a collective psychotic mentality into the enforcement and toleration of eliminatory anti-Semitism.

The first aspect of the loss of normality in relation to the peoples of the earth

There may be no models for the special kind of pain that arises with the loss of one's own national goodness. As far as I know, the classic analytical texts have not yet described grief work focused upon the loss of a collective normality. People who have done severe damage to others, or who have killed, must have experienced feeling the loss of one's own goodness. When reading, thinking through, and ex-posing oneself to the feeling of the horrendous practices within the concentration camps, when visiting a concentration camp such as Mauthausen, the feeling arises that, as a German, one loses one's right to live. The mental and active community of eliminatory anti-Semitism is then subjectively palpable through the presence of other nations. The German community of action exists indissolubly, has had an endlessly painful effect, and has ruined everything. This loss of one's goodness is a miserable loss, and one cannot strive for sympathy from other peoples.

In the presence of other national groups, the typical German paranoid state of guilt is noticeable. One senses the collective equating of "German" and "genocide" as a palpable loss of one's own goodness, including losing the right to live together, discuss, and reflect on the same level of competence with others. Hence, we often feel internationally paralysed, which triggers an uncomprehending vexation in others when we are unable to collaborate with them in a normal way. This mental paralysis of German analysts at international meetings is a true collective symptom lending credence to the above-mentioned belief. It seems that this has been acknowledged in the meanwhile as such.

One's own superego has collective dimensions. I remember the farewell evening, towards the end of the Second Group Relations Conference of German and Israeli analysts in Nazareth 1996, about the "Past in the Present", when the staff members loosened up a bit and, after most of the joint work was completed, joined the other conference members (Erlich, Erlich-Ginor, & Beland, 2009). I felt an enormous pressure from the group to sit down between two members on the sole empty seat. But I did not want to sit there, not at any price. The seat seemed to represent a public condemnation of a destructive perversion, a public revelation of a depravity that was concealed until then. I am fairly certain that no one but me noticed what I was experiencing. It was a collective pressure, unnoticed by the others, that I have to feel concretely and publicly German and, thus, bad, badness with no clear content but which was enormously deep-seated: Nazi-bad, so to speak. I was supposed to acknowledge this judgement, had to think it through at the time and thereafter. I was able to report it in private talks, but not publicly. For one needs other people to come to recognise that "my friends want me to stay on task". One regains life then, when one has already accepted the loss of German goodness.

Although mourning work addressing the loss of one's own goodness as a German might seem to others, and might be criticised, as an almost intolerable narcissistic navel-gazing, nevertheless I am fairly sure that this loss must be accepted and tolerated; otherwise the victims' loss cannot be genuinely felt.

One task can be accomplished, when what is at issue is the loss in value of one's own German identity: one can then acknowledge what one knows regarding the origin of the genocides, its extent, and significance. One can read widely, for example, and gain clarity on the details concerning all facets of the annihilation within the camps, as Sofsky (1992), for example, described them. One can gain clarity about the aims and goals of active cruelty. One can recognise that there was an inventive cruelty within the camps whose intention did not have to be formulated in words as the explicit intentions of a collective, giving a constant, precise formulation concerning all the methods and ways the Jews were to be tortured to death. The goal was the systematic annihilation of the personally organised, individual humanity of each individual. That is why the camp inmates were not allowed to kill themselves to escape incremental physical and psychological destruction. One was supposed to suffer precisely thus: to bear witness to the step-by-step destruction of one's own humanity. The inmates were supposed to die on their own by starvation, freezing, disease, and exhaustion, living in their own excrement, and through the psychological laws of the incremental loss of their own identity, little by little. The final goal was killing, but prior to that, as part of the process, the production of a "Mussulman" existence, of the living dead who had lost everything that constitutes humanity, psychologically and physically, and had become a burden to almost everyone else who still persevered in exemplifying to them their own future.

If one is clear on this intentional goal of annihilation by means of a million-fold forced, terrorised self-destruction, one can more easily understand why, increasingly since the end of the war, and increasing further still since the fall of communism and the end of German partition, there is an unconscious collective current, a deep German conviction as a feeling of identity in relation to humanity, that one has lost normal human goodness, that one no longer possesses the normal goodness of the other nations. Some people have this consciousness so intensely that they believe they have forfeited the right to live. We Germans have become, for centuries, perhaps forever, the nation that wanted to cruelly and insanely annihilate humanity, to kill every Jew.

The second aspect of the loss of normality: the historical roots of the anti-Semitic delusion

If one feels one's way socio-psychologically into the mentalities of the twelve years of the Third Reich, the years of the Weimar Republic before it, and the post-war years, one can only hold one's breath when one takes note of the collective belief in national propaganda, the belief in the hoped-for restoration of national greatness, the collective enthusiasm in the illusory idealisation of the leading persons of state, in anti-Semitic conformity, as a form of licensed mad inhumanity, and the glorification of violence and murderousness. Much of this was of

ancient provenance and customary for centuries, such as the idealisation of authorities and hierarchies, the self-obligation of state-loyal
families to believe in the idealism of the leading political personalities,
and in the good intentions and honest strivings of the elites. For
centuries, there was a ban on discovering the inhumane intentions of
one's parents or authorities, as there was a willing belief in Christian
idealisations; there was also a ban on discovering the objective hypoc-
risy in Christian society, or uncovering systematic political lies. Above
all, for 2,000 years there was the habit of anti-Semitism, a blindness to
the projection of Christians' guilt on to the Jews by the leading personalities of the Church; later, people closed their eyes to the eliminatory
laws to maintain the belief in the purity of Aryan blood, just as there
was an inhibition against realising that the old Church anti-Judaism
had morphed into eliminatory anti-Semitism. There was, and still
is, the lack of depression about abysmally deep damage to the heart
of actually existing Christianity, about Church anti-Judaism, which
began as early as the Gospels, in particular the Gospel of John. For
those who regard the humaneness of lived Christianity as the best
heritage of German and European identity, misgivings about the
justification for continuing to regard this legacy as good are among
the most painful losses of a collective, historically good identity
(Beland, 1991).

The loss of a collective good normality as a result of a history of the collective delusion of Christian groups

It is possible that the catastrophe of the anti-Semitism delusion began
with the first Christians' belief in the resurrection as a hallucinated
defence against denied catastrophic grief. The damage caused by
denying the grief, idealising the collective hallucination, and idealising
the hierarchy and organisation of the Church, might have already
begun. All three forms of damage would explain the projection of
the Christians' guilt, and their envy of a collective, the Jews, whom
they secretly believed were more orientated to reality. I will not ignore
the counter-evidence of successful Christian grief, for example,
Michelangelo's Pietá, which expresses the grief after the crucifixion,
lovingly holding the corpse while nevertheless letting it go, living
through one's own grief. What is good in Christianity, which one could

call the internationalisation of Judaism, is historically always simultaneously present with the deluded prejudices and it is also effective.
Nonetheless, one must dare to formulate the painful facts: Christian
groups and nations have lived since the first century in a history of
reformulated delusion. Perhaps I ought to formulate this more
precisely: since the Crucifixion, Christian groups have lived a history
of delusion. The adherents of the Crucified One could not grieve over
their loss; instead, they denied it in a hallucinatory way, and transformed it into divine life. Not much later, I suspect, the denied guilt
and grief tipped over into the never ending hatred of Jews. Bion, in his
famous fable, spoke of the small band of gifted liars who paradoxically
"carry the morals of the world on their shoulders". They were devoted
to the "elaboration of systems of great intricacy and beauty in which
the logical structure was preserved by the exercise of a powerful
intellect and faultless reasoning" (Bion, 1970, pp. 100–101).

I now leave behind these unfinished considerations, although
they are concerned with extremely important legacies of our historical mentality that have moulded all Western societies, and move
on to one of the historical forms that generated the most malignant
prejudice, the Christian anti-Semitic delusion—one that is no longer a
mere hypothesis. (By doing so, I leave aside the distinction between
Church anti-Judaism and later racist anti-Semitism, because I think
this distinction clings to historical externalities of words and changes
of symbols, and, where it is overemphasised, may defensively,
through a kind of historicism, veil the identity of the deluded hatred
of Jews in all forms of anti-Judaism and anti-Semitism.) The writings
of Saint Augustine provide a manifest example of the rise of the
centuries-long indoctrination of hatred and the exclusion of Jews,
the licence to socially and legally persecute them, and the repeated
terrorising of them, canonised by the highest offices as a doctrinal
obligation, that is, the obligation to delusion. This example can teach
us how the Christian peoples were drawn into a deluded prejudice
whose worst embodiment was ultimately Hitler's hatred of Jews, and
the complete paralysis of the German population's outrage against
this hatred and passive acceptance of, or wilful participation in, it.

It is well known that Augustine of Hippo (354–430) had a tremendous influence on Western theology and philosophy. In his polemic,
Tract Against the Jews, he declared that the Jews were evil, wild, and
cruel. One can observe that Augustine's anti-Semitic assertions

immediately make sense if one reads them *as the projective expressions of the author's unconscious self-judgement.* Augustine's stance and intention in publishing this tract *was* evil, wild, and cruel. He compares the Jews to wolves (which also fits directly with his own predatory intentions to tear up the normality of the Jews), calls them "sinners, murderers, the wine of the prophets turned into vinegar" (as the writer's self-judgement), "a stirred up dirt" (which Augustine here stirs up after he has produced it), "guilty of the monstrous crime of godlessness", of which charge Augustine makes himself guilty in the act of writing this. He denies their status as a people chosen by God, and denies their right to call themselves Jews. Augustine was the first theologian who blamed the Jews of his own time for Jesus' death 400 years earlier, and who determined their punishment, the *perpetua servitus*, and the Jews' never-ending thraldom under Christendom. In 1205, Innocence III adopted this idea as a legal stipulation. In 1234, it was included in Gregory IX's collection of decrees, thereby making them ecclesiastical law.

Augustine's assertions all make sense as unconscious projective statements regarding his own self. As canonised assertions, they permitted the Christians of the following 1,500 years to project on to the Jews all their own states of guilt, which all stem from the same aetiological source, and, thus, must do with their own godlessness and inhumanity.

In the dogmatised texts that, since Augustine, have defined the role of the Jews in Christian salvation history, the projection that always seems to have been the decisive unconscious mechanism for anti-Semitism was made in exactly the same *collectively formative* way as it was earlier formative in the individual. The distorting induction of the dogma calls forth a complementary projective identification among the faithful. (On this socio-psychological mechanism, see Beland, 1992, 1999.) What is projected is guilt; this is evident from Augustine's text as a destructive deed. If a collective then turns such a projection of guilt into dogma, that is, raises it up as an exemplary process towards the collective's effective self-understanding as a group, then it is methodologically correct to treat the collective's dogmatised text as an individual's text. The projection must be read as a statement about the projector, that is, every individual of the entire collective. Here, an aetiological equating actually takes place. The functional identity of the same psychotic mechanism and its pathogenic application is effective as the collective's lasting identity-forming conviction, for all members of the collective. A collective delusion is thereby formed. However, there is always a desire to project one's own evil. This is the case for disbelief in salvation (through the Crucifixion) as well as for the Christians' preached and felt guilt. Because of this, the Christians' double guilt, the Jews are guilty of it projectively, the Crucifixion as the murder of God. The Jews are to blame for the unchanged cruelty of the new Christians, who were supposed to represent the New Israel. In this way, a prejudice arises as a collective delusion; it is offered anew to all members of the Church collectively in every generation, who repeat it, guilt-free, to make Christians projectively guilt-free. Anti-Semitic Christians no longer need to have guilt feelings and belief in forgiveness; they rid themselves of these by employing anti-Semitic projections.

Blaise Pascal, for example, the famous French religious philosopher and mathematician (1623–1662), whom historical judgement generally regards as an especially intelligent and independently thinking man of moral integrity, planned on adopting Augustine's assertions in his book *Apology for the Christian Religion, Proofs of Jesus Christ*. Thus, he noted in his *Pensées* (1958, p. 180):

> It is a wonderful thing, and worthy of particular attention, to see this Jewish people existing so many years in perpetual misery, it being necessary as a proof of Jesus Christ, both that they should exist to prove Him, and that they should be miserable because they crucified Him; and though to be miserable and to exist are contradictory, they nevertheless still exist in spite of their misery.

He might have judged the matter differently if the Reformation had rejected the anti-Semitic delusion as an un-Christian heresy. But the reverse happened, and once again it was the thinking of an influential single individual who re-established and solidified the projective thinking-out of personal motives. Towards the end of his life, Martin Luther exacerbated Church anti-Semitism. Veneration for him had an identity-forming effect in the Churches of the Reformation. They became, or remained, anti-Semitic. The Confessing Church, under the influence of Karl Barth, in the beginning of the 1930s, was the first to distance itself from the inhumanity of this way of thinking, but the numerous Lutheran state Churches did not. The following quotations again prove the generation of prejudice through the mechanism of projective identification. What was projected on to the Jews was a precise, unconscious self-judgement of Christian Nazis.

On 17 December 1941, seven Lutheran state Churches (Saxony, Hessen-Nassau, Mecklenburg, Schleswig-Holstein, Anhalt, Thuringia, and Lübeck) took a position on the law that went into effect on 1 September 1941, stipulating that all Jews within the territory of the German Reich were required to wear a yellow star. They proclaimed the following:

> As organs of the German national community, the undersigned German Lutheran state Churches and heads of Churches stand at the front of the historic defensive battle that, among other things, necessi-tated the Reich Police Ordinance on the marking of the Jews as born enemies of the world and the Reich, just as Dr. Martin Luther, after bitter experience, made the demand to take the severest measures against the Jews and to expel them from German lands. From the Crucifixion of Christ to the present day, the Jews have combated Christianity, or abused and falsified it, to achieve their own self-serv-ing goals. The Christian baptism changes nothing about the racial char-acter of a Jew, his ethnicity, and his biological being. (Church Yearbook for the Lutheran Church of Germany, 60th–71st year, 1976, p. 460)

If we take back the projection and read,

> From the Crucifixion of Christ to the present day, we Christians have combated Christianity or abused and falsified it to achieve our own self-serving goals. The Christian baptism changes nothing about the mental character of a German Christian, his ethnicity, and his biolog-ical being . . .

that is, baptism is completely ineffective, the German Christian remains as destructive as he ever was, then the senseless term "born enemies of the world and the Reich" can also be examined as a projection and then it loses its nonsense as a concept, in that it is *a preconscious self-judgement of the Christian Nazis* as born enemies of the world and the Reich.

Current task of acknowledgment of the past collective psychosis of the Germans

The task of acknowledging the past collective psychosis became especially clear to me when in a small study group during the Fourth

Nazareth Group Relations Conference in Platres, Cyprus 2002 (Beland, 2008). I owe something to the two new Conference participants who participated in my small study group, something that I expected at all the earlier Conferences but did not find: another, perhaps the most crucial, reason for the participation of the Jewish and Israeli members in the Nazareth Conferences on "The Past in the Present". It was always more than clear why we Germans took part. We needed the presence of the Jews to realise our own unconscious entanglements and guilt feelings. But the Israelis? The Jewish analysts who live in Germany? The Jews from the Western Diaspora? I could not adequately grasp the reason for their participation. I thought I knew some of the reasons for my Israeli colleagues on staff: their never explicitly spoken willingness to help us German colleagues; their interest in the utility of the group relations instrument to bring into consciousness unconscious and defended mental trends opposite to theirs; their own German roots that exerted strong pressure for integration and that, on the other hand, also created stressful tensions due to the irreconcilability of positive memories alongside memories of contempt and the threat of annihilation; their native tongue that was corrupted by the Nazis; their first years of life in Berlin, Frankfurt, Hamburg, or Vienna, or the earlier generations of their own families who had lived, worked, married, had children, and died in Germany; their private Holocaust, the murder of relatives, the agony of millions of individuals. But perhaps the Jewish members of the Conferences wanted something else for themselves, something only the Germans possessed. "I want to meet your horror." "You Germans must be monsters. You did monstrous acts. What did it feel like?" These were key sentences for me in Platres. It was Israelis from the younger generation who expressed these thoughts in the little group. I think that can be translated as

> "I need and seek the encounter with the murderous delusion of German anti-Semitism for me, not for you, in order to understand something more about the Holocaust, your goal of annihilation, and your insane, merciless cruelty.
>
> "How does it feel that you, all together, wanted and did something so insane and murderous?
>
> "I am afraid that it is still present and could come to power at any moment. I want to know from you what it consists of. You can know this."

At that time, I answered that I could not (not yet) answer. But I understood that we Germans owed them an answer. I think the task was justified, but I was not up to it. I did not want to experience the murderous delusion as my own, but then I thought we must approach this task as well as possible. Perhaps we do not need to experience this murderous delusion as our own, but we must understand it from the inside. I have an inkling that many individuals find it is necessary to answer, out of introjected identification with German deeds, insane deeds that are accessible to us and that we can feel our way into.

We cannot expect representative, non-German psychoanalytical reflections on our collective German case, our emotional situation, and our dangers. We have to work them out ourselves. One source will lie in our collective memories and in the psychoanalysis of crime. What we can learn there indicates rather unambiguously that crimes are committed in psychotic, projective, and identificatory states of delusion.

So, Rosenfeld's hypothesis became concrete for me in Platres, as a practical task. When Rosenfeld gave his lecture on "Narcissism and aggression" in Wiesbaden in 1984, he compared the psychotic rule of a destructive, narcissistic organisation within the overall personality, to the rule of the Hitler regime over the German nation, hardly any of his listeners could understand him or grasp the importance of his hypotheses. Rosenfeld concluded at that time with the words:

> If the psychotic, all-powerful structure overwhelms an entire nation, then it is very difficult to completely acknowledge insight into this insanity. Perhaps it is only now possible to study the deeper psychological elements that overpowered the German nation more than fifty years ago. I am afraid that a complete cure for this dangerous disease will still cost a great deal of time and demand active support. (Rosenfeld, 1988, p. 391, translated for this edition)

What we can learn from Rosenfeld's analogy between the murderous narcissistic centre of a psychotic pathology and the German governmental structure and mentality is the deluded character of the whole. The industrial logistics of the annihilation of the Jews of Europe and the world, the waging of war with the goal of world domination, and the intention of complete self-annihilation as the unconscious background, were based upon a mixture of deluded fury and rational calculation. What, in my opinion, must be added to Rosenfeld's analogy is a satisfactory insight into the historical genesis of the collective mental subordination, the susceptibility to seduction by propaganda, and the internal terrorism of the power apparatus. The destructive narcissism of the individual has an individual genesis in an infantile catastrophe, for which there is probably no collective equivalent. (For the discussion of "chosen traumas", cf. Volkan, 1999, and below.) For me, collective genesis is best understood so far through the psychoanalysis of anti-Semitism as the projection of what Christians repress; the genesis of the paralysis of outrage over political cruelty is best explained by the mental ban on de-idealising hierarchy through the centuries.

We surely agree that the unsolved developmental and systematic epistemological problems loom oppressively large in dimension and number. For example, it is still unknown whether the terrors of the infantile catastrophe, the later destructive narcissism, and the traumatic threat to a collective is analogous to the absolute cruelty of a truly paranoid political leader convinced of his murderous mission. Bion expressed the problem of the existence of an inner, absolutely cruel power analogous to existing objects as follows: "[It] is violent, greedy and envious, ruthless, murderous and predatory, without respect for truth, persons, or things" (Bion, 1965, esp. p. 111, here p. 102). His words are still an unexploited, systematic treasure of psychoanalytical clinical instruction, and refer to a horror we can all become subjected to as individuals and groups.

Let me conclude by recalling Michelangelo's Pietá again. I am grateful to Joshua Durban for pointing out this work of art of successful, humane grief. In contrast to this grief stands unsuccessful, denied grief. The loss of one's own goodness and normality can be mourned on the model of the Pietá. If many German individuals and our collectives can tie the acknowledgment of the loss of their own goodness to the experience that "they, the nations, want the Germans to stay on task to understand their Holocaust", then these individuals and their collectives can respond more easily to the request: "I want to meet your horror". The sentence has intentions in two directions. We can, alas, repeat the second, meaning it about ourselves as well, and say it to each other.

Note

1. For lack of a better one, I use this term to designate participation in a collective experience of the loss of *bonitas*, and I use it synonymously with the loss of collective normality, loss of a good collective identity, and the loss of humaneness collectively. It is meant as an emotional correlate of a sociological notion for relations of peoples; cf. the Indo-European root meaning of "good": "fitting (within a construction, a human community)" (translated from the Duden Etymologie).

References

Beland, H. (1991). Religiöse Wurzeln des Antisemitismus. In: *Die Angst vor Denken und Tun. Psychoanalytische Aufsätze zu Theorie, Klinik und Gesellschaft* (pp. 317–340). Gießen: Psychosozial.

Beland, H. (1992). Psychoanalytische Antisemitismustheorien im Vergleich. In: W. Bohleber & J. S. Kafka (Eds.), *Antisemitismus* (pp. 93–125). Bielefeld: Aisthesis.

Beland, H. (1999). Die Angst vor Denken und Tun (Oblomows Retreat). In: H. Weiß (Ed.), *Ödipuskomplex und Symbolbildung* (pp. 119–141). Tübingen: Edition Diskord.

Beland, H. (2008). Kollektivsymptome unter verändernden Erfahrungen. Bericht der fünf "Nazareth-Konferenzen" (1994–2006): Von "The Past in the Present" (Nazareth, 1994) bis "Shaping the Future by Confronting the Past" (Zypern, 2006). In: *Die Angst vor Denken und Tun: Psychoanalytische Aufsätze zu Theorie, Klinik und Gesellschaft* (pp. 383–403). Gießen: Psychosozial.

Bion, W. R. (1965). *Transformations*. London: Karnac.

Bion, W. R. (1970). *Attention and Interpretation*. London: Tavistock.

Bohleber, W. (2007). Remembrance, trauma and collective memory. *International Journal of Psychoanalysis, 88*: 329–352.

Durban, J. (2007). Vom "Schrei" zur "Pietá" – Thanatos im Trauerprozeß. In: *Eros und Thanatos*. Herbsttagung DPV 2006 (pp. 57–74). Frankfurt: Kongreßorganisation: Geber & Reusch.

Erlich, H. S., Erlich-Ginor, M., & Beland, H. (2009). *Fed with Tears – Poisoned with Milk. The "Nazareth" Group Relations Conferences Germans and Israelis – The Past in the Present*. Foreword by Archbishop Desmond M. Tutu. Giessen: Psychosozial.

Freud, S. (1968). *Briefe 1873–1939*. Frankfurt: Fischer.

Herbert, U. (1992). Zweierlei Bewältigung. In: U. Herbert & O. Groehler (Eds.), *Zweierlei Bewältigung. Vier Beiträge über den Umgang mit der NS-Vergangenheit in den beiden deutschen Staaten*. Hamburg: Ergebnisse.

Laplanche, J., & Pontalis, J.-B. (1973). The language of psychoanalysis. *The International Psycho-Analytical Library, 94*: 1–497. London: The Hogarth Press and the Institute of Psycho-Analysis.

Mitscherlich, A., & Mitscherlich-Nielsen, M. (1967). *Die Unfähigkeit zu trauern*. München: Piper.

Pascal, B. (1958). *Pascal's Pensées* (Introduction by T. S. Eliot). New York: E. P. Dutton.

Rosenfeld, H. (1988). Narzißmus und Aggression. In: P. Kutter, R. Paramo-Ortega, & P. Zagermann (Eds.), *Die psychoanalytische Haltung* (pp. 375–392). München-Wien: Internationale Psychoanalyse.

Rüsen, J. (2001). Holocaust-Erfahrung und deutsche Identität. Ideen zu einer Typologie der Generationen. In: W. Bohleber & S. Drews (Eds.), *Die Gegenwart der Psychoanalyse – die Psychoanalyse der Gegenwart* (pp. 95–106). Stuttgart: Klett-Cotta.

Sofsky, W. (1992). *Die Ordnung des Terrors: Das Konzentrationslager*. Frankfurt: Fischer.

Volkan, V. D. (1999). *Das Versagen der Diplomatie. Zur Psychoanalyse nationaler, ethnischer und religiöser Konflikte*. Gießen: Psychosozial.

CHAPTER SEVEN

On xenophobic and anti-Semitic prejudices*

Tomas Böhm

Introductory considerations

I start with thoughts about everyday hostile ideas, through the structure of black and white thinking, to take us through the perverse thought systems and individual hatred to gain a better understanding of the complicated phenomenon of prejudices, exemplified eventually by the special case of anti-Semitism. My preliminary hypothesis is banal, gruesome, and decisive in its consequences: the goodness or love of human beings is fragile and hard to rebuild, while the evilness or hatred of mankind is stable and easily aroused.

This might also be based upon the experience that in the ambivalence of human relations, the loving and tender trends are more precarious than the hostile and aggressive trends.

We can also understand the dialectic between goodness and cruelty in terms of the conflict between the depressive position and

---

* This chapter is an elaboration of an earlier paper: "On the dynamics of xenophobic prejudices – with antisemitism as an illustration" (Böhm, 2010), published in *Scandinavian Psychoanalytic Review*, p. 332, which, in its turn, is an updated summary of a book by the author, *Inte som vi* [Not like us] (Böhm, 1993).

the schizo–paranoid position. It seems that we have the tendency to fall back, regress easily under pressure, to the schizo–paranoid position, when the needs or desires of the baby are not immediately met by the mother because she is not there to fulfil them. The absence of the good object is then experienced as the presence of the bad object (Klein, 1984). The bad object is then hated and, in phantasy, attacked. The hated frustrating object quickly becomes persecutory, as it is imagined to take revenge in a similar way to how it is treated. This is why the baby feels persecuted, hence the use of the word "paranoid" in paranoid–schizoid. Gradually, a more realistic view of the self and object evolves, seen as possessing both good and bad attributes, leading to the greater integration and maturity of the depressive position. The schizo–paranoid position corresponds to black-and-white thinking and "us against them" cruelty without empathy. On the other hand, we need psychic work and effort to reach the depressive position, which corresponds to potential goodness (empathy), and because of the effort needed it is precarious. We see this on political levels, too, in how easy it is to destroy democratic societies and how long it takes to rebuild them.

Ideas and prejudices

Every day, all of us work both unconsciously and consciously with our notions and prejudices in a way that usually gives us sufficient control over the ordinary hostility that comes up in relation to others (Böhm, 1993). Hostile ideas seem to make life simpler, but, at the same time, they run into opposition from our sense of reason, which tells us that tolerance of complexity is better and makes it possible for us to keep hateful impulses within manageable bounds. However, even when we are relatively aware of complexity, something happens to our unconscious notions or ideas (what Freud would have called *Vorstellungen*) when they are transformed into prejudices:

1. Instead of being *my notions*, such ideas become impersonal and projected on to external reality.
2. Instead of being *flexible*, they become rigid and less susceptible to dialogue and influence.

3.   Instead of being *notions* or *value judgements*, they become quasi-objective facts about reality: "This is not just what *I believe*, it doesn't matter what you say, this is the way things *are*".
4.   Prejudices are, in this definition, and in my experience, unconscious. We might be conscious in general that we have prejudices, but we are unconscious of our own specific prejudices. Prejudices, thus, do not differ from other unconscious ideas in being unconscious, even if they are more rigid and difficult to reflect upon.

As I see it, prejudices stem from a special, split ego position (Freud, 1940e) and the small child's way of dividing the world into good and evil, a position to which we tend to return in crises. In this schizo–paranoid position (Klein, 1984) that we struggle with all our lives, we do not need to suffer from uncertainty and ambivalence. We seem sure of what is right or wrong. Prejudices contribute to this simplification by giving the illusion of solving problems concerning guilt, conflicts, and moral questions. Morgan (2009) uses a similar concept when she discusses unconscious beliefs in couples' relationships, where the partners have views about the other and the relationship, views that they regard as *facts* until they are questioned and shown to be beliefs. However, I believe that these "facts" are often closer to preconscious fantasies or ideas, since they do not necessarily need to arouse a great deal of resistance if they are questioned. But they can also be on the other side of the spectrum, closer to prejudices, with fierce resistance aroused if confronted. Morgan bases her ideas also on Britton (1998), who discusses the stunned reaction when someone learns that a believed fact was really an idea.

If we go back to notions or ideas (beliefs) we can see that both can be influenced by new information, and originate principally from the following sources:

•   identification with adults or other authorities ("Real men like hunting and fishing");
•   infantile conclusions ("Women like to kiss a lot; Santa Claus really exists");
•   the media tell us of notions that we internalise ("Black people are good at long-jumping; Gypsies like to dance; Jews are good in business");

- myths that survive as cultural ideas or superstition ("Breaking a mirror brings misfortune; redheads have a hot temper").

If anxiety-driven ideas or notions are not questioned, discussed, or tested they might be cemented into prejudices. Here is an example: "Foreigners take all our jobs; they live in first-class hotels on taxpayers' money". What needs to be questioned are also the unofficial word lists, euphemisms, myths, and insinuations about certain groups, denigrating nick-names and codes, which are often devaluations.

Ideologies might also become prejudices, in the sense that they are built up by selected facts, *subjectively* equated with goodness, *and these facts are also interpreted in a selected direction*, driven by certain—often hidden—interests or forces, and inaccessible to argument and questioning. Therefore, most people can predict much of what will be said in political debates and anticipate the use of selective facts by different ideological spokespersons.

Black and white thinking

The allure of simplifying things into black and white (right or wrong) also brings with it thoughts of purity (Volkan, 2004). Most extreme political or religious ideologies express this need. According to this sort of utopian fantasy, a group can make a complete projection of all its evil parts, then root them out (in the external world) in order to reach an imagined state of paradisical harmony. For example, the Nazis projected all evil on to the Jews and other non-Aryans, and not even the risk of losing the war could stop them from trying to stick to their projections and destructive schemes against these "enemies". Stalin placed the evil in the kulaks, later in the alleged enemies of the Party, then in the Jews. Integration meant human weakness for him.

We all seem to have a basic tendency to a sadomasochistic choreography in the schizo–paranoid position (Böhm, 1993), where we group things into superior and inferior. This arouses our paranoia: "Someone is taking my job!" "Immigrants drive around in limousines!" But again, most of us manage to control these simplifications by becoming more nuanced and tolerant.

When we move from fantasies to acts, we can assume that destructive acts—both individually and in groups—are anxiety-driven and that we all have split-off parts of our personalities that drive us to act (Böhm & Kaplan, 2011; Kaplan, 2006).

Some people are humane, "normal" in their daily life, yet can alternate and display a violent or prejudiced part of their personality. They may seem dissociated, as having split parts of their personalities, where the prejudices are kept in a split-off part that is without contact with other efforts of integration. These people might be rigid, violent, or act in strange, contradictory ways in special situations. The preparedness to act on prejudices as though they were "facts" seems to correspond somewhat to what Parens (in Chapter One of this publication) calls "malignant prejudice".

Clinical vignette

A male psychotherapy patient told me, with a somewhat hostile smile, that he assumed I (as a Jew) must feel bad when American Jews are arrested for buying organs for transplantation from poor people. I asked him to elaborate his thoughts, and he said that this corresponded to his impression that Jews looked down upon other people as I must also look down on him. Was it not true that Jews regarded themselves as the chosen people? And that most Jews are richer than the average; and how did they manage to become so rich?

I was surprised that all this came up. I had seen him as a non-hostile, somewhat shy and inhibited man, and had not realised the nature of his fantasies about me. He was not simply ignorant, was he? Or did his ideas reflect ignorance mixed with latent xenophobic ideas?

I said that he seemed to use ideas about Jews to express feelings of humiliation and unfairness against the world and me. Jews had become the vehicle, but I was certain it was about something else. Criminals are criminals, I said, regardless of whether they are Jews or Christians. Did he feel I was using him in any sense, taking his organs away?

He then responded that he had understood I had written books about my work. Wasn't that using patients, and would I use all the sensitive things he had told me?

We were back on a transference track, but it struck me how easily his fear and hatred became expressed along a xenophobic train of thought. Instead of expressing his own feelings and ideas, he expressed quasi-objective facts about Jews being rich, having earned money in dishonest ways, and acting as the chosen people. In these prejudices he seemed certain of what was right or wrong, thereby solving issues about moral conflicts. His choreography was sado-masochistic, and he saw me as trying to be superior and making him inferior.

Orthodoxy and fundamentalism

Orthodoxy can lead to fundamentalist mind-sets. In a pilot study, I interviewed three persons who were orthodox in their religious beliefs (Böhm, 1998). I found it striking how these three, a Muslim, a Jew, and a Christian, appeared to have more in common with each other than with members of their respective religions who were not orthodox. The Christian said so explicitly. The orthodox mind-set, that is to say, a thought structure with absolute truths, as well as a certain degree of contempt for the "lukewarm relativism" of their own non-orthodox fellow believers, seemed to unite them.

Orthodoxy and fundamentalism encourage a split-ego universe by admitting only one way to truth and holding all other ideologies as false, untrue, and perhaps dangerous and threatening as well.

One might think that orthodoxy has higher moral mind-sets. That is what they often claim themselves. They possess the "only and pure" version of whatever the subject is about. Instead, I think it is rather the case that the superego of the orthodox person is strict, inflexible, and works also according to the schizo–paranoid position. "It's either total adherence or none at all." So, the mind-sets are not higher, but merely more rigid.

The movement toward orthodoxy seems to begin with a basic ideology or an ethical, religious, political, or other mind-set that is beyond questioning because it is regarded as sacred or absolute in some other sense that we now recognise as the thought process of prejudices. This goes along with the closed mind's certainty and black-or-white argumentation. Whatever is not right, according to the particular orthodox principles, is wrong. This leads to a disinclination to accept different, but equally valid, interpretations (multiple meanings) of ethical, religious texts, or beliefs. Gradually, the orthodox believer comes to regard other interpretations as inimical to all that is sacred, and, thus, feels that it is legitimate to fight them. This struggle to eliminate the unorthodox gradually supersedes all other human and religious ethics, since it is regarded as sacred.

As Waller (2001) and Volkan (2004), among others, have described, we can note how people are changed in a destructive way, by the process of unchallenged prejudices. Orthodoxy moves towards a more and more radical and intolerant attitude toward other beliefs. The orthodox followers see their beliefs and texts as literal and concrete, telling them to take action (such as eliminating their opponents) rather than symbolic, open to multiple and abstract meanings. In the final step, they let an authoritarian, fundamentalist worldview dominate their thought processes. Purity and simplified single-mindedness distort their view of reality and crowd out its pulsating and complicated multi-dimensionality.

I assume prejudices can constitute the basis for acts of discrimination and intolerance, which are not necessarily seen as such by the perpetrator.

"My own team": splitting and projection

In the world of sports, we cheer for our own team. The other fellows seem awkward or wrong. When they play together with our chaps in the national team they appear quite all right, since they are temporarily transformed into "our chaps" in this new setting. However, on his own team the other person looks different, especially since I do not know him except as a competitor, a rival. The somewhat scary, superficial impression becomes more complex, but might diminish if I get to know him, and then curiosity takes over from fear. But again, the despised other fellow (or person on the other team) unconsciously also reminds me of what is alien and different in myself, something I feel only vaguely (Kristeva, 1991), which increases my fear. To keep that "something" under control, I project it with all my power into him, the other one. During the match between our teams, this is also facilitated by the group dynamics that strengthens the split between us and them, good and bad, so that we can maintain our simplified division.

The benign rivalry between sports clubs seems strongly dependent upon the degree of playfulness, or regression in the service of the (group) ego. As soon as the rivalry becomes some kind of experienced reality, as in orthodox black-and-white opinions (those who are not for us are against us!), the benign quality is lost, and destructive leaders can turn a group quickly away from precarious playfulness.

When we are not protected by reasonable tolerance towards others, the fear and hatred of the unknown may find ways into neutral indifference or latent xenophobia: "We didn't know, and by the way, we thought they were going back to the place they came from"; "If they were attacked they must have done something provocative, otherwise it wouldn't have happened."

What does the border look like between the ignorant person who needs more information, the latently xenophobic individual who expresses his unconscious hatred in hidden ways, and the manifestly xenophobe or racist who ideologically identifies with his hatred and is not willing to question it?

There are people who experience social anxiety about being caught, rather than feel genuine remorse for their hostile actions. But most of us gradually become disillusioned in our grandiosity during childhood and develop an inner, relatively stable conscience and ego ideal. However, if a "brilliant" leader enters the stage, he can activate the old wish of merging ego and ego ideal—especially to a susceptible group—that can switch off the subject's conscience. The leader transmits the ideological illusion (Chasseguet-Smirgel, 1985) that the impossible is possible. Power, dominance, rivalry, and even violence suddenly seem possible and necessary. Ideology is always presented as something good and pure. Who could be against pure goodness?

Immigrants and self-image

The newcomer influences the society into which he inserts himself. His presence upsets the moral, political, and scientific ground rules of the receiving group. People may feel influenced in their cultural identity, language, beliefs, and group identity. Grinberg and Grinberg (1989) speak of a "catastrophic change".

Franz Kafka (1992, pp. 71–72) described how "the villagers" must dehumanise the stranger who has moved in with them: ". . . your ignorance of the local situation is so appalling that it makes my head go round to listen to you and compare your ideas and opinions with the real state of things". Kristeva (1991) reminds us that we are strangers to ourselves. We hold together different parts or identities that we must tolerate as contradictory or pluralistic. She is herself an example of what I call a "hyphen-identity". A Bulgarian-French psychoanalyst–linguist–author who shows us the way from a totalitarian, schizo–paranoid position, in which you are either Bulgarian or French, psychoanalyst or author, not *both*, towards a depressive, integrated position where different ambiguous parts are tolerated and held together by hyphens.

In a dialogue (Böhm, 1993, p. 47) between a female teacher and sixteen-year-old boys from a class consisting of students training to become construction workers, the teacher asked what they thought about immigrants and refugees, and they answered: "They should leave, all of them!" All the myths about foreigners flourished. Thinking about the two immigrant boys in the class, the teacher asked, "What about Veikko and Ibrahim?"

"Oh no, not them, they are OK!"

"So who should leave then?"

"Well, all the others, that's obvious!"

Levitt (2010), in a personal communication, remarked that these comments from the boys reminded him of the top Nazi's claims about providing exemptions for specific Jews: "Wer Jude ist, bestimme Ich" ["I will determine who is a Jew"].

These boys—especially as a group—could not keep the different arguments within themselves as an internal conflict. If the others have to leave, what is so different with Veikko and Ibrahim? Instead, they made a split between "our guys", Veikko, Ibrahim, and "myself" or us, and the others whom we do not know and who must leave. The group dynamics help to simplify matters. The teacher explains that someone, often a kind of leader, turns around and says, "And this is what we think, all of us, isn't it?" But when she asks them individually, they become more uncertain.

During spring lessons, this teacher read children's books to them, books meant for twelve-year-olds. They were sitting outside in the sun. She brought some cakes and juice. While she was reading, a big, tough boy said to her (Böhm, 1993):

"This is like it was in day care."

"Does it matter?" she asked.

"No", he murmured.

She felt touched, and remarked that these boys needed so many more basic things than talking about what was wrong with immigrants. Their cultural and emotional poverty was obvious in the stereotyped prejudiced thinking they had regarding immigrants.

The difference in looks seems especially important, with regard to psychological distancing from strangers. This distance also brings with it projected and envious myths about alleged character traits, such as black people and their "musicality, potency, and running ability", Jews and their "interest in money, perversions, and unreliability", the "cunningness" of the Arab, or "sadism" of the Japanese.

The individual and hatred

The schizo–paranoid position creates the basis for separating different phenomena from each other, while the depressive position is the basis for integrating parts within a whole, thereby enabling us to grieve and offer reparation. Brenman (2006) discusses the infant's wish to possess his mother, who must be present in an optimal way. The child learns to tolerate separation as the mother remains in its memory and he knows that the mother will keep him in her mind as well. The human truth is that people need each other, and this truth outweighs the total dominance of primitive defences and fears, such as cannibalistic impulses and projected persecutory anxiety against cannibalistic monsters. On a societal level, the unintegrated, primitive phenomena are often connected with totalitarian ideologies that regard us as totally right and the others as completely wrong. In a fundamentalist world, hatred dominates instead of reflection, and prejudices instead of depressive grief.

Fonagy (1998) asserts that an alienated self exists in us all, as the consequence of the inevitable deficiencies of the normal care-taking we experienced. This self is normally covered by self-representations that we can create from good new experiences. However, the alienated self becomes dangerous when later traumatic events, within the family or the close social environment, force the child to dissociate and split off a part of the experienced pain by identifying with the aggressor. In these cases, the covered deficiencies in care-taking are filled with images of the aggressor, and the child experiences himself as destructive and, in extreme cases, as monstrous. Brutal behaviour from attachment objects generates intense shame, and we can assume that this also applies to one's close social network. Early parenting deficiencies might contribute to a lasting vulnerability in the child that can be very destructive if later experiences are unfavourable (Fonagy, 1998; Fonagy, Gergely, Jurist, & Target, 2002).

As a consequence, some people deny that they need others. Instead, they become preoccupied with grievances. They may also substitute the need for love with sadomasochistic relationships and perversions. Everyone is experienced as hateful, and the world is seen as populated by unpredictable, cynical people. Thus, the alienated self can become filled with hateful prejudices, identifications with one's care-taker's prejudices, as well as hateful identifications with the aggressor.

Roth (2005) differentiates between "frustrated hatred" born from neglect or abuse and the inherited, transgenerational hatred that the care-takers transfer both consciously and unconsciously. The content of these two kinds of hatred include xenophobic prejudices. Roth states that inherited hatred is hard to influence through psychotherapeutic interventions, since it is largely unconscious.

A patient in psychoanalysis, K, was an academician highly motivated for analysis, both on account of his research interests and for personal reasons. He distanced himself from his father, who was brought up in Germany and was a member of the *Hitlerjugend* (Hitler Youth) as a teenager. K had left-wing, liberal, and pro-Jewish opinions. During a session after a weekend break, he confessed, under intense embarrassment, that he had a passing thought that I was a dirty, unreliable Jew for having left him alone during the weekend. He said that he did not know where it came from. It had no connection to his conscious thoughts about me, or the weekend break, and our only possible guess was that it came from a deep identification with his father's opinions. His alienated self was filled with both frustrated and inherited hatred that gave rise to, and used, transmitted unconscious prejudices as vehicles of hatred.

When hatred and prejudices dominate within the personality, certain typical characteristics are created: to feel empathic with the other person becomes impossible, if the other is *different*, is identified with the other, evil, *weak* side, and reminds me of my own denied weakness and lonely alienation; the *needy* side reminds me of my own denied needs connected with weakness, the *nuanced* side is felt as a diffuse lack of decision making and weakness, and the *emotional* side is perceived as unmasculine, risking a breakthrough of my own sadness, "femininity", and homosexuality.

Envy adds a destructive quality to everyday life (Joseph, 1989). Envy tries to destroy the good qualities of the other person. It can hide as critical comments, making the other ridiculous, or as provocations. Alberoni (1991) also adds gossip and devaluation as common masks for envy.

It seems as though *difference* by itself is sufficient to provoke hateful and envious reactions. In the latency years, children want to look the same and follow the rules of the game in their social training. This is also a way to master envy, by creating total "anal" justice. No one is different, everyone looks the same in their anus; they will produce the same shit.

We tend to fall back into the schizo–paranoid position throughout all our lives. It seems difficult to tolerate a contradictory, unclear, and ambiguous world and self-image. We are always tempted to glide back into a perspective where the evil may be placed somewhere else (Igra, 1988). Children who had good enough mothering, and at least an average expectable environment during their course of development, can probably tolerate difference in a somewhat more relaxed and self-affirming way, even if no one is totally protected against prejudices and acts of revenge. Even well-protected individuals can risk being swept along by large group dynamics and destructive leaders.

The special case of anti-Semitism

Anti-Semitism is an old example of ideas and prejudices about a defined group of people. Some of these ideas are an ego-syntonic part of everyday life. Where I grew up as a child, the owner of a clothes shop (who might have been Jewish) was called "the clothes Jew". Friends who were greedy or careful with their money were said to be "greedy as Jews". The ones with big noses had "Jewish noses". Today, you might hear that a Jew has a "nose for business". These people might not have met a Jew in reality. If a Jew reacts to these ideas, he might be regarded as oversensitive or lacking a sense of humour. However, he knows or feels that these ideas belong to the anti-Semitic "word list". These words are transmitted through invisible, peculiar ways into the word lists of families, friends, and teachers.

> For Jews, anti-Semitism is something concretely expressed. For example, there are anti-Semitic words, pictures, and statements. Whether the person is an anti-Semite "in his heart" is irrelevant . . . we need only to look at what they have said or written. An ontological state of "being an anti-Semite" is not a necessary condition for being able to either say something anti-Semitic or assume responsibility for what one has said. (Wolkoff, 1992, translated for this edition)

As illustrated by the extract above, prejudices are expressed in actions, though these actions and the ideas behind them are blamed on the victims; in the case of anti-Semitism, on the Jews themselves. Thus, anti-Semitism is seen as something that has to do with Jews and their characteristics, not with the needs and distorted views of the anti-Semites (Jakubowski, 1992).

Freud (e.g., 1939a) had several ideas about the psychodynamics of anti-Semitism: Jews aroused envy in other people by being the first-born children of God; Jews are circumcised and, thereby, arouse unconscious fear of castration; Jews are regarded both as castrated and weak, but also as having unusual sexual power and expressing cruel perversions. Historically, Jews were also accused of spreading leprosy, which Freud regarded as a fantasy projection, as if they were thinking "they separate from us as if we had leprosy" (my wording). Freud also speculated that many Christians were "misbaptised" (Freud, 1939a, p. 91), meaning that they had kept the polytheism of their forefathers under a thin veneer of Christianity. The grievance is then projected upon the source of their Christianity. Freud noted that the Jews are accused of having murdered Jesus Christ, who, in spite of being a Jew himself, became a victim of cruelty.

A more modern view on anti-Semitism comes from Arieti (1981). He points to a few characteristics of the persecution of Jews: the God without image is seen as a provocation to images of Gods. The Jews are accused of deicide, killing the Gods. This is also connected to the accusation concerning the killing of Jesus and the ritual murder of Christian children. Chasseguet-Smirgel (1985) underlines the fact that the Jews, in contrast to many neighbouring peoples, did not sacrifice children. Other peoples continued such practices, and projected this accusation on to and against the Jews.

Arieti also discusses endocracy, which signifies an internalised, unconscious commandment to obey that is grounded in childhood. The obedient person thinks he is doing the only possible thing, out of his own free will. Eichmann, for example, seems to have felt minimal guilt for his deeds during his trial. The fully "endocratised" person is doing what he thinks is the only possible act. Himmler is regarded by most historians as an inhibited, extremely authoritarian personality (Longerich, 2008). Nothing from his childhood seems to point to other gross abnormal character traits. However, the whole authoritarian atmosphere within his life circumstances must have influenced this emotionally and relationally inhibited person, and might have contributed to an endocratic experience of inner commands without apparent guilt feelings.

Power is also an ingredient in a society built upon codes of honour and hierarchy. Some individuals are born to rule and some to obey. Arieti (1981) describes how one idea might be that "my life will be less restricted if I take your freedom, if you obey me". (Arieti, 1981, p. 291) On the basis of Western notions of human rights, it is difficult to understand how the old codes of social hierarchies could pervade entire countries.

The perverse thought system

At this point, I follow a line of thought beginning with what Chasseguet-Smirgel (1985) writes about: the perverse system. She emphasises that there are two basic differences that are difficult to acknowledge for most children: the differences between generations, and between the sexes. For some persons, differences in themselves are provocative. Accordingly, everyone should be the same and exchangeable. Nothing should be impossible (such as changing sex), and neither should you have to wait for something (such as growing older). Good and bad should be the same, as should life and death, sexuality and torture, men and women, adults and children.

Idealisation is an important part of underlining that this system of thought is superior, compared to the "genital universe", where there are differences and conflicts.

Certain leaders convey ideologies that promise that the impossible is possible. These leaders are like parents who deny their genital and generational realities.

When someone with prejudices and a perverse thought system hears about a Jew, he associates this with someone who is different and has another background. Already this difference might provoke distancing, envy ("he thinks he is someone special"), paranoid fantasies, and hatred. To this is added the complex identity of the Jew, at least when it is experienced as too complex for someone who wants *simplified* answers.

The Jew has a mixed identity: national and Jewish, maybe even immigrant-national-Jewish. Since the Jews also have a mythology connected to their identity, they attract racists like a magnet!

Mixtures consisting of intact different aspects are like a red flag for someone with a perverse thought system. Integration is not felt as possible, and the notion of purity is a consequence of this difficulty. Typical ideas in such persons are: "pure Aryans", fears of racial mixtures, "soon there will be no blue-eyed children left here!"

Finally, there is within the racist with the perverse thought system the *obsession for power and superiority*. This follows the sado-masochistic notion of a social system with vertical, authoritarian hierarchies as its basic model, including a fear of inferiority. Thus, the Jews attract interest as a weak, different group, a complicated mixture of identities, which implies an impure and feared collectivity with a mythology that is connected to evil.

The power of the group

Freud underlined (1921c) that the group becomes more intolerant, irrational, and illogical compared to the individual. Freud discussed the regression that is sometimes characteristic of individuals within large social groups and institutions. However, groups in general are themselves often regressed. The group sometimes has a lower moral level of norms and behaviour, which implies that the ego ideal of the group's members has become more primitive. Something within the relationship among group members obliterates the individual's free thought and judgement. The egos of the individuals seem paralysed by the new group ego ideal when this is projected on to the leader, common idea, or ideology. In addition, the group is more easily influenced than the autonomous individual, who can keep his critical faculties more or less intact when he is challenged.

We have to distinguish between nationalism, feelings of national identity, and a sense of unity (national feelings) (Ambjörnsson, 1992).

National feelings have less to do with history and the heroic past than nationalism. Nationalism can transform feelings into actions and distort the emotions in the name of all kinds of action-orientated, chaotic inner feelings. However, how does one make the chaotic emotions the object of working through, instead of acting them out in a murderous way?

Perhaps democracy is one of the best mental blocks against acting out primitive aggressive feelings. However, a democratic system also requires some kind of equality within the distribution of resources and wealth in a society as a resistance against envy.

In *Group Psychology and the Analysis of the Ego* (1921c), Freud suggests that the demand for equality (equal love) among children could be seen as an idealistic reworking of the situation in the primal horde, where the brothers were equally feared and persecuted by the father. Further, culture plays an important part in working through difficult emotions, internally or within a transitional mental space.

Conclusion

The combination of authoritarian socialisation and undemocratic views of society are deadly. They must be confronted at the earliest signs of their appearance. The hostility and intolerance of prejudice is always there as a potential threat, because of our never-ending tendency to fall back upon splitting and projecting our unwanted sides, even if these tendencies and our ability to resist them is variable. It seems preferable to prevent hateful violence from starting, rather than to ask how it starts. Thus, the fight against these destructive phenomena will continue because there is no final solution for it. Suffice to say, safe people who are members of well-organised groups with democratically elected leaders (who are not sadists) do not commit violent crimes based upon prejudices and fantasies of revenge. On the other hand, there are plenty of destructive and totalitarian political leaders with uncontrolled narcissism who show their lack of empathy and aggression (Wirth, 2009). These destructive leaders use prejudices as the fuel and the vehicles for group aggression within disorganised groups.

I conclude with an extract from Arieti (1981, p. 296):

A person should not be required to be a victim for following his faith, even if he is ready to be a victim for it. A person should not be hated for retaining his faith, or for what was linked long ago, with his faith. Power should not be allowed to be uncontrollable. Surplus of endocracy should not be permitted to develop and reduce people to blind followers. Sadism should be prevented or treated as soon as possible. No sadist should ever be allowed to become a political leader.

References

Alberoni, F. (1991). *Avund* (Envy). Gothenburg: Korpen.

Ambjörnsson, R. (1992). Nationen är en historisk konstruktion (The nation is a historical construction). *Dagens Nyheter*, 14 April.

Arieti, S. (1981). The prerequisites of Nazi barbarism. *Israel Journal of Psychiatry and Related Sciences, 18*(4): 283–297.

Brenman, E. (2006). *The Recovery of the Lost Object*. London: Taylor & Francis.

Britton, R. (1998). *Belief and Imagination*. London: Routledge.

Böhm, T. (1993). *Inte som vi* (Not like us). Stockholm: Natur & Kultur.

Böhm, T. (1998). *Att ha rätt* (To be right). Stockholm: Natur & Kultur.

Böhm, T. (2010). On the dynamics of xenophobic prejudices: with anti-semitism as an illustration. *The Scandinavian Review of Psychoanalysis, 33*: 32–39.

Böhm, T., & Kaplan, S. (2011). *Revenge: the Dynamics of a Frightening Urge and Its Taming*. London: Karnac.

Chasseguet-Smirgel, J. (1985). *Creativity and Perversion*. London: Free Association Books.

Fonagy, P. (1998). Attachment, the Holocaust and the outcome of child psychoanalysis: the third generation. Paper presented to the Third Congress of the European Federation for Psychoanalytic Psychotherapy in the Public Sector, Cologne, Germany, 28 March.

Fonagy, P., Gergely, G., Jurist, E. L., & Target, M. (2002). *Affect Regulation, Mentalization and the Development of the Self*. New York: Other Press.

Freud, S. (1921c). *Group Psychology and the Analysis of the Ego. S.E., 18*: 65–143. London: Hogarth.

Freud, S. (1939a). *Moses and Monotheism, S.E., 23*: 1–137. London: Hogarth.

Freud, S. (1940e). Splitting of the ego in the process of defence. *S.E., 23*: 271–278. London: Hogarth.

Grinberg, L., & Grinberg, R. (1989). *Psychoanalytic Perspectives on Migration and Exile*. Newhaven, CT: Yale University Press.

Igra, L. (1988). *On Life and Death* (På liv och död). Stockholm: Natur & Kultur.

Jakubowski, J. (1992). The Jew as a metaphor. *Judisk Krönika*, 2: 2–3.

Joseph, B. (1989). Envy in everyday life. In: *Psychic Equilibrium and Psychic Change* (pp. 181–192). London: Tavistock/Routledge.

Kafka, F. (1992). *The Castle*. New York: Schocken

Kaplan, S. (2006). Children in genocide: extreme traumatization and the 'affect propeller'. *International Journal of Psychoanalysis, 87*: 725–746.

Klein, M. (1984). *Envy and Gratitude and Other Works 1946–1963*. London: Hogarth.

Kristeva, J. (1991). *Strangers to Ourselves*. New York: Columbia University Press.

Longerich, P. (2008). *Heinrich Himmler. Biographie*. Munich: Siedler.

Morgan, M. (2009). Unconscious beliefs about the relationship and the other. Presented to a seminar on Family Therapy, Stockholm, November 2009, unpublished.

Roth, E. (2005). *Emerich är mitt namn – hatet, förnedringen, kärleken* (Emerich is my name – the hatred, the denigration, the love). Stockholm: Carlsson.

Volkan, V. (2004). *Blind Trust: Large Groups and Their Leaders in Times of Crisis and Terror*. Charlottesville, VA: Pitchstone.

Waller, J. (2001). *Becoming Evil: How Ordinary People Commit Genocide and Mass Killing*. London: Oxford University Press.

Wirth, H.-J. (2009). *Narcissism and Power*. Giessen: Psycho-Sozial.

Wolkoff, R. (1992). Budet att minnas gör oss till experter [The commandment to remember makes us experts]. *Dagens Nyheter*, 4 April.

CHAPTER EIGHT

A Peruvian case of prejudice

Jorge Kantor

S igmund Freud clearly established a universal trait among humans in *Group Psychology and the Analysis of the Ego* (1921c, p. 101):

> Every time two families become connected by a marriage, each of them thinks itself superior to or of better birth than the other. Of two neighbouring towns each is the other's most jealous rival; every little canton looks down upon the others with contempt. Closely related races keep one another at arm's length; the South German cannot endure the North German, the Englishman casts every kind of aspersion upon the Scotchman, the Spaniard despises the Portuguese. We are no longer astonished that greater differences should lead to an almost insuperable repugnance, such as the Gallic people feel for the German, the Aryan for the Semite, and the white races for the coloured.

Freud's description is quite applicable to the culture of these latitudes. Coastal peoples despise the peoples of the mountain; people from the mountain feel the same antipathy towards those from the jungle. The common Peruvian citizen hates Chileans, Ecuadorians detest Peruvians, Chileans resent Argentina, and so on. Colonial Spanish America left behind a legacy that is extremely difficult and complex.

In spite of that, what I find most relevant in Freud's thinking, in relation to the Peruvian case, is found in his first statement cited above: "each . . . [family] thinks itself superior to or of better birth than the other".

It is important to note that, in these regions, many of these two disdaining families carry that difference to a radical extreme; it is as though with each marriage, one family places itself in a position of superiority and the other is located in a corresponding position of inferiority. However, it is not only that people in families always judge their own family superior to others; there is a generally accepted social convention that designates one of them superior and the other inferior.

The assessment of these differences between two families may be debatable, in any given case; however, it is usually obvious to both which one is more valued socially, culturally, economically, and racially. The fact that the white population as a whole is not considered part of the popular classes makes the difference in skin colour and the accompanying socio-economic class distinctions that are conflated with it effective. Ultimately, every child born in this land comes to identify with one aspect of his or her origin, in terms of superiority–inferiority.

Anthropologist and historian Juan Carlos Callirgos (1993) noted that in Peruvian society there is an identifiable correlation between race and class. Consequently, when individuals are classified in racial terms, they are automatically classified both socio-economically and culturally. These characteristics are stratified into a hierarchy of relationships, where it is assumed that European attributes, or provenance, are more valuable than those traits or heritages imputed to belong to other ethnic groups.

Anthropologist Nelson Manrique (1999) noted that in other parts of the world, such as North America and Europe, there is a strong and rigid dichotomy between blacks and whites, or between whites and other minority groups. In Peru, however, there is a broad spectrum of racial categories that are difficult to define as they have varying degrees of *mestizaje* (miscegenation). In the American case, on the other hand, the rigid opposition between whites and blacks, for example, allows the discriminator to see the discriminated as an "other", entirely different from himself. In Peru, *mestizaje* makes such objectification almost impossible.

In Peru, it is impossible as an "objectification" of discrimination, because the subject discriminator cannot be separated from "object" discriminated. In Anglo-Saxon countries, white racism against blacks, is reliant upon the ability to "objectify" the one who is discriminated against: the "white" discriminator feels the "black" as somewhat alien and foreign to himself, a subject on to which he can download prejudice, hatred, and contempt; *mestizaje* presents a rather different situation in those latitudes.

Many Peruvians use the term "Indian" to insult one another, even if they themselves have some Indian blood in their veins, thus implying a denial of a part of their own identity; discrimination, hatred and loathing form constituent elements of the self.

In other words, in order to discriminate against someone for being "Indian or *mestizo*", one must deny the "Indian" aspect of the self, which constitutes a denial of one's identity. This is an important feature of our racism, which makes it such a heart-breaking and negative aspect of the formation of both individual and collective identity. It is a radical alienation: the inability to recognise and accept your own face in the mirror. This produces a form of racism that is deeply complicated and difficult to understand (Manrique, 1999).

In Peru, a person can easily pass from being a discriminator to being discriminated against or *vice versa*, according to the circumstances at any given time. The positions change according to the environment, the same person being considered as a member of one race or another, depending upon who does the classifying.

The consequence is paramount, as the socially desirable group differs so fundamentally from the majority of Peruvians; racism in this situation can, in this way, also become self-referential. That is what makes it so perverse and corrosive. Racism of this sort prevents us from accepting ourselves for what we are, which makes our racism so tragic.

As pointed out by the psychoanalyst Max Hernandez:

In Peru, there was always the anxiety of not being a country with a clear identity. On the one hand we had *mestizaje* and, second, two clearly defined peoples, one Indian and another European. . . . When one looks down upon the other ethnic groups, the individual internalises that contempt. To mediate social and psychological conditions, the subject may make a creative elaboration of the meeting and resolve the trauma. In the absence of such mediation, the individual only deceitfully camouflages, as an alternative, one part, with serious detriment to his self-estimation, or lives in a permanent split. (Max Hernandez, as cited in Gilio, 2010, p. 119, translated for this edition)

Callirgos (1993), quoting anthropologist Gonzalo Portocarrero, who observed that there is a ritual around the newborn, gives an interesting example of how this situation materialises within social custom: relatives and friends try to highlight the white racial traits of the neonate, and encourage the idea that the baby will be white, while the features revealing *mestizaje* characteristics are discreetly passed over in silence. To this ritual we must add the dispute over white racial traits: relatives and friends trying to determine from whence the features of infants and children come. If there are clear eyes or light hair, as a result of maternal genes, the father tries to prove that these are characteristics of his own family. If there are features that indicate *mestizaje*, then blame is imputed to the other family. These disputes can go on indefinitely.

Nobel Prize winner, Mario Vargas Llosa, in his autobiographical novel *El Pez en el Agua* (1993, p. 14) wrote about this type of thinking, "One is always white or *cholo* (*mestizo*, half-breed) with respect to someone else, because one is always placed better or worse than others".

He continues, explaining,

This categorisation decides a large part of personal destiny; it is maintained thanks to an effervescent structure of prejudices, feelings— disdain, contempt, envy, resentment, admiration, emulation—which is often below the ideology, values, and prejudices, the deeper explanation of the conflicts and frustrations of Peruvian life . . . Most often it is unconscious, born of a self that is hidden and blind to reason, breast milk, and started becoming formalised from the first wails and gurgles of Peru. (Vargas Llosa, 1993, p. 14, translated for this edition)

Portocarrero (2009) noted that, in the process of socialisation, Peruvians are trained to recognise and simultaneously to hide racial differences. Given the complexity of race in Peru, Peruvians have developed a sharp sensitivity in recognising physical variations.

The children of these families inherit a psychic structure that incorporates elements of discrimination, creating a transgenerational configuration that psychoanalyst Noberto Marucco (2006) calls a "passive primary identification". Parents and older family members pass on their prejudices, values, and negative valuations to the younger generation through the course of socialisation, and eventually a child's beliefs are shaped by their parents' attitudes. From a psychoanalytic point of view, both the superego and ideal ego are constructed through primary identification with these significant figures.

Psychoanalyst Jorge Bruce (2007) calls attention to Peruvian clinical practices that tend to ignore associations, experience, or circumstances relating to racism. He thinks that this omission enables us to observe the infiltration of a covert racist ideology in the psychoanalyst's mind. He recommends that we explore this ideology in the intimacy of the analytic couple, both in the transference and the many non-transferential experiences found when working with patients.

With this in mind, I present four vignettes from the psychoanalysis of a young man. I think they will illustrate the psychodynamics of prejudices. This analysis to which I refer took place during the early 1990s. John was then twenty-three, single, and a literature major in college.

Case illustration

John's paternal family belongs to the upper class and owns several businesses; their surnames indicate that they originally come from northern Europe. The mother's family belongs to the lower strata of the middle class, a migrant from the central highlands to the city of Lima.

When his father and mother were approximately twenty years old, driven by forces greater than the differences of class, they met at an intersection of neighbourhoods, where young men from the upper classes sought girls from the lower classes on Saturday nights. John believes that the "primal scene" in which he was conceived occurred in his father's car, after several beers.

When his mother became pregnant with John, his father doubted the child's paternity. His mother, finding no other alternative, travelled back to her family's land in the mountains, where John was born. A few months later, John's mother left him in the care of an aunt, and returned to work in the city of Lima.

According to John's account, he did not see his mother again until five years later when he was first brought to Lima. Two temporal sets were opened, "before and after", two clearly defined times, with a different maternal presence in both.

John's reconstruction of the first of these periods is set in a country atmosphere rich in the affection and attention of his maternal relatives. As he was the only child at home, he remembered himself receiving a loving and generous treatment from his maternal family. Even the memories associated with events related to the discovery of sexual differences, as well as memories of childhood sadism, are pleasantly located in this temporal and spatial set.

At the age of five, he came to Lima. Although he did not know it at the time, he was brought to reside in his mother's house. His mother lived with a partner and their son, his half-brother, two years of age. John has some memory of his departure from his aunt; seeing her in the interprovincial bus window, going back to a different location than where he would live. Holding his mother's hand, he understood that he would stay with her in Lima. The dark roads and avenues, the dim and lonely nights, stayed with him as an uncomfortable fascination. Under this compulsion, John emerged into a new family structure that awaited him.

At that time, his mother was in contact with his father. Shortly after arriving in Lima, he came to know his father, and remembered that when he saw him enter the door of his house, he was struck by his appearance; his father was completely different from all the people he had known. John, although much different in skin colour, had features very similar to those of his father.

"This man is your father," he was told.

Later, he was legally recognised by his father. Unlike the first temporal period, this time set was felt and remembered dramatically. The adjustment process, the new family, and the city were experienced with difficulty and distress. He associated memories of this period with episodic sadness, humiliating situations, and the discovery of adult sexuality, bursting in an aggressive way into his life at six years of age, when a neighbour, a tailor, touched him. Recalled (reconstructed) later, in the midst of the anxiety in which he lived, he understood that these sexual aspects, in his words, "opened all doors".

Fondled by an adult and an observer of sexual scenes on several occasions, in Lima he lost the protection he once enjoyed and experienced a lack of control over his immediate environment. Neither his mother nor the family structure associated with her, nor the existence and importance of his father, gave him the sensation of having a secure base.

The relationship with his father's family took hold gradually, through his paternal grandmother. The medium was an evangelical Christian group to which she belonged. Eventually, John, his mother, and half-brother entered this religious cult. This religious structure provided by the grandmother traced the intersection of the encounter between the two families (however, the father was not a member of this group).

At age twelve, John complained to his father of the ill-treatment he supposedly received from his mother, hoping to move in with his father. However, he was sent to his paternal grandmother's home instead. Shortly after that, John and his grandmother moved to the USA, where they stayed until he was sixteen years old. When he returned to Lima, he asked to live with his mother.

When he was eighteen years old, his father, who was in psychoanalysis at that time, recommended that he start psychotherapy. In describing the reasons that brought him to my office, what stood out in his mind most was his father's suggestion to seek therapy and his dilemma with regard to the religious group, in the sense of not knowing whether he wanted to continue integrating into the group or start working part time, since these were two incompatible aspirations. The analysis started four years after this first meeting. During this period, I saw him two times per week, but this was interrupted for a year and a half because he went to work in the family business outside Lima. Eventually, he left the religious group, lived alone, and began his university studies. The following vignettes are drawn from the first year of his psychoanalysis.

Vignette 1

John: Do you want to know what I feel about the explosions in Miraflores? I feel resentment, resentment towards Miraflorinian snobbishness, towards Lima. First I thought that someone had thrown a dynamite stick into a supermarket; that they had thrown it into a window, and then I knew . . . I can put myself into the shoes of those guys; I imagine driving the car, then the running away in flight.

Analyst: You spoke of resentment towards Lima, of the Miraflorinian snobbishness.

John: It's a term that I don't like, "Miraflorinian snobbishness", and Lima is so big.

Analyst: That's how big it must have felt.

John: They say in the highlands, I was a happy, playful child. That's how my aunt remembers me. On the other hand, in Lima they say I was hard, tough, and solitary. My mother always tells a story: one day, when I ate my first ice-cream, I don't know, I must not have liked it, I threw it away, my mum hugged me, and it seems that I didn't let her, and I told her "bad boy, bad boy!"

John refers to an incident that happened on the night before the session. ("Do you want to know what I feel about the explosions . . .?") The terrorist insurgent group, "Shining Path", exploded a car bomb with a load of about 500 kilos of ANFO mixed with dynamite, in a street of an upper middle-class neighbourhood (the city of Miraflores), killing twenty-five people and destroying several buildings.

He posed the question to the analyst: "Do you want to know?" My office is located in the city of Miraflores; to talk about it in that way with respect to the bomb attack could be seen as an aspect of negative transference. However, when I enquired about the resentment, he displaced it and widened it to include the big city of Lima (Miraflores being a part of it). Then, after I related the feeling of the day before with the mind-set of when he was a little boy ("That's how big it must have felt"), he linked this experience to his past experience of moving from the mountains and his difficulty in establishing a connection with his mother in the city of Lima.

Traces of this configuration came from three different time periods. The first is told through the representation of the aunt, the time in the mountains: "They say that in the highlands I was a happy, playful child." The second is a memory provided by the mother, the first representative of the city of Lima: ". . . they say that I was hard, tough, and solitary." The third time was his identification with the bombing of the previous night and the terrorists of Shining Path. The "bad boy", the way he described himself when he tasted ice-cream for the first time with displeasure, puts him in the same set as the other "bad boys", that is to say, the terrorists of Shining Path: "I can put myself into the shoes of those guys"; both seem unable to accept the city of Lima.

Vignette 2

John: When I arrived there was no place to park; a car was coming out and I saw the girl in the rear-view mirror, "it is good, the car"; I thought, I do not know why, but I make myself say "fucking car". And when I enter the room, I barely see you and suddenly it came to my mind: "prostitute". I've just come from a class on Italian literature. Dante saw in just the same way that the . . . [he said the name of the evangelical Christians] sees the Catholic religion, the "prostitute" with the kings, the temporal power beyond the spiritual, which is what its competence is. I'm also reading *The Leopard*, which is a novel about a nobleman. And they posit the opposition between the nobility and the crude bourgeois without manners. Then, I come and say to you: "prostitute". Because of the girl who was here before, I guess. It was a natural embarrassment, when you come across someone who is in analysis with the same person, and showing respect for others as well: "do not look at his face"; it's even a little maternal.

Analyst: You mentioned the opposition of the nobles with the vulgar bourgeois, and now you're talking about the noble courtesy of the person who . . .

John: (interrupting) No, it is fundamentally that "she does not greet me". Maybe it is shyness or she may not like my face. She is not seeing that things are this way. . . . I feel I am growing a belly, feeling chubby. I feel that somehow I associate with my father's belly, and I think I could . . . not in an ugly sense, but rather more strongly, more potently. Yesterday, I was thinking what it would be like to fuck Amalia and I thought, "Amalia, the little girl", I suppose also "the little dark girl" that was also in this fantasy and it was like having the Leopard on top of her. The Leopard, really a big man, a tremendous man, like my old man, as if I was becoming like him. And Amalia is dark like my

mother, a dark woman and I. But this feeling of being an
infiltrated *cholo* (*mestizo*) and that is the real reason why that girl
did not greet me.

First, John felt deeply hurt by the fact that his "sister in analysis"
did not recognise him. This engendered in him the need to insult me,
but in a very precise sense "I thought, I do not know why, but I make
myself say 'fucking car'. And when I enter the room, I barely see you
and suddenly it came to my mind: 'prostitute'." It is important to note
that she is a white woman.

From a logical point of view, psychoanalysts and prostitutes could
be put into a common propositional characteristic: we both charge
money for our attention. But it is difficult for John to attack me
directly and he tries to back off. When I pointed it out, he made his
feelings of rejection conscious: "she does not greet me".

Then we can appreciate how he elaborated an alternative in which
he places himself into a superior position, invoking the representation
of his father: "The Leopard, really a big man, a tremendous man, like
my old man, as if I were becoming like him", and to achieve his
goal he needs a woman to reproduce the "primal scene" like Amalia,
someone dark like his mother.

However, this compensatory construction does not accomplish its
purpose; he cannot avoid feeling inferior. At the end, although
painfully, he can connect with this feeling: "But this feeling of being
an infiltrated *cholo* (*mestizo*) . . . that is the real reason why that girl
did not greet me."

Vignette 3

John: Yesterday I met a patient of yours in the street. I felt uncomfortable, and I made a bow like you make to a public figure.
What did she think? A familiar face, an instant . . . What sucks
is to talk about her, my impressions, I have nothing against her,
a little compassion, maybe empathy; she looks scared. Not a
very white person; she has a vulnerable look. I'm afraid you
would tell me, "What do you think, asshole, a whiter tone?" I
must be jealous.

Analyst: Fearful that I want to protect her from your jealousy.

John: It's the only painful thing. This morning I went running; it was great, although I am still scared of dogs, when I see one on my way, I go to the other side of the street. Speaking about this danger is like realising that they do not want to fuck me: my friends, my father. After running, I don't want to masturbate, or take a drink; I only want healthy food.

A new encounter with another "sister in analysis" illustrates the importance that John gave to classifying himself as part of my set of patients. For now he placed himself in the superior position, although he still felt uncomfortable. Immediately, the racial classification is activated: "Not a very white person." He is afraid of my reaction; he fears that I would confront him with his *mestizo* origin: "I'm afraid you would tell me, 'What do you think, asshole, a whiter tone?'"

The racial aspects, in terms of social hierarchy, as these vignettes show, were a constant source of concern for him. Undoubtedly, they refer to a complex configuration regarding personal background as well as current identity.

The dogs could be seen as a projection that points out the threat of a part of the self that hates and could attack him. After all, the original etymological meaning of the word *cholo* is, precisely, "dog" (Callirgos, 1993).

Interestingly, he mentions that he felt that he was acquiring a sense other than a configuration of superiority–inferiority in which those in power over him want to subjugate him: "it is like realising that they do not want to fuck me: my friends, my father." It might be possible for him to place himself within a pattern in which things could be felt in a different way.

Vignette 4

John: I think, "Jorge is being cautious with me," in English it would be "to take care" [he said this in English]. There is also a racial thing: "the Czar of all Russia". A little love from me to him.

This short vignette is helpful in understanding how John's thought moves in racial terms: "There is also a racial thing." John represents the figure of the analyst as a powerful figure: "the Czar of all Russia", a powerful image, but also a despotic one: a kind of primordial father. In any case, it signifies more protecting than caring.

It is worthy of note that the mention of the Czar came after he acknowledged that he felt his analyst was concerned about him, and before he expressed a positive transference statement. Interestingly, he refers to the analyst in the third person, thus putting some distance in his loving, saying, "A little love from me to him", as though he could not make an affectionate remark directly. Even when he refers to me, he used my name, also as a means of putting some distance between us. He did not say, "You are cautious with me", or "A little love from me to you". I think that he chose the third person not only because of a transference issue, in the sense that it is difficult for him to address me directly, but for the reason that I represent in the transference a mighty figure just like his father.

I think that the meaning of his statement in English "to take care" is not the only one that is implicit in his first expression: "Jorge is cautious with me". It sounds to me more like what the Spanish meaning indicates, that is, the need to take precautions. The tricky distinction between the Spanish and English languages about "caring" and "caution", and the difference that appears in my countertransference between the Czar and the pogroms that my ancestors suffered in pre-revolutionary Russia, emphasises the dangerous hierarchical structure in which John placed himself (and me).

Conclusion

Although John's birth does not provide an exact example of the encounter between two Peruvian families fighting over who is less *mestizo* than the other, his life does dramatically epitomise the fact that Peruvians live in two different worlds at the same time, or, more properly, in the same place. Somewhere between these two spaces, John is trying to find, with the help of psychoanalysis, his own evolved place.

The "passive identifications" to which children are subjected by their elders, includes in John's case a destination that began five years after he was born with the redirection by his maternal family, and through the link that John opened with his paternal family: the hope for a better social and economic situation. John constructed in his psyche two completely different sets, paternal and maternal, in which he was the only connection: an extraordinary kind of passageway.

It is also remarkable how John sexualised his relationship with the world; it was as if the world was to be fucked or that he would be fucked by it. This is a patent example of what the psychoanalyst Elisabeth Young-Bruehl (1996) calls "hysterical prejudice", that is, a way to "act out in the world forbidden sexual and sexually aggressive desires".

Interestingly, his sexual and aggressive associations in the analysis never included his father's family (he had a wife and children). Perhaps the importance that he imputed to his father was so mighty and powerful that he could not fantasise about them in that way. It is possible that the representation of John's father had not yet become the father of the Oedipus ordeal, but, rather, symbolises the terrible father of the primal horde.

John's psychic apparatus could only produce associations that communicate at the level of primary process. The Shining Path bombing, the fear of dogs, his hard to get position in class status, among other things, are unconscious products and artefacts set deeply within his psyche. The vignettes illustrate the operation of features of a racial radar in which Peruvian people are placed into different worlds; a kind of gradient of colour and ethnicity, in which the paternal family is positioned at one end and the maternal family at the other.

John's psychoanalysis is an example of how the racial hierarchy between the maternal and paternal families is played out within the self through identification; the self is divided into the two opposing sets, the discriminated against and the discriminator. Psychoanalysis offers us a vantage point from which to understand the complexities of the vicissitudes of prejudice, when the subject's identity is split into these two opposing camps; the subject is forced to maintain the tension between these two sides in order to retain his identity, oscillating from one to the other in a perpetual conflict.

It might take the general population many years to move to the level of secondary process thinking, in which Oedipus can become manifest. Instead, primary process thinking rules over racial prejudice and representation.

Although the psychoanalytic relationship is part of that equation, and the analyst is inevitably placed somewhere within the racial gradient, it is also an opportunity to live a process that, at least in this particular case, could accelerate the general time set, and people like John would move forward with a perspective that they could overcome the "passive identifications" in which their psychic apparatus was set up. The psychoanalyst may accomplish this as well.

References

Bruce, J. (2007). *Nos habi_amos choleado tanto: Psicoanálisis y racismo.* Surquillo, Lima: Universidad de San Martín de Porres, Fondo Editorial.

Callirgos, J. C. (1993). *El racismo: la cuestión del otro (y de uno).* Lima: DESCO, Centro de Estudios y Promoción del Desarrollo.

Freud, S. (1921c). *Group Psychology and the Analysis of the Ego. S.E., 18*: 69–143. London: Hogarth.

Gilio, M. E. (2010). *Cuando los que escuchan hablan: Conversaciones con grandes psicoanalistas.* Buenos Aires: Libros del Zorzal.

Manrique, N. (1999). *La piel y la pluma: Escritos sobre literatura, etnicidad y racismo.* San Isidro, Peru: CIDIAG.

Marucco, N. (2006). Actualización del Concepto de Trauma en la Clínica Psicoanalítica. *Revista de Psicoanálisis, LXIII(1)*.

Portocarrero, M. G. (2009). *Racismo y mestizaje y otros ensayos.* Lima: Fondo Editorial del Congreso del Perú.

Vargas Llosa, M. (1993). *El pez en el agua: Memorias.* Barcelona: Seix Barral.

Young-Bruehl, E. (1996). *The Anatomy of Prejudices.* Cambridge, MA: Harvard University Press.

PART IV

CONCLUSION: REALISTIC EXPECTATIONS

CHAPTER NINE

The future of prejudice and the limits of psychoanalytic intervention[1]

Cyril Levitt

From its beginning, psychoanalysis was forced to confront both popular and academic prejudice, not only on account of its supposedly prurient and lurid subject matter,[2] but also on account of the Jewish background of almost all its early adherents, practitioners, and many of their patients. The large psychoanalytic literature on the topic of prejudice and related matters (including racism, anti-Semitism, discrimination, ethnic and racial violence, genocide, and ethnic cleansing) provides analysts with an armamentarium in confronting prejudice in their clinical work, and in their understanding of its psychodynamic causes and development. Yet, in spite of this rich and burgeoning literature on prejudice and related issues, there have been relatively few attempts by analysts and psychoanalytic institutions to educate non-analytically orientated professionals who come up against issues of prejudice in their daily work. I include among these groups of professionals teachers and educators, social workers, jurists and legislators, mediators and arbitrators, police and military (in democratic countries), as the most prominent.[3]

Although I strongly favour this kind of outreach and participate in it enthusiastically, this chapter explores the obstacles in the path of developing an effective strategy for understanding and combating prejudice more generally, and attempts to answer the question why prejudice remains such a serious social problem and a threat to civil peace within many countries and regions of the world. Why does it continue to be such a destabilising force, in spite of decades, if not centuries, of enlightenment, the spread of democratic institutions and practices, the rule of law, and the growth of equality and tolerance? It seems as though the advancement of these welcome developments is accompanied world-wide by far too many examples of hostile, malignant collective prejudice, hatred, and violence.

In the preceding chapters, distinguished analysts show the power of psychoanalytic approaches to understanding the dynamics of hostile and malignant prejudice, as well as describe the techniques they employ with their patients, their interventions in childhood regarding expressions of prejudice and violence, their work with manifestations of large group prejudice in the realms of ethnic, religious, and national hatreds and conflicts, and their integration of psychoanalytic concepts and various philosophical approaches to the problem of hatred and violence. Each of them speaks powerfully with regard to the positive and encouraging results of these psychoanalytic approaches to the problems they have confronted. I applaud them for their efforts and encourage them to expand their horizons. Nevertheless, in conclusion, I hold up the mirror of reality to reflect the difficulties, mostly practical,[4] to achieving better results in this important area of social concern. In general, I argue that even though the psychoanalytic approaches outlined here represent important and significant contributions to the understanding, analysis, and struggle against hostile and malignant prejudice, their practical applications on a large scale are limited and partially blocked by psychological, cultural, political, institutional, interest-group obstacles as well as historical trends and realities which militate against the full implementation and success of our theoretical and practical achievements.

The problem

In the fifth chapter of *Civilization and Its Discontents*, Freud (1930a) writes about what he considered the innate human inclination to aggression, and illustrates it by means of several historical examples:

The element of truth behind all this, which people are so ready to disavow, is that men are not gentle creatures who want to be loved, and who at the most can defend themselves if they are attacked; they are, on the contrary, creatures among whose instinctual endowments is to be reckoned a powerful share of aggressiveness. As a result, their neighbour is for them not only a potential helper or sexual object, but also someone who tempts them to satisfy their aggressiveness on him, to exploit his capacity for work without compensation, to use him sexually without his consent, to seize his possessions, to humiliate him, to cause him pain, to torture and to kill him. Homo homini lupus. Who, in the face of all his experience of life and of history, will have the courage to dispute this assertion? As a rule this cruel aggressiveness waits for some provocation or puts itself at the service of some other purpose, whose goal might also have been reached by milder measures. In circumstances that are favourable to it, when the mental counter-forces which ordinarily inhibit it are out of action, it also manifests itself spontaneously and reveals man as a savage beast to whom consideration towards his own kind is something alien. Anyone who calls to mind the atrocities committed during the racial migrations or the invasions of the Huns, or by the people known as Mongols under Jenghiz Khan and Tamerlane, or at the capture of Jerusalem by the pious Crusaders, or even, indeed, the horrors of the recent World War – anyone who calls these things to mind will have to bow humbly before the truth of this view. (pp. 111–112)

We could, alas, augment these historical references, penned eighty-five years ago, with more than a few additional examples that would make Freud's illustrations pale by comparison in scope and brutality. However, even if we take issue with Freud's anchoring of aggression in the invariable instinctual disposition of humankind, there is no denying the seeming intractability of the phenomenon, as it has frequently manifested itself in the historical record.

Parens (above, pp. 5–6) traced the origins of prejudice from the multi-trends theory of aggression to the foundational relationship between mother and child, the formation of identity, and the generation of "stranger anxiety". Thus,

(t)his multi-trends theory of aggression holds that the trend, which is neither inborn nor biologically generated, and is constituted of the range of affective expressions of hostile destructiveness (HD), that is, from anger to hostility, rage, hate, etc., is structured, along lines proposed by Kernberg (1966) by experiences of excessive psychic pain (Excessive Unpleasure) in the context of object relatedness.

The degree and character of the individual's expression of hostile destructiveness is related to the nature and degree of the psychic pain or excessively unpleasurable experiences within the child's significant object relationships. The young child develops a special and preferential relationship with his or her mother (or primary care-giver) and, by extension, to other family members. Faces[5] and voices are, thereby, not all perceived in the same way by the infant and toddler. It is the quality and intensity of these relationships that constitute the foundation for developing tolerance of difference and the capacity to live within a multi-cultural society and world. The distinction that the infant and toddler make between such elements as the face, voice, composure, communication, and body language of their mother, other close care-givers, and strangers is one of the bases for prejudices that we all have as a matter of course. Parens refers to this kind of ubiquitous and normal prejudice as benign, because it does not necessarily malign others or lead to discriminatory behaviour and violent attacks against them. It is benign prejudice to support one's national team at the Olympics. Not all expressions of national or local favouritism and preference are malevolent. In spite of globalisation, international trading blocs, and military alliances, nationalisms both soft and hard continue to flourish, some benevolently, others malevolently.

The question that Parens pursues concerns the active factors in transforming benevolent prejudice into the hostile and malignant varieties. One of the important factors is found within the child's response to his or her own ambivalent trends in relation to mother and early care-givers. Displacement, inhibition, and splitting towards the end of the first year, followed by projection, rationalisation, and denial somewhat later, may lead to "reality distorting defences" just prior to the onset of latency. These, in turn, may become some of the organising factors in hostile and malignant prejudice, in combination with other influences. Parens believes that traumatic experiences may help create a need to discharge the hate engendered by the excessive pain induced by trauma in the form of revenge (Gilligan, 1997), and help formulate within the traumatised individual's psyche "the need to have enemies" (Volkan, 1988). Finally, Parens considers the important role of education and "socialisation into identifications", which may coerce the development of malignant prejudice from the more common and normal benign variety. In contrast to such empirically based work within psychoanalysis of the last five decades, in *his* ambitious attempt to interweave psychoanalysis and anthropology in *Totem and Taboo*, Freud sought to elucidate the phylogenetic basis for collective violence in the murder and cannibalism of the primal father by his sons within the primal horde.[6]

Psychoanalysis can help us understand hostile and malignant prejudice, and provide methods for treating its psychopathological manifestations in clinical practice. It can assist professionals in those fields in which expressions of malignant prejudice and hostile destructiveness are daily fare by helping them understand and deal with them practically. Psychoanalysis, however, cannot treat outbreaks of massive forms of hostile destructiveness built upon malignant prejudice once a critical point is reached. Freud and his generation of analysts were helpless, and perhaps more than a little naïve (we can say in hindsight), in the face of Nazism in Germany and Austria, and it was only by the counter-force of arms that the hostile destructiveness unleashed by the Nazis, fascists, anti-Semites, and militarists were successfully subdued. But the necessary alliance against the Axis powers quickly led to geopolitical tensions between the Western democracies, the Soviet Empire, and, somewhat later, Communist China and North Korea. It was against the background of this conflict that the relinquishing of the last vestiges of colonialism led to the formation of new states and new alliances, the course of which was accompanied by a good deal of hostile destructiveness, both domestically and in relations between states. One need only mention the problems of many African countries, the Middle East wars and conflicts, the brutal events surrounding the break-up of the former Yugoslavia, mass murder and violent repression in Latin America, the Cambodian and Rwandan genocides, the civil wars in Sudan, Nigeria, and Ethiopia, terrorism in the former Soviet Union, northern China, and the USA, and the wars in Iraq and Afghanistan, to illustrate the scope and extent of hostile destructiveness in the last half of the twentieth and the first decade of the twenty-first centuries.[7] The acquisition of weapons-grade nuclear capacities and long-range delivery systems by Iran, and the real possibility of such material being acquired by non-state terrorist actors in the near future, promises to raise the threat of yet more egregious acts of hostile destructiveness to a level hitherto unknown.

Vamık Volkan, whose valuable contribution also appears above, has dedicated much of his research to these larger questions of inter-state, inter-ethnic, and interreligious conflicts within our world. His chapter, based in part upon his early experiences as a Turkish child in Cyprus suffering aggression at the hands of elements of the Greek-Cypriot population, is juxtaposed in my mind with the accounts of a close friend regarding his experiences as a *Greek* child in Cyprus around the same time, suffering, in his account, aggression by elements of the Turkish population. Of course, one could substitute for Turkish and Greek any number of other conflicting ethnicities, religious groups, or states, all representing the same conundrum. How is it that we can adjudicate in a fair and objective manner con-flicts in which even the most intelligent and well-intentioned individ-uals are found on both sides, holding passionately to their opposing narratives? Henri Parens, in his contribution to this volume, has called this the Janus dilemma: someone who is a terrorist in the eyes of one community is a national or religious or ethnic hero in the eyes of another community. This is one of the most formidable obstacles to successfully mastering malignant prejudices and its attendant violence. The depth and exasperatingly stubborn intractability of the problem is perhaps best expressed in a joke that I heard in Jerusalem many years ago. A vendor of *tschochkes* (*bric-à-brac*, souvenirs) near the Western Wall of the Temple noticed that day after day, week after week, year after year a certain pious Jew would appear at the Wall and fervently pray for several minutes and then leave. The vendor, after several decades at his post, decided to retire. But his curiosity got the better of him and he decided to approach this pious individual who appeared with Kant-like regularity at the Wall to ask him about the meaning of his private ceremonial. He addressed the man as follows: "Sir, I have noticed over the years how every day at the same appoin-ted time you approach the Wall and engage for several minutes in fervent prayer. Can you tell me why you do this?" The man replied, "I am praying for peace in the Middle East." "And what has your experience been through these years of fervent prayer?" "It's like talking to a wall," the man replied. At this point in time, we have little hope of solving this vexing dilemma.

Parens takes some comfort in the fact that the countries in Europe, North America, and Japan were able to develop friendly relations after recurrent warfare. The question naturally arises: can such reciprocal changes in identity required of enemies for peaceful coexistence come about before extended conflict on a mass scale occurs? (One is reminded here of Heine's saying, cited by Freud (1930a, p. 110n): "One must, it is true, forgive one's enemies – but not before they have been hanged.") Could France and Germany have evolved to their present day co-ordination and co-operation without the Franco-Prussian War, the Great War, and, ultimately, Germany's near complete destruction during the Second World War? One could also argue that Japan would never have been willing to sue for peace without suffering the horrific experiences of Hiroshima and Nagasaki. Furthermore, we shudder to think what the world would have been like had the Axis powers prevailed.

We ought to ask ourselves why it is that the achievement of an objective, rational assessment of situations in which we are embroiled often seems beyond our grasp. Anthropology supplies us with some explanations for this phenomenon; psychoanalysis complements anthropology in this regard. Surely, we recognise, and, in much of the West, celebrate, religious, national, cultural, and ethnic differences, but remain dedicated to overarching ideals applying universally to people everywhere. These notions of universality and objectivity are true Enlightenment ideals which most of us embrace. Yet, as empirical anthropology has shown, no one is human in general, just as no one speaks "language" *per se*. Even those who understand and speak many languages speak only a small number of possible real languages, given the plethora of language-speaking communities in the world. Esperanto, as an experiment involving the development of a common universal language, was a failure largely because there is no concrete society of generic human beings, speaking one common language, with the same culture, social and political institutions, value systems, etc.[8] The human being, as such, remains an abstraction, that is, an ideal construction composed of abstractions from real, living human beings with different cultures, language communities, or religious traditions, etc.

Even those societies, most, if not all of them Western, which are positively multi-cultural *de facto* or *de jure*, not only allow but encourage all their component communities to practise their traditions, educate their children in their own schools (as long as they observe the minimum curriculum in subjects such as science, mathematics, and civics), or even attempt to proselytise others through argument or example. These rights that are protected by means of the law stand opposite signs of growing conflicts in recent years between group rights, individual rights, and the competing rights of different groups. No multi-cultural societies are free of ethnic, racial, and religious conflicts.[9] If anything, these conflicts are increasing, voices are becoming more strident, and acts of violence are occurring more frequently.

Some may argue that it is a matter of time before intermarriages, unions of people from different ethnic, religious, linguistic, and class backgrounds will make "nationalism", ethnocentrism, religious particularism, etc., and the thinking and attitudes that arise on these bases, obsolete. However, it is difficult to see how this can happen— at least in the short term—for several reasons. The largest populations in the world by far—in China, India, Africa, Latin America, and the Middle East—tend to be homogenous within larger sub-groupings in terms of language, religion, and ethnicity. Furthermore, the rate of intermarriage between the largest populations is very low, and will continue to remain low into the foreseeable future. Even in "multi-cultural" countries, such as the USA and Canada, the intermarried couple does not automatically enter into a universal culture, sharing universal institutions and values, speaking an international and universal language.

A married couple formed, for example, by one member from a Greek-speaking and Orthodox background and the other from a Turkish-speaking Muslim background constitutes a unit that is either isolated unto itself and seeks to divest itself of both cultures trying to lead a "normal", that is, secular or civic life within the country in which they live, or tries to balance the claims that their respective families and communities make upon them and their children in terms of language, religious and cultural practices, and affiliations in relation to such matters as cuisine, social, political, or moral values, membership of clubs, ethnic and religious institutions, etc. They might even associate with other intermarried couples from different backgrounds, on the basis of their common intermarried status or some other mutual interests.[10] However, the homogeneous ethnic communities will remain dominant, for at least the next several decades. Strauss (1962) had already adumbrated an argument of this sort in relation to the Jews.

Finally, as we have seen, psychoanalysis contributes a unique answer to the question concerning the barriers to objectivity, on the part of "interested parties" to group conflict. The predilection for "our own" arises from our earliest attachments, identifications, object relations, projections, and projective identifications. Our judgements are never pure and "the facts" can be interwoven into various cultural narratives which include moral, religious, historical, and cultural grids through which they are constructed, deconstructed, and reconstructed. This plasticity of factual integration often causes the parties to engage in conflict with, and to talk past, one another. The results of the recent elections to the European Parliament which became known as this book was in the process of publication is an alarming reminder of the seriousness of these matters.

Individual rights vs. group rights in relation to hostile and malignant prejudice

France is one example of a country that seems to have drawn a line against group rights in favour of individual rights, arguing, with some cogency, that this is to align with the tradition of its revolutionary past.[11] It is worthwhile to consider the words of Stanislas de Clermont-Tonnere, a deputy in the French Chambre, in a speech on the 23rd of December, 1789, in which he referred precisely to the question of group rights in the French Republic. Although he refers explicitly to the Jews at the time of the Revolution, it could equally apply to the large Muslim minority in France today. I cite it at length because it is consonant with the sense of current French thinking:

> There is no middle way possible: either you admit a national religion, subject all your laws to it, arm it with temporal power, exclude from your society the men who profess another creed and then, erase the article in your declaration of rights [freedom of religion]; or you permit everyone to have his own religious opinion, and do not exclude from public office those who make use of this permission. . . .

> Every creed has only one test to pass in regard to the social body: it has only one examination to which it must submit that of its morals. It is here that the adversaries of the Jewish people attack me. This people, they say, is not sociable. They are commanded to loan at usurious rates; they cannot be joined with us either in marriage or by the bonds of social interchange; our food is forbidden to them; our tables prohibited; our armies will never have Jews serving in the defence of the fatherland. The worst of these reproaches is unjust; the others are

only specious. Usury is not commanded by their laws; loans at interest are forbidden between them and permitted with foreigners. . . .

This usury so justly censured is the effect of our own laws. Men who
have nothing but money can only work with money: that is the evil.
Let them have land and a country and they will loan no longer: that is
the remedy. As for their unsociability, it is exaggerated. Does it exist?
What do you conclude from it in principle? Is there a law that obliges
me to marry your daughter? Is there a law that obliges me to eat hare
and to eat it with you? No doubt these religious oddities will disappear; and if they do survive the impact of philosophy and the pleasure
of finally being true citizens and sociable men, they are not infractions
to which the law can or should pertain.

But, they say to me, the Jews have their own judges and laws. I respond
that is your fault and you should not allow it. We must refuse everything to the Jews as a nation and accord everything to Jews as individuals. We must withdraw recognition from their judges; they should
only have our judges. We must refuse legal protection to the maintenance of the so-called laws of their Judaic organization; they should
not be allowed to form in the state either a political body or an order.
They must be citizens individually. But, some will say to me, they do
not want to be citizens. Well then! If they do not want to be citizens,
they should say so, and then, we should banish them. It is repugnant
to have in the state an association of non-citizens, and a nation within
the nation. . . . In short, Sirs, the presumed status of every man resident
in a country is to be a citizen. (Hunt, 1996, pp. 86–88)[12]

We read or hear these words and we are jarred by their intolerance
of communal or cultural difference, and policies of multi-culturalism.
However, in less stringent ways, they continue to influence our
politics, laws, and social relations. France bans the burqa and the
government of the Province of Quebec will not serve women wearing
the niqab, while the Toronto District School Board frees Muslim
students from their classes and clears the school gym to enable these
students to pray at appropriate times, while female Muslim students
are not allowed in the same area as the male students. In Québec, the
formerly ruling separatist Parti Québecois proposed a "Charter of
Québec Values" (which would ban the headscarf and other religious
symbols such as the yarmulke, the turban, a large cross in public
(except in the Provincial Legislature or on top of Mont Royale since
these are "cultural artefacts" rooted in Québec history). In France,

according to a report by Kramer (2011), Elisabeth Badinter continues to defend a somewhat modernised version of Enlightenment thinking in her contrarian feminism and strongly supports the burqa ban. Some New Yorkers want to forbid the construction of a mosque several blocks away from Ground Zero; others want to encourage strip clubs to open beside the mosque.

I find Clermont de Tonnere's speech amazing, not only because it seems to express the sentiment behind much of the current debate in France, but also because it grates on some of us as it violates our multi-cultural sensibilities. It sounds extreme to our modern, or, rather, postmodern ears. I also believe that it was the predominant sentiment in the Western democracies down to the end of the Second World War. I further believe that the sea-change in relation to group rights occurred as a direct response to the Holocaust, racism in the American South, apartheid in South Africa, the legacy of colonialism, oppressive and discriminatory practices (under which I include pater-nalistic and care-taking practices) in relation to indigenous peoples, in short, various aspects of wrong and injury inflicted upon groups, resistance to which was couched in the language of group rights. When the powerful feminist critique became a juggernaut beginning in the mid-1960s, following on the heels of the civil rights movement in the American South, group rights and freedoms began to dominate public discourse.

However, it would be false to characterise the present situation from the point of view of the conflict between individual and group rights alone. Even if we were to accept the shift to group rights as legitimate and necessary, we will find that what has resulted is a new conflict between the rights and sensibilities of various groups.

Anthropology

The concepts of humanity, human nature, and human rights, are not very ancient. They probably had their origins in the West around the time of Alexander, when the large number of diverse populations needed laws and "language" to facilitate and regulate commercial and other forms of social intercourse with one another. It roughly corresponded with the rise of koine Greek, Ελληνιστική Κοινή in the same Alexandrian period as the language of common speech across different speech communities within the empire. In Rome the *ius gentium* provided a similar legal framework, facilitating contact between and among Romans and foreigners within the empire. The *lex naturalis*, or natural law, originated from the Socratic distinction between φύσιζ (physis) and νόμοζ (nomos), or the laws given by God or Nature binding on all men universally and the laws of social convention that are variable and amendable.

As Krader (1966, pp. 51–52) has expressed it,

> The expression of the nature and identity of mankind in the abstract, however clear it may be as a concept, is neither well thought out nor fully explored; hence it is at once the triumph and defeat of speculative and empirical anthropology. To be human is to participate in mankind in general, and to participate in a particular culture; it is the latter which is known best. Objectively, the individual achieves his or her human nature only through the channel of the particular culture, not through that of mankind in general; in this sense we speak of particular human nature. The unity and uniqueness of mankind as the culture bearer, while having gained formal expression, has been given little substantial content. Moreover, the concept of the abstract concept, the totality as unity, has few consequences in relations between peoples and between social classes. The individual identity of man is engendered by the expression of his being of his own kind as opposed to the being of those other nations and classes, and as opposed eventually to the being of the other; this mode of achieving identity is counter-posed to the concept of the unity of man, and the unity of the separate human group with mankind as a whole . . . The conditions which have made possible the concept of mankind as an abstract unitary, objective totality, impede the realization of the concept.

Many speech communities studied by anthropologists do not have a word for humanity or human being as such. Very often their self-designation is a word or phrase that means "true people" or "the people",[13] or it refers to some geographical location or an activity or characteristic for which the community is known or prides itself.[14] As Krader (1966, pp. 52–53) has expressed it,

> In primitive society, on the other hand, the concept of man in general is frequently lacking, or incompletely conceived and expressed; man, the category of genuine man, will then refer to the members of the speaker's social group, to people of like language or culture, and the

further extension of the notion is vague, even possibly including only some members of the group or language community, excluding others, stopping short of its outer limits, which are therefore not considered to be an absolute unity by its members. As a consequence, some members of the same people (conceived as an absolute ethnic unity by civilized men, the anthropologists) may be treated as outsiders, as others, albeit not as a thing or as something other than human, subhuman. In primitive circumstances, the expression of the identity of man is not conceived in the abstract as mankind, self-conscious social man, man as a member of the human kind in general. On the contrary, the conscious awareness of the primitive society in question is barely developed, and therefore its identity is weakly expressed, while the identity of other men, man outside one's own social group, man in others societies, the other (man and society), and mankind as a whole, may not be given expression at all. Within primitive society, oppositions between own and other, between man and man, man and society, group and group (as a whole society and part of a society), and next between man and nature, are poorly developed and expressed. There is no thought of contradictions within primitive society as these are conceived abstractly by civilized man; these may only be discovered post hoc by civilized man, who is in fully contradictory relations himself, and then traced back to their roots in primitive society, or by primitives who are so no longer, having come into contact with civilized societies.

Our modern concepts of humanity, human dignity, and human rights have their origins in part in the political theories of the social contract, in the writings of Hobbes, Locke, Rousseau, and the formalistic universalism of the Enlightenment as it applied the method of science and mathematics to social and political issues. All particularisms were to fall before the impartial judgements of reason and empirically based argument. Quantity trumped quality as all aspects of nature were rationalised, mathematised, and systematised.

I am outlining, rather than championing, a stream of historical development entirely relevant to our theme of hostile and malignant prejudice. Here, I think that psychoanalysis can provide us with some help.

The empirical and clinical work of Henri Parens, over more than forty years with babies, toddlers, and children with their mothers, has convincingly demonstrated the importance of the quality of early attachment in later expressions of hostile destructiveness and malignant prejudice. To this, I would like to add something regarding the importance of identification and education to ego and superego development. Before I do this, however, I want to look at the reaction to the Enlightenment views I presented earlier.

Our contemporary understanding of human rights has its origins in the formation of the United Nations during the Second World War, as a reaction to Nazi race theories and practices, and the racialist militarism of the Axis powers, more generally. In the past several decades, the struggle for human rights has become politicised, and the United Nations itself has muddied the waters significantly with Durban I, II, and III. This state of affairs is yet another step backwards, and makes the work of combating malignant prejudice that much more difficult. Orwell might have referred to the new language of human rights, with justification, as a kind of Newspeak.

Anthropology, psychoanalysis, and malignant prejudice

Anthropology had its modern beginnings in the writings of Giambattisto Vico, Johann Gottfried Herder, Immanuel Kant, and Charles-Louis de Secondat Baron de Montesquieu, among others. It was taken up by Hegel, and steered into a different direction by Ludwig Feuerbach and Karl Marx. In the aftermath of the evolution-ist revolution, at the hands of Charles Darwin, Herbert Spencer, and Alfred Russell Wallace, it was brought into the positivist orbit under the aegis of evolutionism in the latter half of the nineteenth century. The evolutionists, for the most part, were true to the Enlightenment project of applying invariable natural laws to human affairs, and, accordingly, they devised various schemes that outlined the supposed necessary stages of human development. For example, the American lawyer and anthropologist Lewis Henry Morgan (1877) published his major work, *Ancient Society*, on the lines of human development from savagery, through barbarism, to civilisation.[15] Their work was based upon evidence supplied mostly by missionaries and colonial government officials, as well as by travellers to exotic places, such as Francois Bernier (1891), the French physician who travelled to Mogul India and recorded his impressions and his historical understanding of India in the late seventeenth century.

As many critics have pointed out, evolutionism in anthropology went hand in hand with colonialism, imperialism, and even Karl

Marx, one of the more sophisticated evolutionists, was not above using racial epithets. The notion of higher and lower races and stages of social development reflected the attitudes of colonialist powers and offered them, willingly or unwillingly, an intellectual framework to justify their policies. Franz Boas and his students in the USA, and A. Radcliffe Brown in the UK called evolutionism in anthropology into serious question. The link between evolution and human progress was challenged in practice by the perfection of the machine gun, and the introduction of the tank and the aeroplane on the battlefields of the First World War.

With the exception of a few outliers in the discipline, Western anthropology rejected evolutionism as a framework and focused on empirical studies of specific communities and societies. Along with the general attack on structuralism and modernism in the arts and other social sciences, anthropology largely moved away from what post-colonialists and postmodernists call "essentialism", according to which group and individual characteristics are reduced to certain essential qualities which define who they are and, thus, limit the possibilities for change and growth. In addition, the categories which are used to analyse individuals and groups, such as, "race", "class", and "gender", are themselves relativised, so that no one element is considered "foundational" to the exclusion of the others. The philosophical and logical problems of this turn in anthropology are significant, but cannot be followed further within the context of our work here. Suffice to say, there is a strong anti-Enlightenment, indeed Romanticist, thrust behind this turn in anthropology.

A Jewish-American anthropologist that I knew many years ago was once asked, by a colleague from a different department of the local university, whether he was planning to attend a meeting at the Jewish Community Centre for a discussion regarding a matter of some concern to the local Jewish population. His reply was, "I would never take part in such atavistic activities." The next day, he was observed on campus sitting in a Native drum circle beating upon an Iroquois Water Drum. Going native, although presented as identifying with an oppressed indigenous group, might, in fact, be seen as a demeaning and derogatory expression of the "simplicity" and "primitiveness" of the indigenous people themselves, and lead to a double standard. "What can you expect from these simple people who have been traumatised by colonialism and imperialism?" Excusing terrorism on the part of some extremist members of indigenous groups may let them off the hook, because, after all, *they* cannot be expected to adhere to "civilised" norms, which has led to the very oppression and struggles of these indigenous groups. They not only get a huge pass, but the source of every evil is now seen as stemming from Western capitalist societies, which, thus, become the repositories and source of all that is wrong with the contemporary world.

When I was a student in the 1960s, I took a class on the sociology of genocide taught by a former German-Jewish refugee. We were to read a book about the round-up of the Jews in France after the German occupation. There was a young boy in the book who was not Jewish, but was arrested and interned in the Vichy French camp at Drancy.[16] One of the students in the class, when attempting to read her report on the book, became distressed as she talked about this boy mistakenly thought of as a Jew. She trembled, started to cry, and rushed out of the room. Several of her friends went out after her to calm her down. When she had returned to the class somewhat composed, the professor asked her what it was in her report that so distressed her. "Don't you see," she said. "He wasn't Jewish. It wasn't meant for *him*."

The anthropologist who considered the traditions of his own people atavistic while participating in and celebrating a traditional practice of indigenous people, and the student who became upset when the non-Jewish boy was treated as a Jew, that is, when the death sentence was not meant for him, were giving expression to a similar double standard. It is perfectly acceptable to participate in atavistic practices, as long as the group is indigenous, victimised, and relatively "primitive". It is not fair that a non-Jewish boy is caught up and treated like a Jew, and sent for deportation to the East for "resettlement", since it was not meant for him.

Contemporary forms of conflict concerning hostile and malignant prejudice

There are two polarities that seem to be crystallising in North America and Western and Central Europe. The one pole represents a collection of people who are orientated to the past, who want to preserve *their* language, culture, and their way of life by limiting or restricting expressions of minority languages, cultures, religions, etc. At the other extreme, there are those who argue that there can be no legitimate critique of, or opposition to, a minority culture, religion, or value system from within the dominant culture, religion, or value system. If a minority community through immigration or a high birth rate becomes the majority, so be it.

There is something hallowed about indigenous cultures, minority religions, ethnic traditions, and practices that put them above reproach. This polarity is generally understood as coming from the left. But it has its intellectual predecessor in the Romantic tradition on the right. The social and political facts that underlie these growing extremes are related to large Muslim minorities in Europe and, to a significantly lesser degree, in Canada and the USA. Given the higher birth rate within these minority communities, concerns in Europe especially are heightened in regard to the future of Europe's indigenous languages, Christian heritage, and culture. Recent events in Norway (not only the Breivik case, but increasing electoral support for far right parties) are poignant and alarming reminders of the passion and potential violence surrounding these questions.

One must also consider that the Muslim world is not homogenous and monolithic; the same holds true for the Arab states as well. Sunni, Shia, and Christian tensions will not, it seems, be ameliorated, not even with the settling of the Israeli–Palestinian conflict, to wit the bloody civil war in Syria, which has polarised, or, rather, given palpable expression to, the polarisation within the Muslim world itself.

Psychoanalysis and group prejudice

I return now to psychoanalysis and what it tells us about the nature of group attachments and out-group tensions. Henri Parens tells of the importance of identification in relation to attachment, separation–individuation, object constancy, and stranger anxiety.

Freud originated his ideas on identification in the 1890s in relation to hysterical symptoms, referring largely to his patients' identifications with parents, authority figures, persons generating envy, siblings, and the like. In works such as *Three Essays on the Theory of Sexuality* (Freud, 1905d) and *Totem and Taboo* (Freud, 1912–1913), he links identification with orality and oral incorporation. With the development of his theory of narcissism, he distinguished between hysterical and narcissistic identification in "Mourning and melancholia" (Freud, 1917[1915]) and *Group Psychology and the Analysis of the Ego* (Freud, 1921c). In the latter work, Freud wrote about identification as the most primitive form of love. The little boy in his example admires his father, wants to emulate him, be like his father, do the things his father does, and step into his father's shoes both literally and figuratively. Freud seems to have been unclear in his own mind as to whether this father admiration and emulation immediately assumes a hostile colouration, or whether the hostile trend develops along with the triangularity of the Oedipus complex. However, without doubt, the young child's identifications with people such as parents, siblings, close relatives, or authority figures are central to the development of the child's character.

Parens refers to the fact that the child comes to learn that the way things are done in his or her family is different from the way they are done in the families of his or her friends and others. I am suggesting further that the differences are internalised and varied in character formation as well. Freud also argued that identifications are absolutely central in the formation of the superego. The critical agency of the ego is composed of elements of the identifications with parents in the wake of the dissolution of the Oedipus complex. The moral aspect of our being is largely a result of these identifications and their vicissitudes in the process of making what we inherit from our parents our own. Freud was fond of citing Goethe in this regard.

In any population, there is a great deal of variation in terms of healthy ego and superego development. Freud (1930a, p. 144) raised the question concerning the possibility of pathological development of an entire culture at the conclusion of *Civilization and Its Discontents*, and recognised that that would require some point outside the culture from which to make such judgements. Freud preferred to leave this question to the future:

> But there is one question which I can hardly evade. If the development of civilization has such a far-reaching similarity to the development of the individual and if it employs the same methods, may we not be justified in reaching the diagnosis that, under the influence of cultural urges, some civilizations, or some epochs of civilization – possibly the whole of mankind – have become 'neurotic'? An analytic dissection of

such neuroses might lead to therapeutic recommendations which could lay claim to great practical interest. I would not say that an attempt of this kind to carry psycho-analysis over to the cultural community was absurd or doomed to be fruitless. But we should have to be very cautious and not forget that, after all, we are only dealing with analogies and that it is dangerous, not only with men, but also with concepts, to tear them from the sphere in which they have originated and been evolved. Moreover, the diagnosis of communal neuroses is faced with a special difficulty. In an individual neurosis we take as our starting-point the contrast that distinguishes the patient from his environment, which is assumed to be 'normal'. For a group, all of whose members are affected by one and the same disorder no such background could exist; it would have to be found elsewhere. And as regards the therapeutic application of our knowledge, what would be the use of the most correct analysis of social neuroses, since no one possesses authority to impose such a therapy upon the group? But in spite of all these difficulties, we may expect that one day someone will venture to embark upon a pathology of cultural communities.[17]

It is at this point that "education" becomes an important variable. By education, I refer to all those elements by which a society or a community imposes its values and prejudices upon individuals in subtle or coercive ways. Such impositions may be done by means of police and military oppression and suppression, but the more effective and more insidious ways are by working through identifications involving the ego and superego. We love our country, our flag, our religion, our values, our history, our ideals, our way of life, our leaders, etc., and there is nothing intrinsically wrong in this, especially, as Freud would say, when our leaders are compassionate and lovers of justice, our country promotes the highest ideals, our religion is generous to those outside the faith community, etc. However, these values and ideals can be twisted in jingoist, chauvinist, racist, and hateful ways under specific conditions, which may go beyond the citizenry's control.

I refer only to two such conditions with real historical referents that are applicable here.

The one condition, obtained in Germany during the Weimar Republic, is that of economic, political, and social crisis, the features of which include high and rising unemployment, widespread hunger, anomie, de-idealisation of traditions, or current leaders and political elites. The second condition characterises the Israeli–Arab conflicts and concerns resentment born of shame, humiliation, and envy from the different histories of contending peoples. Let us consider this example a little further, since it is much in the news.

Zionism, in part, was born out of the fear, shame, and humiliation of Jewish populations in Europe and elsewhere as a result of widespread and at times organised oppression, discrimination, violence, forced conscription, pogroms, unfair taxation, restrictions on the practice of profession, and the ownership of land. The fear, humiliation, and shame felt by the Holocaust victims and the desire for not just a national home, but a homeland on their ancestral territory, in which their fate was and once again would be vested in their own hands, fuelled a popular movement among Jews in the 1930s and especially during, and in the aftermath of, the Second World War. In addition, there was a good deal of sympathy all over the world for the Jews more generally at this time.

The Yiddish expression—*azoy vi es christelt zich, azoy yiddelt's zich* (as it goes with the gentiles, so it goes with the Jews)—has been attributed rightly or wrongly to Heinrich Heine. Zionism was fuelled by a number of European influences, in addition to its roots deep within Jewish culture: there were Tolstoyan and Nietzschean impulses, Romantic and Enlightenment streams, Marxism and other forms of socialism, and psychoanalytic thinking. The following vignette, recalled by the Zionist student, Shmaryahu Levin (Levin & Samuel, 1930, pp. 248–249), at the University of Berlin a few decades after the event described, captures the flavour of the mixture of socialism and the response to anti-Semitism by European Zionism. A popular socialist agitator, Alexander Parvus (born Israel Lazarevich Gelfand), was attacking nationalism. In the crowd was the socialist-Zionist student, Nahum Syrkin:

> Parvus was thundering . . . against the meaninglessness of nationalism. He cited Marx, history and philosophy, and then, feeling that these arguments were too vague and academic, he grabbed hold of his own coat and roared: "The wool in this coat was taken from sheep which were pastured in Angora; it was spun in England, it was woven in Lodz; the buttons come from Germany, the thread from Austria: is it not clear to you that this world of ours is made up of the labour of ten different races?"

The argument and, still more, the illustration, was effective. You could almost feel the stream of intellectual sympathy turning in Parvus's direction. Hands were lifted to applaud—and then something unexpected happened. Parvus's coat was too small for him. In the fury of gesticulation, and while he pulled his coat about to illustrate his argument, he had ripped the right elbow, which now showed a stretch of white shirt. Right opposite Parvus sat Nachman Syrkin, whose eyes burned with rage and contempt. Just at the moment when Parvus completed his argument, Syrkin, unable to contain himself, rose to his feet and shouted, "And the rip in your sleeve comes from the pogrom of Kiev!" The effect of that interjection was marvellous. Parvus had worked an hour to come to his climax of the international coat. Syrkin had undone him with a sentence. The hands that were lifted to applaud Parvus seemed to swing over. You knew they were applauding Syrkin now. A fearful tumult rose in the hall. Idiotically, Parvus roared that he had never been in Kiev, and that at the time of the famous pogrom he had been in the Baltic countries. Nobody cared where he had been. For that evening, at least, he was undone.

Judea Pearl (2009), the father of Daniel Pearl, the journalist murdered by Islamic terrorists in Pakistan who broadcast his son's beheading online, has argued that anti-Zionism, although not the same as anti-Semitism, is yet more insidious, because it denies to the Jewish people the right to a state, the right to which it accords to other peoples.

> Anti-Zionism earns its discriminatory character by denying the Jewish people what it grants to other historically-bonded collectives (e.g. French, Spanish, Palestinian), namely, the right to nationhood, self-determination and legitimate coexistence with other indigenous claimants.

> Anti-Semitism rejects Jews as equal members of the human race; anti-Zionism rejects Israel as an equal member in the family of nations . . .

> Given this understanding of Jewish nationhood, anti-Zionism is in many ways more dangerous than anti-Semitism. First, anti-Zionism targets the most vulnerable part of the Jewish people, namely, the Jewish population of Israel, whose physical safety and personal dignity depend crucially on maintaining Israel's sovereignty. Put bluntly, the anti-Zionist plan to do away with Israel condemns 5.5 million human beings, mostly refugees or children of refugees, to eternal defenselessness in a region where genocidal designs are not uncommon.

Secondly, modern society has developed antibodies against anti-Semitism, but not against anti-Zionism. Today, anti-Semitic stereo-types evoke revulsion in most people of conscience, while anti-Zionist rhetoric has become a mark of academic sophistication and social acceptance in certain extreme yet vocal circles of U.S. academia and media elite. Anti-Zionism disguises itself in the cloak of political debate, exempt from sensitivities and rules of civility that govern inter-religious discourse, to attack the most cherished symbol of Jewish identity.

Finally, anti-Zionist rhetoric is a stab in the back to the Israeli peace camp, which overwhelmingly stands for a two-state solution. It also gives credence to enemies of coexistence, who claim that the eventual elimination of Israel is the hidden agenda of every Palestinian.

One might speak of Jewish exceptionalism in regard to the absence of a sovereign territory for 2,000 years, a story of national survival without land, or, as Berlin (2000, p. 143) once put it,

It was once said by the celebrated Russian revolutionary, Alexander Herzen, writing in the mid-nineteenth century, that the Slavs had no history, only geography. The position of the Jews is the reverse of this. They have enjoyed rather too much history and too little geography.

Vamık Volkan has written of the chosen traumas of different peoples in their specific ressentiment[18] in relation to others. Sometimes, however, the traumas choose the people, as I would argue is the case with the Holocaust, which makes it different from the battles of Culloden or Bila Hora,[19] since some of the survivors are still alive, as are most of their children and grandchildren, and the direct effects of that horrendous experience is still active in an immediate way. The success of Zionism in some ways is linked to the Holocaust, and it is no accident that discrediting the Holocaust appears necessary to both neo-Nazi and Islamist movements in their de-legitimisation of the State of Israel.

On the Arab side, anti-Zionism was fuelled first by fear of Jewish immigration into Turkish-Palestine, which related to economic competition, xenophobic and religious animosity, and, later, post-1948 humiliation over the loss of part of what was regarded, at least *de facto*, as Arab, more generally of Muslim, land in what later came to be known as Palestine, Syria, and Jordan, political constructs foisted upon the locals as a result of the Ottoman Empire losing this territory to France and Great Britain in the wake of the First World War. Then being defeated by the Jews in successive wars added to the humiliation and shame that combined with the seething envy of the fledgling Jewish state's successes. The Jews' historical powerlessness, their lack of modern military prowess, their sufferings as victims during the Holocaust, and their second-class citizenship everywhere (*de jure* or *de facto*) made the military defeat of the Arab armies all the more bitter (Landes, 2014).

The local Arab population within Jewish Palestine either left their homes on account of the fighting, some out of fear, others in the hope of a swift victory by invading Arab armies, or were expelled or threatened by on-site Hagana/IDF or Irgun fighters.[20] The local Arab populations observe the anniversary of the State of Israel's establishment as the *nakba*, or catastrophe, and their grievance is further politicised by rejectionist and revanchist Arab and Muslim states.

What we have here and elsewhere are competing narratives of humiliation, shame, and envy, which work through the ego and superego identifications of large masses of people, encouraged by governments, leaders, and sympathisers. I think the common element in these times of crisis, of the mobilisation of national, religious, and ethnic revanchist movements, which threaten war, ethnic cleansing, or genocide, is the threat of annihilation physically, spiritually, or culturally. It becomes a struggle of shamed and humiliated communities who feel they must move on to victory, however they define it, or death.

What can we learn from this? It seems that we ought not to have high expectations in terms of our involvement in helping to avoid large-scale conflicts. The United Nations, through Durban I, II, and III, along with the membership on the UN Human Rights Council of states, whose own policies on human rights are more than suspect, and the imbalanced voting record in the General Assembly, have severely weakened the moral authority of that international body. Had aliens from outer space visited the earth and learnt of the earth's most pressing issues from the United Nations, they might well conclude that Israel is the primary cause of the world's misfortunes. In short, human rights have become politicised at the international and national levels.[21]

In my opinion, the two areas where we can work most effectively are: (1) in small-scale groups of infants, toddlers, children, and their

192 HOSTILE AND MALIGNANT PREJUDICE

parents, the efficacy of which Parens and others have so clearly demonstrated[22] and (2) in providing psychoanalytic insights regarding hostile and malignant prejudice to professionals who work in fields where they are frequently engaged with such problems, professionals such as teachers, social workers, police, jurists, or legislators, and to parents who provide the material and help shape the ego and superego identifications that are so crucial for both character development and, on the group level, for shaping the contours of the larger polity in which character development is embedded.

Conclusion

Some may find what is written here unduly pessimistic. However, I believe it is realistic. Despite recent trends in psychoanalytic thinking, I continue to maintain that one of the foundations of psychoanalytic work remains the distinction between reality and illusion or delusion. We should not overestimate our capacity to solve the seemingly intractable problems of hostile and malignant prejudice and violence. However, I also caution against undue pessimism and defeatism.

I do not believe in an eschatological vision of salvation or destruction. I do, however, advocate careful analysis and the dedicated and slow but steady work that moves us slowly forward in addressing one of the most insidious, enduring, and pressing problems of human civilisation.

Notes

1. I would like to thank Louis Greenspan and Abe Fuks for their helpful comments on this concluding chapter.
2. In a public lecture at McMaster University, in Hamilton, Ontario, Canada, in the 1980s, Bruno Bettelheim told an autobiographical story of how his purchase of psychoanalytic literature at a small bookstore in Vienna during the First World War was always placed discreetly in an opaque paper bag, since it was understood by the general population to be pornographic.
3. The former Committee on Prejudice (Including Antisemitism) of the IPA has prepared relevant literature for non-analytically orientated professionals as a major part of its outreach effort in line with the commitment

of the IPA to a general outreach programme, aimed at making psycho-analysis relevant within the larger community. To date, we have prepared four pamphlets for distribution to non-analytic professionals. See Böhm (2013), Heenen-Wolff (2013), Parens (2013), and Volkan (2013).

4. Henri Parens has demonstrated successes in his work with mothers and their young children. However, these mothers were a self-selecting group of volunteers and do not constitute a representative sample from the population from which they emerged. Would mothers suffering from common psychiatric problems—depression and anxiety disorders, for example—do as well with their children without extensive medication or psychotherapy?

   In addition, one must consider the enormous cost in training com-petent specialists, such as Henri Parens and his colleagues, to work with millions of mothers and their children. Furthermore, such extensive inter-ventions in parenting would surely become a political hot-button issue for libertarians and others, who are, in principle, opposed to any kind of government-sponsored programmes that are imposed upon families. These are the practical problems that militate against the widespread implementation of the excellent work that Parens and others have done and continue to do.

5. Neuroscience has recently discovered some of the brain physiology that subtends the mental experience of attention to the face. See Kandel (2012).

6. Freud focused on the phylogenetic basis of the Oedipus complex, in which the collective murder of the primal father is repeated onto-genetically by subsequent generations in unconscious fantasy and to a much more limited degree in action, and forms the core complex of the neuroses. However, in subsequent works, such as *Group Psychology and the Analysis of the Ego* (1921c) and *Civilization and Its Discontents* (1930a), he examined prejudice and aggression under the heading of the "narcissism of minor differences" which arises out of the necessity of binding communities together in such a way that hostile impulses are directed against those outside of communal bonds. In *Civilization and Its Discontents*, Freud (1930a, p. 114) writes,

> It is always possible to bind together a considerable number of people in love, so long as there are other people left over to receive the manifestations of their aggressiveness . . . When once the Apostle Paul had posited universal love between men as the foun-dation of his Christian community, extreme intolerance on the part of Christendom towards those who remained outside it became the inevitable consequence.

This raises a question within Freud's thought concerning the relation between patricide and fratricide. In the last sections of *Totem and Taboo* (1912–1913), Freud considered the fate of Jesus, the son, in terms of the expiation of the patricide committed by the band of brothers. Through the resurrection, the victory of the son over the father is guaranteed, and in the establishment of Christianity in which the object of worship is the son in place of the murdered father.

René Girard has challenged Freud's primacy of patricide in his theory of mimetic violence, according to which the stability of a community can only be established and reaffirmed by the periodic sacrifice of an innocent from within the ranks. More recently, the historian Russell Jacoby (2011) developed an explicit thesis that implies that most of the horrendous violence in human history is related to the narcissism of minor differences, and that the bloodiest of wars are civil or fratricidal wars. Avoiding mention of Freud's death drive, he traces the roots of these impulses back to the fear of women and anti-Semitism to the Jewish practice of male circumcision, citing the work of Otto Weininger as an important reference in these connections. Stephen Pinker (2011) has argued that the violence of the past in fact has been in recent decline.

7. This is not to suggest, of course, that the causes of these conflicts are only psychological. There are economic, political, historical, religious, as well as psychological motives that are at work, and must be included in any thorough analysis of particular situations.

8. One might compare the attempt to introduce Esperanto with the success- ful revival of Hebrew as the national language of the Yishuv, the Jewish settlement in that part of the Turkish Empire called by the Romans Palestina, later in the British Mandate of Palestine, and then of the State of Israel. It was a great success, because it represented the needs and aspirations of the Jews who settled there for a common language linking them all to the tradition that they all shared which overcame the divi- sions—although such divisions still exist—occasioned by their different diaspora experiences that they internalised. They could not have embraced Esperanto with the same passion and sense of urgency.

Speakers of Yiddish refer to it as *mameloshn*, mother tongue, but this was true for only a part—albeit a large part—of world Jewry. Hebrew was conceived in the Zionist project as the true mother tongue of the Jewish people as a whole. The amazing re-establishment of the Hebrew language in less than a century proves the success of this linguistic revival. It has not only become the language of millions within Israel and around the world, but has given rise to a world-class literature—poetry, prose, plays, song—and science, some examples of which have captured international awards, including the Nobel Prize.

In a way, English has become a sort of international, if not universal, language that has occurred organically and not as an artifice imposed or voluntarily accepted by a population. Of course, international English is not spoken by any non-English group in place of the native language, but is driven by commercial interest and especially by the Internet. The development of language is akin to an organic process that moves quietly, unreflectively, and unconsciously over time.

The early development of Modern Hebrew is exceptional. After its initial introduction, it developed in the same unconscious ways as other languages. Much of the slang, for example, is derived from Arabic. The development of language is reminiscent of the debate in law between Friedrich Karl von Savigny and Justus Thibaut, concerning the possibility of developing a national set of laws for Germany in the aftermath of the Napoleonic wars. The latter supported a national civil code of law for all the German states as artifice, created by a group of legal minds *ad hoc* in a systematic way; the former believed such a civil code could only evolve organically over time reflecting the traditions of a people.

9. A friend who worked in an agency of government in Canada that supported multi-cultural activities and programmes told me that most minority workers in the agency believed that their minority was the most aggrieved and that, from time to time, derogatory comments were made about the other minorities. The irony in this situation, which Freud already knew, was that an agency that was explicitly created to serve minority communities in a positive, multi-cultural way became a hot-spot of group hostility and tension.

10. There are more complicated kinds of intermarriages that require greater sensitivity on the parts of both partners. For example, marriages between members of groups that have traditional enmity toward one another, such as Turkish and Greek Cypriots, Arabs or other Muslims and Jews, Hindus and Muslims, or Chinese and Japanese, may feel greater tensions that they can only overcome through mutual understanding, tolerance, and maturity from both sides. This will, however, vary from case to case.

Someone who is nominally Jewish, a graduate of a prestigious university, would have fewer domestic difficulties marrying someone of a nominal Christian background who is a graduate of a similar prestigious university. World literature, art, opera and the theatre, psychoanalysis, etc., and the moral values that may be derived from these may provide significant substitutes for the domestic solidarity formerly provided by the more provincial bonds of ethnicity, nationalism, and religion. However, this applies to a very small percentage of the world's population at the present time and in the near future.

11. Nevertheless, there can be no doubt that such measures are surreptitiously aimed at the public expression of Islamic rituals and customs.

12. On the tensions between this Enlightenment view of equality and the various forms of multi-culturalism, refer to the excellent study by Eriksen and Stjernfelt (2012).

13. As is the case for the Ainu of northern Japan and far eastern Russia, the Inuit of Northern Canada and Alaska, the Nez Perce of the American Pacific Northwest, the Yupik of Central Alaska, the Tanaina of Southern Alaska, the Kets of Siberia, and many, many others. The Germanic tribes did not have an endonym that included all the Germanic tribes to the exclusion of all other peoples. They did have a name for non-Germanic peoples with whom they came into contact, "walha".

14. Such as is the case among the Koyukans of Alaska, the Han and Kutchin tribes in Alaska, the Northwest Territories, and the Yukon, the Chippewas, and many others. See Campbell (1997).

15. Friedrich Engels' later work, *The Origins of the Family, Private Property and the State*, was based upon Marx's excerpts from, and glosses on, Morgan's book. See Krader (1972).

16. Drancy was run by the French police until 3 July 1943, when its administration was taken over directly by the SS.

17. Erich Fromm, among others, attempted such a pathology of America: more broadly, the capitalist culture of acquisitiveness and war. See the intellectual biography of Fromm by Friedman (2013).

18. I use this term in the way that Nietzsche and Max Scheler employed it, as a kind of unrequitable hatred related to an experienced treachery, grand insult, or abuse on the part of some political, ethnic, racial, or religious group. It is the hatred of the slave for the master, for example.

19. Volkan does not claim that the Holocaust is a chosen trauma of the Jews in his contribution to this volume; he sees it rather as an ethnic marker.

20. There is a large body of literature on the question of the expulsion or voluntary leaving of Arabs from Israel, both before and during the War of Independence. In his controversial book on the origins of the Palestinian refugee problem, Morris has documented the role of the military expulsion of local Arabs, especially in Lod and Ramle, by the Hagana, or IDF, and the fear engendered by the sporadic excesses of the Israeli military, as a cogent reason for Arab flight. In his more recent work on the subsequent historical developments in the relations between Israel

and the Palestinians, however, he articulates the view that full and actual implementation of the right of return would necessarily imply the end of Israel as a Jewish state. Taking Morris's work as a whole, I believe that it represents the most convincing historical account of the Israeli–Palestinian conflict. More recently, he argued that all opportunities for peace have been pursued, and that Israel has done what it had to do to ensure its survival. In this regard, see Morris (1989, 1994, 2004a,b, 2010). Ari Shavit (2013), correspondent for Ha'aretz, has taken a similar, if less forceful, view of Israel's foreign policy in terms of the bottom line of its survival, especially in the chapter "Lydda". For two distinctly anti-Israel views see: Pappé (2006) and Tyler (2012).

21. Vamık Volkan has worked for years with various groups who have historical antipathies to one another, examples of which appear in his chapter above. One never knows, of course, whether one or more of these participants from the diplomatic core, high-ranking military, helping professions might influence the great course of events in some minor or major crucial way. Admittedly it is better to have them meet under conditions organized by Volkan regardless of the palpable impact.

22. Although Henri Parens has demonstrated the efficacy of his work with the mothers and their children, there are a number of practical difficulties in translating his path-breaking work into national programmes to reduce the potential for hostile and malignant prejudice and violence. First, the mothers within his group were self-selecting and probably more involved in the concern and care for their children's futures than mothers within the general population. Second, the amount of money, state and private, required to train, equip, and deploy the number of professionals to institute these programmes on a large scale would be astronomical. Third, a significant number of mothers who could benefit from participating with such programmes have psychological and emotional issues of their own. They might not be able to participate in these programmes without first obtaining treatment for their own issues. Here, we encounter a programme that has proved its effectiveness but has come up against enormous practical problems of implementation.

References

Berlin, I. (2000). The origins of Israel. In: *The Power of Ideas*, H. Hardy (Ed.) (pp. 143–161). Princeton, NJ: Princeton University Press.

Bernier, F. (1891). *Travels in the Mogul Empire, A.D. 1656–1668*. London: Constable.

Böhm, T. (2013). *Resistance Strategies Against Prejudice*. Geneva: IPA.

Campbell, L. (1997). *American Indian Languages: The Historical Linguistics of Native America*. New York: Oxford University Press.

Engels, F. (1942). *The Origin of the Family, Private Property and the State: In the Light of the Researches of Lewis H. Morgan*. New York: International.

Eriksen, J.-M., & Stjernfelt, F. (2012). *The Democratic Contradictions of Multiculuralism*. New York: Telos Press.

Freud, S. (1905d). *Three Essays on the Theory of Sexuality. S.E., 7*: 123–245. London: Hogarth.

Freud, S. (1912–1913). *Totem and Taboo. S.E., 13*: 1–162. London: Hogarth.

Freud, S. (1917e). Mourning and melancholia. *S.E., 14*: 237–258. London: Hogarth.

Freud, S. (1921c). *Group Psychology and the Analysis of the Ego. S.E., 18*: 69–143. London: Hogarth.

Freud, S. (1930a). *Civilization and Its Discontents. S.E., 21*: 57–145. London: Hogarth.

Friedman, L. (2013). *The Lives of Erich Fromm: Love's Prophet*. New York: Columbia University Press.

Gilligan, J. (1997). *Violence: Reflections on a National Epidemic*. New York: G. P. Putnam.

Heenen-Wolff, S. (2013). *Psychoanalysts Against Prejudice: The Case of Sexual Orientation*. Geneva: IPA.

Hunt, L. (1996). *The French Revolution and Human Rights: A Brief Documentary History*. Boston, MA: Bedford Books of St. Martin's Press.

Jacoby, R. (2011). *Bloodlust: On the Roots of Violence from Cain and Abel to the Present*. New York: Free Press.

Kandel, E. (2012). *The Age of Insight: The Quest to Understand the Unconscious in Art, Mind, and Brain, from Vienna 1900 to the Present*. New York: Random House.

Krader, L. (1966). Primary reification and primitive mythology. *Diogenes, 14*(56): 51–73.

Krader, L. (Ed.) (1972). *The Ethnological Notebooks of Karl Marx: Studies of Morgan, Phear, Maine, Lubbock*. Assen: Van Gorcum.

Kramer, J. (2011). Against nature: Elisabeth Badinter's contrarian feminism. *The New Yorker*, July 25, 44–55.

Landes, R. (2014). Why the Arab world is lost in an emotional nakba, and how we keep it there. *Tablet Magazine*, 24 June 2014, available at: http://www.tabletmag.com/jewish-news-and-politics/176673/emotion-alnakba?all=1#.

Levin, S., & Samuel, M. (1930). *Youth in Revolt*. New York: Harcourt, Brace.

Morris, B. (1989). *The Birth of the Palestine Refugee Problem, 1947–1949.* Cambridge: Cambridge University Press.

Morris, B. (1994). *1948 and After: Israel and the Palestinians.* Oxford: Clarendon Press.

Morris, B. (2004a). *The Birth of the Palestinian Refugee Problem Revisited.* Cambridge: Cambridge University Press.

Morris, B. (2004b). The Tantura "Massacre" Affair. *The Jerusalem Report,* February 4.

Morris, B. (2010). *One State, Two States: Resolving the Israel/Palestine Conflict.* New Haven, CT: Yale University Press.

Pappé, I. (2006). *The Ethnic Cleansing of Palestine.* Oxford: Oneworld.

Parens, H. (2013). *We All Have Prejudices. But, Why?* Geneva: IPA.

Pearl, J. (2009). Is anti-Zionism hate? *The Los Angeles Times,* March 14.

Pinker, S. (2011). *The Better Angels of Our Nature: Why Violence Has Declined.* New York: Viking.

Shavit, A. (2013). *My Promised Land.* New York: Random House.

Strauss, L. (1962). Why we remain Jews: can Jewish faith and history still speak to us? A lecture given on February 4, 1962 at the B'nai B'rith Hillel Foundation of the University of Chicago. Study of Jewish Community Organization.

Tyler, P. (2012). *Fortress Israel.* New York: Farrar, Strauss, & Giroux.

Volkan, V. D. (1988). *The Need to Have Enemies and Allies: From Clinical Practice to International Relationships.* Northvale, NJ: Jason Aronson.

Volkan, V. D. (2013). *Us and Them: Shared Prejudice.* Geneva: IPA.

INDEX

abuse, 12–13, 16, 90, 129, 145, 196
   sexual, 62
affect(ive), 63, 75, 96
   bonds, 49
   expressions, 5, 171
aggression, xiv, xvi–xvii, xxi, 3–4, 7,
     61, 144–145, 158, 171, 174, 193
   associations, 165
   cruel, 171
   desires, 165
   development of, 3–4
   feelings, 150
   group, 150
   massive, 62
   measure of, xiv
   passive, 6
   patterns of, xxv
   profile, xiv, 4–6
   theory of, 4–5, 171
   trends, xvii, 135
Aichhorn, A., 4, 13
Akhtar, S., 11, 18
Alberoni, F., 146
Alderdice, J., 68, 78–79
Ambjörnsson, R., 150
American Psychoanalytic
   Association (APA), 68
anger, xiv–xvi, 5–6, 10, 171
Annan, K., 19
anthropology, 37, 173, 175, 179,
    182–183
   cultural, 30
   empirical, 180
anti-Semitism, xii, xxiii–xxiv, 19, 32,
    46, 61, 122, 125–128, 130, 132, 135,
    146–147, 169, 188–190, 192, 194
   Christian(ity), xxii–xxiii

delusional, 122, 125
eliminatory, 121–122, 125
exterminatory, xxii
racist, xxii, 126
theories of, xxiv
anxiety, xxiv, 37, 46, 50, 58–59, 61, 91,
    97, 103, 105, 109, 155, 158
   castration, 69
   childhood, 58
   disorders, 193
   -driven, 138
   persecutory, 144
   professional, 79
   separation, 9
   social, 142
   stranger, xiv, 7–10, 50, 171, 185
Anzieu, D., 61
Appleyard, K., 4
Apprey, M., 67
après-coup, xxi, 89, 93, 98, 102, 105,
    107, 111–113
Arendt, H., 32, 35, 39–40
Arieti, S., xxiv, 147–148, 151
Arlow, J., 61
Ast, G., 63, 73
attachment, 3–5, 7–10, 14–15, 21, 62,
    71, 177, 185
   child('s), xiv, 9
   early, 181
   evolving, 9
   favourable, 6
   group, 185
   infant's, 9
   object, 9, 10, 145
   quality of, 6
Auschwitz, 41, 101, 106
Awwad, E., 20–21